D1548692

Peter De Vries
and Surrealism

Peter De Vries and Surrealism

Dan Campion

Lewisburg
Bucknell University Press
London: Associated University Presses

813.52.
De Vries

Associated University Presses
440 Forsgate Drive
Cranbury, NJ 08512

Associated University Presses
25 Sicilian Avenue
London WC1A 2QH, England

Associated University Presses
P.O. Box 338, Port Credit
Mississauga, Ontario
Canada L5G 4L8

The paper used in this publication meets the requirements
of the American National Standard for Permanence of Paper
for Printed Library Materials Z39.48-1984.

Library of Congress Cataloging-in-Publication Data

Campion, Dan, 1949–
    Peter De Vries and surrealism / Dan Campion.
        p.   cm.
    Includes bibliographical references (p.) and index.
    ISBN 0-8387-5311-6 (alk. paper)
    1. De Vries, Peter—Criticism and interpretation. 2. Surrealism
(Literature)—United States. I. Title.
PS3507.E8673Z59   1995
813'.52—dc20   95-5571
                                                                    CIP

To my father
Raymond E. Campion

and in memory of my mother
Wilma Frances Dougherty Campion

I fear chiefly lest my expression may not be *extra-vagant* enough, may not wander far enough beyond the narrow limits of my daily experience, so as to be adequate to the truth of which I have been convinced.

—Thoreau, *Walden*

Thoreau said he never saw a man 100% awake, just as Freud, fifty years later, was to find no one ever wholly asleep.

—Chick Swallow in *Comfort Me With Apples*

Contents

Acknowledgments

This study was abetted by Peter De Vries, who responded to my letters and early drafts with the grace and wit abundant in his works but not reasonably to be expected by an importunate correspondent. His generosity and kindness, like his literary gifts, are greater by far than my ability to describe them.

I am thankful for all the help provided by Jan De Vries, who has been very kind in taking time to discuss this study with me and very generous in allowing me to quote extensively from her father's works.

I am indebted to Ed Folsom for advice and encouragement that guided and sustained me during the course of this study. To Paul Baender, Paul Diehl, Ruedi Kuenzli, and Brooks Landon I owe many critical insights and editorial improvements. I am deeply grateful for their friendship and their generosity of time and spirit.

Saul Bellow, Brendan Gill, James Laughlin, Frederick Manfred, and Edouard Roditi graciously replied to my inquiries with illuminating remarks. I am thankful to all the writers who over the years have kept up a stimulating discussion about Peter De Vries, and I am personally obliged to several of them: Ralph C. Wood offered valuable research ideas and editorial suggestions, and Edwin T. Bowden and Bernard van't Hul very graciously answered my requests for information. Richard Boston allowed me to quote extensively from his *Anatomy of Laughter*, Roy Newquist from his *Counterpoint*, and David Gascoyne from his *Short Survey of Surrealism*.

From my friend Joan Fallert I learned to trust my own sense of humor and that of a sympathetic reader. My colleagues Candace Noble and Sherri Miller have given consistent support and good counsel. The University of Iowa Library staff provided superb research assistance, and Jim Bass, Renee Huntley, Sister Dolores Koza, and Jim Perlman supplied a variety of helpful sources. I was fortunate to receive also the kind help of Helen Klaviter of *Poetry* and Herbert J. Brinks of the Calvin College archives.

I am grateful for the valuable advice provided by Pauline Fletcher of Bucknell University Press and by Julien Yoseloff, Michael Koy, and Evelyn Apgar of Associated University Presses, and I appreciate the thoughtful copyediting of Diane D. Burke.

9

André Breton's penetrating vision provided the occasion for this study. The inspiration is provided by JoAnn Castagna, who, in our partnership in reading Peter De Vries as in everything besides, is reading several pages ahead of me.

The following publishers and individuals have generously given permission to use extended quotations from copyrighted works: From "Secular Elegies II," by George Barker, in *George Barker: Collected Poems*. © 1987 by George Barker. Reprinted by permission of Faber and Faber Ltd. From *An Anatomy of Laughter*, by Richard Boston. © 1974 by Richard Boston. Reprinted by permission of Richard Boston. From "Surrealism," by Kenneth Burke. © 1940 by New Directions. Reprinted by permission of New Directions Publishing Corporation. From "Late Song," by Peter De Vries, first published in *Poetry*. © 1938 by The Modern Poetry Association. Reprinted by permission of Jan De Vries and the Watkins/Loomis Agency and of the Editor of *Poetry*. From "Fusion and Confusion," by Peter De Vries, first published in *Poetry*. © 1938 by The Modern Poetry Association. Reprinted by permission of Jan De Vries and the Watkins/Loomis Agency and of the Editor of *Poetry*. For "Mirror," by Peter De Vries, first published in *Poetry*. © 1939 by The Modern Poetry Association. Reprinted by permission of Jan De Vries and the Watkins/Loomis Agency and of the Editor of *Poetry*. From "The Reader Writes," by Carl Crane (Peter De Vries), first published in *The New Yorker*. © 1939 by The New Yorker Magazine, Inc. Reprinted by permission of Jan De Vries. From *But Who Wakes the Bugler?* by Peter De Vries. © 1940 by Peter De Vries. Reprinted by permission of Jan De Vries and the Watkins/Loomis Agency. From "Poetry and the War," by Peter De Vries, first published in *College English*. © 1943 by the National Council of Teachers of English. Reprinted by permission of Jan De Vries and the Watkins/Loomis Agency. From "James Thurber: The Comic Prufrock," by Peter De Vries, first published in *Poetry*. © 1943 by The Modern Poetry Association. Reprinted by permission of Jan De Vries and the Watkins/Loomis Agency and of the Editor of *Poetry*. From TIME Reading Program Introduction to *Lions, Harts, Leaping Does and Other Stories*, by Peter De Vries. © 1963 by Time-Life Books Inc. Reprinted by permission of Time-Life Books Inc. For Peter De Vries's statement included in *Authors Take Sides on Vietnam*, edited by Cecil Woolf and John Bagguley. © 1967 by Simon & Schuster, Inc. Reprinted by permission of Jan De Vries and the Watkins/Loomis Agency. Also © 1967 by Peter Owen and Simon & Schuster Inc. Reprinted by permission of Peter Owen Publishers, London. From *Forever Panting*, by Peter De Vries. © 1973 by Peter De Vries. Reprinted by permission of Jan De Vries and the Watkins/Loomis Agency. From *The Garden of Disorder*, by Charles Henri Ford. ©1938 by New Directions. Reprinted by permission of New Directions Publishing Corporation. From "Humour," in *The Collected Papers*, vol. 5, by Sigmund Freud. © 1961 by The Institute of Psycho-Analysis and Angela Richards. Reprinted courtesy of Sigmund Freud Copyrights, The Institute of Psycho-Analysis and The Hogarth Press for permission to quote from *The Standard Edition of the Complete Psychological Works of Sigmund Freud*, translated and edited by James Strachey, and by permission of HarperCollins Publishers Inc. From *A Short Survey of Surrealism*, by David Gascoyne. © 1935, 1982 by David Gascoyne. Reprinted by permission of David Gascoyne. From *The Poetry Anthology 1912–1977*, edited by Daryl Hine and Joseph Parisi. Copyright © 1978 by The Modern Poetry Association. Reprinted by permission of the Editor of *Poetry*. From *Thurber's Anatomy of Confusion*, by Catherine McGehee Kenney. © 1984 by Catherine McGehee Kenney. Reprinted by permission of The Shoe String Press, Inc. From *James Thurber*, by Robert E. Morsberger. Copyright © 1964 by Twayne Publishers, Inc. Excerpted with permission of Twayne Publishers, an imprint of Macmillan Publishing Company. From *Counterpoint*, by Roy Newquist. © 1964 by Rand McNally & Company. Reprinted by permission of Roy Newquist. From "Talk With Peter De Vries," by Lewis Nichols. © 1956 by The New York Times Company. Reprinted by permission. From "How Shall My Animal," by Dylan Thomas, in *The Poems of Dylan Thomas*. © 1938 by New Directions Publishing Corporation. Reprinted by permission of New Directions Publishing Corporation. Also in *Dylan Thomas: The Poems*. © 1971 by J. M. Dent & Sons Ltd. Reprinted by permission. From *The Years with Ross*, by James Thurber. © 1959 by James Thurber. Reprinted by permission of Little, Brown and Company. From "As I Knew Them," by John Timmerman. © 1975 by Calvin College Communications Board. Reprinted by permission of *Dialogue*. From "Peter De Vries: Being Seriously Funny," by Ben Yagoda. © 1983 by The New York Times Company. Reprinted by permission.

Peter De Vries
and Surrealism

1

Introduction

Pᴇᴛᴇʀ De Vries wished to be known primarily as a humorist,[1] much as Ben Jonson wished to be thought of as a humourist, and he gave us the richest concentrations of humor produced by any recent American writer. These works merit study in their own right as products of a civilized mind, and careful readings of them instruct us in comic ends and means of central importance. Kenneth Burke proposed in his "Definition of Man" that "mankind's only hope is a cult of comedy,"[2] and De Vries's work offers a unique comic alchemy. But why "Peter De Vries and Surrealism," a linkage some readers may find a surreal juxtaposition? *Surreal,* after all, is a word that, already depleted from hard use in its careless application to mere trendiness in the arts, is becoming shopworn as a label for a wide variety of uncanny events and sensations, most of them awful.[3] Yet *surrealism* is more than a mere label for scandal, and the surrealist movement, meliorist in its own way, contributed powerfully to De Vries's uniqueness. Before he committed himself to the refinement of comedy, De Vries once thought about taking a run for Chicago alderman as a reform candidate.[4] Later, his characters would talk about "running on the Surrealist ticket."[5] De Vries's career became, in fact, a series of experiments in extravagance, a run on a Surrealist ticket: a surrealistic tour of America and a constructive Americanization of surrealism.

Peter De Vries wrote twenty-three novels, two novellas, a play, and many stories, poems, essays, and reviews. Born in 1910 into an ultraconservative Dutch Calvinist enclave on Chicago's South Side and to what one of his heroes might call "an upbringing he chafed under," De Vries lived for most of his life in the cosmopolitan and secular East. Thus he has been characterized as a "culturally displaced person," endowed with a unique perspective on modern American culture.[6] Indeed, the titles of his novels (*I Hear America Swinging, Slouching Towards Kalamazoo, The Prick of Noon*), while they suggest wit, erudition, bawdiness, and irreverence, are perhaps most notable for proclaiming an exotic clownishness, and his narrators often

15

are fastidious vulgarians determined not to share embarrassment provoked by their impudence. De Vries's satires are held to be mild rather than flinty, and he is classed as an urbane, *New Yorker*-style raconteur of bagatelles.[7] Leading critics have lauded his works in the prestigious reviews of England and America. His books have sold well, to enthusiastic notices in *Time*, *Newsweek*, and *People*. Many of the author's proponents see him as an eloquent apologist for Christianity in a secular era.[8] Others regard him as an antiromantic, conservative ironist defending secular conformity.[9] Still others emphasize De Vries's darker side and ally him with the absurdists and black humorists.[10] His career among commentators has been protean, his popular success considerable, and his critical acclaim high.

As I have read Peter De Vries's works over the years, I have sensed in them an undercurrent of surrealist subversiveness. This undercurrent has seldom been discussed by writers on De Vries, who tend to ignore, slight, or deny surrealist elements in his work—even though he refers to surrealism and surrealists in all but two of his twenty-six books.[11] My introduction to De Vries came in 1967, when I read an excerpt from *The Blood of the Lamb* in Douglas M. Davis's anthology *The World of Black Humor*;[12] the first De Vries novel I read was *Madder Music*. In both, the presence of surrealistic elements seemed unmistakable. Later, I found it striking that so few critics had noticed the surrealism in De Vries, and that none had discussed it in depth. Nevertheless, when I set about writing on De Vries, I expected difficulty in making a case based mainly on intuition and at odds with able critics who had revealed De Vries's mainstream literary sources and identified his concerns as essentially those of his Calvinist upbringing. As I read De Vries's first novel, *But Who Wakes the Bugler?* (1940), however, and became acquainted with its witty thirty-year-old author, I learned that De Vries was actually engaged with surrealism in the 1930s and 1940s and voiced his interest in his early work. Gauging De Vries's involvement with surrealism proved to be an education in "connoisseurrealism."

Admittedly, the author dismissed his first three novels as exercises,[13] and a young writer's experiments can scarcely be held to dominate his mature works. I do not claim that De Vries ever thought of himself as a Surrealist. He appears to have been inoculated against isms by his experience with Calvinism. What I wish to show is that surrealism contributed an important dimension to De Vries's writings, providing useful forms, important themes, an imaginative carte blanche, and inspiration for his novels' exuberance—which, like the energy in avowedly surrealist works, is undeterred even by absurdity, cruelty, and catastrophe from detecting and transmitting the marvelous.

De Vries's works answer when challenged in surrealist terms. Although De Vries might not have especially welcomed recognition of his links with a movement that in America is usually misrepresented and misunderstood, it seems an absurdity worthy of a De Vries plot that his books have more often been studied in the afterglow of his religious childhood than in the bright light of his formative years as a writer.

Interpretative approaches to De Vries's works have been primarily biographical (Ter Maat, 1963), theological (Hoffman, 1970; Jellema, 1966), thematic (Boyd, 1971; De Roller, 1976; Down, 1986), and broadly descriptive (J. H. Bowden, 1983).[14] With the exception of Jack Kent Boyd and a few of De Vries's many reviewers, critics have done no more than express appreciation for (or, occasionally, deplore) De Vries's most immediately evident and deeply characteristic trait: his playful, allusive style. No close reading of a De Vries novel has been published. Reading De Vries's work with the intention of selecting a novel for such a treatment, I came for the first time upon *But Who Wakes the Bugler?* and discovered confirmation there that De Vries had from an early date been interested not just in surrealism broadly understood as the unusual or bizarre, but in André Breton's movement. It became clear that the novel for close study was this lesser-known, revelatory work.

My growing interest in the early De Vries led me to his first published poems, stories, and essays, and also to the volumes of *Poetry* magazine from 1938 through 1946. During this period, De Vries was connected with the magazine as associate editor and coeditor.[15] The details of his editorial engagement with *Poetry*, which firmly establish his connections to surrealism, have never been taken into account by commentators. Neglect of this phase in De Vries's development has created an array of misconceptions. The early writings have been dismissed as "apprentice work" even though De Vries was publishing in *Esquire* in its golden era and was an editor for a major little magazine. He has been portrayed as a rough provincial whose real literary career began with his move to New York and *The New Yorker* in 1944, whereas by that time he had already found his vocation in six years at *Poetry*. He has been held accountable for trying and failing to achieve convincing realism, plausible plot, and rounded character development, when his surrealist-influenced technique was developed precisely out of an effort to go beyond those criteria. He has been likened to British comedians of wit, some of whom he has never referred to, for using gambits that were more readily available to him in surrealist works he is certain to have read. He is held to have carried the bedrock of his childhood Calvinism, with considerable naivete, to New York, when in fact he brought an ironic perspective born of the strictures and rationalism of Calvinism and the license and irrationalism of surrealism. The young author of 1940 deserves to be reread—he has much to tell us about how to read Peter De Vries.

A close reading of *But Who Wakes the Bugler?* may not persuade readers that it is a great novel, but *Bugler* surely deserves recognition as part of what Constance Rourke called "the extravagant vein in American humor."[16] This first novel has De Vries bringing together many elements and influences into a new form that is best designated *surrealist farce*. Invention of this form places De Vries in a unique relationship to the surrealist-absurdist tradition: aiming to comprise accessibility and complexity, close to the mainstream and close to the occult stream of surrealism, skeptical of both tradition and the avant-garde, De Vries tumbles his readers through the cultural currents and gives a new spin to our perceptions. Whatever one's convictions or complacencies, De Vries will jostle them.

Aldo Leopold, in another connection, wrote "There are some who can live without wild things, and some who cannot."[17] Some readers of Peter De Vries would prefer not to recognize the wildness in his works. They insist his "outer humor" is underlain by an "inner seriousness," and they emphasize the latter both to defend De Vries from the charge that he is frivolous and to legitimize their own interpretations. De Vries's works are meditations in emergencies of faith and of history—and of consciousness itself. I admit I am one of those who could not read a sententious De Vries; I read his works because of the conflict of chaos and order, the play of antinomies, there. De Vries has a familiar domesticated side, but he has an as yet largely unexplored anarchic side as well. The order in his work is often imposed for the sake of being knocked down, to take delight in disorder and a free play of ideas within and beyond the text. This dynamic use of the text as springboard, a surrealist method, De Vries shares not only with the American tradition of extravagant humorists but also with the authors of "Brahma" and "Song of Myself." *Walden* is an archetypal meditation on the transactions between gentility and wildness, and De Vries's works are not so far from continuing Thoreau's "*extra-vagant*" experiment as they might at first appear: there may even be a faint family resemblance between *Walden's* Irishman, John Field, and *Forever Panting's* Stew Smackenfelt ("Taste-for-the-field"). "Let us not mince words," said André Breton, "the marvelous is always beautiful, anything marvelous is beautiful, in fact only the marvelous is beautiful."[18] That declaration is not far afield from Thoreau's, in his manifesto "Walking":

> In literature it is only the wild that attracts us. Dullness is but another name for tameness. It is the uncivilized free and wild thinking in Hamlet and the Iliad, in all the scriptures and mythologies, not learned in the schools, that delights us. As the wild duck is more swift and beautiful than the tame, so is the wild—the mallard—thought, which 'mid falling dews wings its way above the fens.[19]

If De Vries summons up a character to inquire "Why a duck?" he does so not to dress down the original but to overcome the weight of priority—to make wild again what threatened to slide into sententiousness, to become the property of "the schools."

Chapter 2 collects the published information about De Vries's literary career, adding to it facts about his boyhood, his reform politics in 1930s Chicago, and his *Poetry* years. Chapter 3 discusses De Vries's earliest published writings and relates De Vries to 1930s surrealism in preparation for the reading of his first novel in Chapter 4. Chapters 5 and 6 reappraise selected De Vries works in light of surrealism. It is my hope to show the influence of surrealism on the works of Peter De Vries and thus to place them in their proper perspective. In the process, I hope to suggest how large but neglected has been the importance of surrealism in American literature since 1930.

Formal study of De Vries is done at hazard because De Vries often joked at the expense of literary criticism:

> I'm spending the summer puzzling over reviews that keep saying I write about the suburbs and commuters. Not a soul in "Comfort Me With Apples" commuted. Not a soul (or psyche) in "The Mackerel Plaza" commuted. I tried to shake the label in "The Tents of Wickedness" by laying it on the line: "Decency, Connecticut, is *beyond the commuting limits, outside suburbia, exurbia, and all the rest.*" No use. In roll the notices speaking of "satirist of commuterland," "chronicler of timetable culture," etc. Why? Probably because critics tend to take the same train of thought over and over again once it's been set going in [their] heads.[20]

De Vries was not a serious complainer about reviews. He recognized that "responses to humor are so personal. To one reviewer you're the greatest thing since sliced bread, and the next one is calling you a bum."[21] Among the sliced-bread reviewers have been Kingsley Amis, V. S. Naipaul, Martin Marty, Paul Theroux, Anthony Burgess, and George Will; detractors have included Hugh Kenner, Michiko Kakutani, and Malcolm Forbes.[22] Praised or blamed, De Vries is likely to be seen as a commuter, not a bum. In 1971, *The Penguin Companion to American Literature* still identified De Vries as "the comic laureate of suburbia," a portrayer of "commuters in grey flannel suits," and referred to his "steady obsession with religion."[23] Ten years later, the *Dictionary of Literary Biography* persists in calling De Vries an analyst of "the modern moral and philosophical predicament as it is evidenced in suburbia."[24] In 1990 he turns up as the "mass produce[r]" of "short, witty books that do not get confused with 'Anna Karenina'" and is introduced in *The Oxford Book of Humorous Prose* as the author of "many sparky, sophisticated novels mainly about morals and manners in Connecticut."[25] Yet throughout his career, De Vries was writing about surrealism. In *Bugler* and *Peckham's Marbles*, surrealism is satirized; in *Madder Music* and *Consenting Adults*, it is befriended. Often, surrealism, dada, Breton, Dali, de Chirico, Picasso, Tanguy, Ernst, Magritte, and Miró are simply part of the fictional landscape. References to surrealism are the purloined letters of De Vries commentary. A window to the "lightning-filled night of dreams" has been one of his constant frames of reference.

Writers on De Vries have differed on every significant aspect of his work except one. He has been portrayed as a master plotter and a bungler; an earnest molder of rounded characters and a blithe scissorer of cut-outs; a Christian artist and an agent of "pagan holidays"; a melioristic secular humanist and a despairing black humorist; a defender of reason and a reveler in absurdity; a contemptuous satirist and a compassionater; an upholder of conformism and a celebrator of diversity. He is read with gratification by liberals and conservatives, atheists and believers. But however different the writers' interpretations, and though seldom naming it as such, virtually all have testified to the surrealism in De Vries's technique.

Even the many religionists who have found in De Vries a Christian soldier cannot avoid the surreal elements in his novels. Horton Davies, who values De Vries for ridiculing "liberal and social Christianity," has to acknowledge how "deliberately exaggerated and fantastic . . . this extravagance is meant to be."[26] Roderick Jellema, who refers to De Vries as a "Clown of God," speaks also of De Vries's "audacity" and "*phantasmagoric comedy.*"[27] John Timmerman, discussing the search for "saving grace" in De Vries, also sees that a crucial symbol "arises from the subconscious, unwilled and unexpected."[28] Ralph C. Wood admits that "to regard De Vries's wildly comic fiction as a parable of the Gospel may seem to do violence both to theology and to art. De Vries himself is unapologetic about his own unbelief." Nevertheless, Wood concludes that "De Vries may consciously intend to create a comedy of human sufficiency. He provides, in fact, a parable of divine redemption."[29] Is the comedy divine or surreal? Was Shakespeare a Puritan? De Vries's works playfully illustrate the unproductiveness of disputes between believers and nonbelievers. But the experience of reading him may not differ for the two groups, as Wood's first paragraph suggests:

> Peter De Vries is so funny a writer that it may seem inappropriate to take him seriously. His puns are unabashed. Like the cleaning lady, he says, we all come to dust. The mere thought of cremation turns one of his characters ashen. De Vries's aphorisms are no less outrageous. The American home, we are told, is an invasion of privacy. Never put off until tomorrow, we are advised, what you can put off indefinitely. What is an arsonist, we are asked, but someone who has failed to set the world on fire? De Vries's vignettes are even more discerningly surreal. A chiropractor attending a patient throws out his own back. A husband who demands that his wife explain why she bought a mink coat is told that she was cold. Another wife sues her husband's mistress for alienation of his affections, and asks for $65 in damages.[30]

Being "discerningly surreal" is an insufficiently explored De Vries characteristic. Some deny the trait: J. H. Bowden claims that De Vries has no "major recourse to surrealist techniques."[31] Others, like Wood, insist that De Vries's chiding of "secular self-sufficiency" entails "an oblique affirmation of the very faith which author and character alike would seem to have abandoned."[32] They seem unaware of De Vries's declaration, in an essay on Charles Péguy, that

> [T]hat kingdom which man seeks and which he must sometimes think forever lost, is, as ever, within him. From every side come the old cries, Lo here, Lo there. Redemption. No, education. You are a sinner. Rather a fool. Half beast, half angel. No—half-witted. You must be saved! No, you must learn![33]

De Vries celebrates Péguy for refraining from these "old cries." It is fanciful to suppose that De Vries offers them up. In De Vries, neither belief in divine transcendence nor in human self-sufficiency avails. His works are protests lodged against things as they are, in the name of things imagined. In De Vries, the romantic irony of a De Quincey works in collusion with the stringent candor of a Calvin. The *style* that De Vries has evolved, and Anthony Burgess has paid him the compliment "a major stylist,"[34] is the vehicle for a fresh and subversive vision.

* * *

De Vries's most characteristic effect is of detonation, of order flung violently apart.—Max Byrd[35]

De Vries's style in his surrealist farces is a heady mixture, and
critics have had trouble reckoning with it. They usually stop just
short of calling it surrealist. "He uses his puns and fantasies to mask
a sometimes frighteningly keen observation of suburban and creative
mores in one of those southern Connecticut communities populated
by the Babbitts of Bohemia," said Al Hine of *The Tunnel of Love*. Of
Comfort Me With Apples, Whitney Balliett said its characters move
through a world "always slightly askew," speaking "in the finest tradition of the English literature of nonsense." Its protagonist, Chick
Swallow, is a "curiosity" wrapping two "inapposite types [do-gooder
and lover] into one," and the work as a whole is "Mr. De Vries'
rococo dream." Al Hine said of this novel that De Vries's "delight
in word-play . . . reminds you of some of the prose of Dylan
Thomas," that it was a "serious attempt at new ways in fictional
humor by a writer of importance." *The Mackerel Plaza* was welcomed
by W. M. Frohock for examining the contradictory American drives
toward conformity and disaffection and "the latent comic possibilities
of the uneasy juxtaposition" between "inner-directed" and "outer-
directed" individuals.[36]

An avant-garde magazine in 1963 praised De Vries for "almost-
insane irresponsibility." Although Kingsley Amis in his 1964 celebration of De Vries insisted that satire is inevitably "on the side of
reason," Melvin Maddocks in 1965 differed:

It is when things run away from Mr. De Vries's studied control that his
genius, almost against his will, makes itself felt. For his humor has a kind
of headlong compulsiveness to it. . . . Farce snowballing with a kind of
attendant horror—Kafka crossed with the Keystone Kops—this is what
one reads Mr. De Vries for. . . . He is a punster thunderstruck at his own
puns, a moralist whose homilies, to his distress, go amok.

Don Coray admitted, "Even critics who laud De Vries are scratching
their heads to come up with principles by which to appraise him," but
he did his best: *Let Me Count the Ways* reads "as though a manuscript by
Thomas Hardy were freely rewritten by Oscar Wilde, with some
editorial help from Saint Paul and Groucho Marx." Charles Child
Walcutt enjoyed in *The Tents of Wickedness* the verbal "craziness" and
admired the novel's "impudently outrageous plot" and "fantastic set
of human relations" as reflections of modern chaos.[37]

In 1971 Joy Rome claimed that De Vries "has achieved a greater control over his satirical-surrealistic material," but she does not elaborate. Wesley Kort aptly describes De Vries's hero Don Wanderhope as turning from "the rationalism and hypocrisy" of both "religious and non-religious worlds" and claims for De Vries's comedy two primary roles: "to prick illusion or to laugh down what is grotesque in American life and to provide his protagonists with a stouthearted stand against a cruelly intimidating and disappointing world." Kort credits De Vries with inventing "quasi-religious forms of word and ritual," as De Vries claimed for Charles Péguy. Lacking the surrealist frame of reference, though, Kort gets tangled:

> separated structures in our conscious worlds give testimony to a totally disunified world of the imagination in its sheer potentiality, and . . . beyond our conscious world of structures or events separated or in conflict with each other is the quiet of their imagined reconciliation and unity.

What is Kort describing but surreality, a Bretonian sense of "disappointment," and the tonic of surrealist laughter? Penelope Gilliatt, reviewing *Mrs. Wallop*, says simply "The story deals exclusively in the outrageous."[38]

Paul Showers, writing in 1972, says

> De Vries's comedy is the spectacle of a literate mind tottering good-naturedly on the brink of disintegration. Even when he has tied himself down to a formal narrative line, his thought keeps shooting off at wildly divergent tangents, like a basketfull of exploding skyrockets.

Penelope Gilliatt points to De Vries's juxtaposed perspectives:

> It is De Vries's Dutch Reformed background in the Christian form of conflict, mixed with an exquisite knowledge of what everyone doesn't know about Freudian theory, that helpfully makes him an onlooker in this land. His funniness is also aided by the angle of the tangent that he has chosen to write from . . . doomed but cheerful.

Alan Green ventured, "It's as though Dali were a subtle genius and you'd almost walked on past the painting before realizing that the watch was beginning to melt imperceptibly along one finely painted edge." William Walsh, joining a long line of English admirers, noted that De Vries is

> most commonly known for . . . an extraordinary range of comic linguistic devices, an amalgam of Euphues, Hood, Sidney Smith, Oscar Wilde,

Mark Twain, the English parodists and the American practitioners of the wise-crack: except that the wise-crack in De Vries is not the sharply-tagged, puncturing nail we're used to in American comic writing. It connects with an attitude, is continuous and organic, and more like a mode of speech or dialect dedicated to a barely sustained and desperate frivolity. In the De Vries attitude we see an intellectual process which is like something moving and turning back, like in an Hegelian dialectic running backward through a projector. . . .

The delirium of the opposite is a condition many of De Vries's characters escape or collapse into.

The context for such traits is surrealism. When Walsh says De Vries has "the humorist's faculty of seeing the weird in the familiar extravagantly developed," he might well have substituted "surrealist's." Refuting the critics who see only the suave De Vries, Walsh observes that his writing,

> which has the surface elegance of Santayana, is never too creamy or too pat—one senses something turbulent, violent, agitating underneath—and it is why this funniest writer since Oscar Wilde (though one with an immensely superior intellectual equipment) is so serious. One hears something tearing as the satin sentences elaborate.

In Walsh's opinion the "tearing" is the anguished cry of a man who "wants to judge society from the standpoint of good and evil when these categories have been reduced to mental health and psychosomatic disorder." That assessment seems just, but to "religious attitudes" and "dogma" that De Vries has "intellectually discarded" but for which he retains "the sympathy, the taste, the point of view" must be added the humanism of a Stephen Spender and the wit of an André Breton.[39]

Fred Rodewald in 1973 tries to get at what is "unique" in De Vries by claiming he "fuses" the alazon and eiron, thus blurring "the lines between comic detachment and tragic involvement." Simultaneous detachment and involvement also characterizes dreams. Similarly, when in 1974 Craig Challender remarks that in De Vries's novels "the world is unpredictable, incomprehensible; our attempts to order it are necessary, futile, funny," he inadvertently acknowledges De Vries's surrealist slants. Calvin De Vries in 1975 describes *The Blood of the Lamb* in surrealist imagery: "Belief becomes not a fixed position but an oscillation between the magnetic fields of hope and despair." Ordinary compasses won't work in De Vries's world: "He has a franchise on a certain kind of twisty, quirky, misbegotten world that's easy to lose your bearings in," wrote Robert M. Strozier in 1976.

Many disorientations in De Vries's books are sexual: as Max Byrd wrote in 1976, "women often release in De Vries's men a stream of surrealistic fantasy that he likewise shares with Thurber." But Byrd does not elaborate on the "surrealistic fantasy."[40]

Reviewers in the 1980s continued to appreciate the surrealistic elements in De Vries without exploring them and while scarcely ever naming them as surrealistic. In *Consenting Adults* De Vries invents "situations that invert the natural order of things" and animates an "anti-anti-hero."[41] *Sauce for the Goose*, a "crazy quilt of rhetoric and randiness," is "one more evocation of the Last Judgment as reflected in a fun-house mirror."[42] The allusions that "garland" De Vries's books are noted—except for the surrealists.[43] Reviewers of *Slouching Towards Kalamazoo* celebrated De Vries's "unique eccentricity," "continuing enjoyment of contradiction and ambivalence," and "ability to be simultaneously outrageous and urbane" but also reverted to mentions of "Wodehousian whimsy . . . with a whirl of madcap inventions."[44] Reviewers of *The Prick of Noon* referred to it as "deftly improvised confusion" that while "considerably dirtier" than vintage De Vries was a bracing excursion to "De Vriesland" and an exercise in "paronomasiamania."[45] By the time of *Peckham's Marbles*, *Time* referred dutifully to "De Vries's unusual comic novels" and "freewheeling manner."[46]

Several academic critics have come the closest to De Vries's surrealism. Joseph M. De Roller mentions, without exploring, De Vries's mixture of "slapstick and surrealism" in his later novels. Nancy Down detects a generic "surrealism" in De Vries. Jack Kent Boyd mentions dada and surrealism (in footnotes). As appreciative as he is of De Vries, Boyd tends to undervalue him, denying De Vries status as a "major writer" and asserting that most of his works are "marred." Boyd says *The Blood of the Lamb*, for example, "lacks the tonal coherence of fully-achieved art." De Vries is unrepentant for the book. Boyd admits "I sense that De Vries's work reflects, *in extremis*, a changing sensibility of the times for which there is not yet a proper theoretical and critical apparatus." De Vries's work has waited long enough. The philosophy *in extremis* of surrealism (Jacques Lacan appears on at least one surrealist "roster") suggests a rereading that obviates any need for apologetics. De Vries's books have been closely reading their readers for decades, discovering the sanguine tastes of the most staid and the phlegmatic yearnings of the most restless.[47]

2

The Literary Life of Peter De Vries

> Though every prospect pleases,
> And only man is vile
> —Reginald Heber, "Missionary Hymn"

PETER De Vries was born in Chicago on 27 February 1910, coming in with "perhaps Chicago's greatest literary decade," a "Chicago Renaissance" that would prompt H. L. Mencken, in 1920, to declare the city "literary capitol of the United States." A major impulse toward this renaissance was "a new concept, bohemianism," which "was to become a major philosophy in the 'Windy City.'"[1] But that influence would pain De Vries's parents. In the milieu in which Peter De Vries was born, the writing of novels was a worldly vanity. His parents had it in mind that their first and only son would become a minister.[2]

Joost De Vries and his wife, Henrietta (née Eldersveld), were stern Calvinists. Both had been born in small towns in the Netherlands province of Groningen and had emigrated in youth around the turn of the century. They married in Chicago in 1904.[3] They and their children, Engeline (b. 1904), Peter, and Anna (b. 1912), were bilingual. Joost De Vries, unlike his wife, never lost his Dutch accent, a fact his son was to find curious and somewhat embarrassing.[4] Mr. De Vries owned a horse and wagon, with which "he entered the commercial jungle."[5] He was for a time iceman in summer and coalman in winter, and then furniture mover, to the southside Englewood community, which was "harshly circumscribed,"[6] as Peter De Vries recalled in a 1964 interview with Roy Newquist:

> I was born in Chicago in 1910 into a Dutch immigrant community which still preserved its old-world ways. My origins would have been little different had my parents never come to America at all, but remained in Holland. I still feel somewhat like a foreigner, and not only for ethnic

reasons. Our insularity was twofold, being a matter of religion as well as nationality. In addition to being immigrants, and not able to mix well with the Chicago Americans around us, we were Dutch Reformed Calvinists who weren't supposed to mix—who, in fact, had considerable trouble mixing with one another. We were the elect, and the elect are barred from everything, you know, except heaven.

I wasn't allowed to go to the movies, to dance, play cards, go to the regular public schools or do anything much that was secular, even on weekdays. On Sundays we went to church (usually three times) and in between services we sat around and engaged in doctrinal disputation, in which we became adept at a very early age. It was said about us, "One Dutchman, a Christian, two Dutchmen, a congregation, three Dutchmen, heresy." We accepted and even repeated this without any apologies or any suggestion that there was anything wrong with this religious pugnacity. We were the product of a schism, and we produced schisms.

One such schism would soon be Peter De Vries's cleaving from the remainder of the community; he came to consider himself "a dissenting voice . . .; a splinter group of one, you might say."[7] Such a sundering must have been clamorous. The Christian Reformed Church of America, in which Peter De Vries was raised and in whose schools he was educated, was and is theologically and doctrinally the most conservative of the Dutch Calvinist sects. In 1890 the church broke away from the more moderate Dutch Reformed Church and became renowned for ferocity in its schisms, fundamentalism in its approach to the Bible, "terribly cerebral and frigidly unevangelical" relations with the secular world, and richness in "theologians by instinct."[8]

In 1916, Peter, beset by a stammer he would not conquer until high school, entered Englewood Christian, a Dutch Christian Reformed Church school.[9] De Vries once summed up the tenor of his formal education: "I did have the full Dutch Calvinist upbringing, from parochial schools right through college, which was Calvin College in Michigan. Good schools they were, too,—I should say, 'are'—for the Dutch Christian Reformed still maintain their own institutions and keep themselves unspotted from the world."[10] Although his school was doubtless a good one, De Vries did not long remain spotless. It is plain that he was soon getting an unofficial education.

When I was 10, I was the only Dutch Reformed boy in a solidly Irish Catholic parish which (trouble being my *first* name) my family had settled in the very heart of. Our own sort saturated an adjoining ward, but my father had moved out of it for financial reasons (poverty); there were more than enough furniture movers there, and so he drove his horse and wagon, and us, over the border into country religiously dissonant but commercially promising. For his office he rented a store on South Halsted Street and as a family we stowed ourselves in three rooms behind it.[11]

While the admission of a mischievous nature need not be taken too seriously, it would be foolish to underestimate the impact of this 1920 move upon De Vries's developing outlook. As the color-coded ethnographic maps posted in Jane Addams's Hull House attest, as do my own father's recollections of growing up several blocks west of Halsted Street on the corner of Harrison and Loomis Streets, a move out of one's own neighborhood was a virtual emigration. Thus, though De Vries has frequently been described as a provincial deracinated by his move to the East in 1944, he was uprooted for the first time twenty-four years earlier. The imagery of De Vries's recollection is striking: his father "settled" his family in another "country" after "crossing the border" in his "horse and wagon." "Pioneers, O Pioneers!" one might exclaim, except that the pilgrims are entering the territory of the old, unreformed religion. In fact they can see the wall of St. Leo's church from their new home: "Behind [our three rooms], in turn, separated from our kitchen windows by a few feet of Chicago alley, loomed the rear of St. Leo's. This church was what I saw as I ate beaten turnips and boiled beef, musing on the fish the other kids got at least once a week. Weekdays it offered a rampart against which to bounce a handball."[12] The large St. Leo the Great Church building, located at 7747 South Emerald Avenue, was dedicated on 22 April 1906, and in the 1920s presented an imposing facade.[13]

De Vries grew nostalgic about his childhood in a 1962 interview: "'We had nothing to do with anybody else. We were not allowed to go to movies. Card-playing was out. We eschewed all forms of worldliness. In adolescence this was revolting to me,' said De Vries, 'but now, of course, I would like to hear my old Dutch language services again and the Dutch congregation sing the old Dutch songs. It would also tear my heart out to hear them, you know.'"[14] The nostalgia seems to apply to De Vries's first ten years: English became the language of Dutch Christian Reformed Church services around the time of World War I, and the years of having "nothing to do with anybody else" were few. Although De Vries's life may have been "hermetically sealed"[15] before the move to Halsted Street, afterward it was not:

Since my playmates were all Catholic, I had, inevitably, some sense of their religious habits and the general apparatus on which these were framed. Conformity soon had me tipping my cap as I passed the front of St. Leo's; curiosity soon had me peering past its portals into the glimmering gloom of the interior, then venturing forward for closer scrutiny. The wood and stone to which my young friends bowed down soon lost their spell; but far more durable was that cast by the confessionals—in which, in fantasy, my Calvinist training presently had me making revelations of a sort hardly envisioned by the manufacturer.

The featured doctrine of my own denomination was, of course, that of Total Depravity, with the Atonement running it a close second. Since all our righteousness was as filthy rags, it would seem no quibble at all to slip into those booths and confess one's good works. I don't know whether it was this or the normal childhood desire for approval, denied me by my own spiritual overseers on the aforementioned grounds, that made me steal in fancy into the cool seclusion of those dark boxes where my playmates said you might freely unburden yourself, and whisper into hospitable ears, "Father, I have done my sums without being told, I have honored my father and my mother, I have stolen no apples from the grocer like other boys I might mention. . . . Wait, Father, there is more, I helped an old. . . ."

Perhaps a quick-witted priest would have elliptically prescribed a penance for the sin of pride. I just don't know. I know I had more curiosity about my playmates' religion than they had about mine. Our church was clear in another ward, and if our street wanderings ever took us there, we should only have found the doors locked. Still I like to think I was more far-ranging—more catholic, if you will—than they in my tastes and interests. Thus my fascination with St. Leo's and my grasp of what went on inside it—including, of course, the basement where I was sure the rifles were stashed in preparation for the revolution that would seat the Pope as temporal head of the country.[16]

The fantasy about the confessional, the phobia about the church basement, the us/them and me/them attitudes, and the unorthodox interests express a complicated youth. Even allowing for defects or manipulation of memory in De Vries's reminiscence, we can see an insurgent curiosity, in the interest of which he is willing to transgress the conventions of his own sect by entering the Catholic church; imaginativeness; an elevation of himself (more "catholic" than they?); a wish to be accommodating, to belong (tipping his cap); a keen sense for skewed perspectives, natural in his anomalous position; and an inclination to extract humor from the exasperating incongruities of his situation.

However curious and outward-looking De Vries was, he was still a Dutch boy from the South Side. He continued to attend Englewood Christian School, "crossing the border" to his old neighborhood to do so, until graduation in 1923. In that year his older sister, Engeline, died. The sorrow was borne in very different ways by the parents. "My father became very, very religious, so that even the prayers at the table and the school were not enough. We had to end the day by kneeling on the kitchen floor with our elbows on the chairs. My mother never sang in church again after my sister died. We had the minister over one time and he brought that up. He said, 'Mrs. De Vries, I never see you sing.' She started to cry." As for Peter, "from the start, there were problems between him and the church. They were exacerbated."[17] In 1962 De Vries admitted, "For some years I affected a religious belief I did not have,"[18] and it is reasonable to suppose there was more affectation than faith after Engeline's death.

* * *

Noble are the impulses of opening manhood, where they are not utterly ignoble: at that period, I mean, when the poetic sense begins to blossom, and when boys are first made sensible of the paradise that lurks in female smiles.—*Confessions of an English Opium-Eater*

In the fall of 1923, Peter De Vries entered Chicago Christian High School, which was operated by the Reformed and Christian Reformed Churches. Evidently there was already a family plan that he should study at Calvin College in Grand Rapids, Michigan, for at Christian High "he set out to groom himself for the Michigan Intercollegiate extemporaneous speaking championship."[19] This he did, while struggling to overcome his childhood stammer, by "participating in debating and public speaking."[20] Attaining his full height of six feet two inches, he also played on the first team in basketball in his sophomore, junior, and senior years, and he was high scorer on the 1927 team, which went ten and three for the season. His nickname was "Dew Point."[21]

Joost De Vries's trek "across the border" had proved to be a prudent business move. Irish families fleeing "the troubles" after World War I were flocking to the Auburn Park neighborhood, prompting a building boom of "spacious two-flat buildings" in the 1920s.[22] Joost gradually was building up his "one-horse outfit" to a "sizable warehouse business," in which he would eventually own three warehouses.[23] But relative prosperity and Peter's forensic and athletic success did little to assuage the irritations at home or prevent a widening rift between parents and son. He wrote to J. H. Bowden in 1976 that "Talk of a Generation Gap today makes me laugh." [It is] "Child's play . . . a mere chink in the fencepost compared with the Grand Canyon that divided us." He added that perhaps his could be compared with the religious familial tensions and conflicts of present Jewish-American writers, which could be read as the "Same thing in another vein: to wit, the all-or-nothing point of view postulated from the parental side of the household, religiously based." De Vries describes his father as "an extremely complex mixture of opposites: nervous, temperamental, religiously austere and repressive, inflexible; but . . . also emotional, kind, sensitive, outgoing, generous." His mother had "'the same disappointments, anxieties and tensions, but was less articulate. Poor soul.' She was 'a submerged and mute member of this highly provincial, narrow, insulated Dutch-American, Calvinist community in the heart of "worldly" Chicago, in which she lived till 69 [i.e., until her death in 1950].'"[24] Neither parent was at all prepared for a new direction their son now took.

After Peter's disaffection from Christian Reformed strictures, his openness to new surroundings and new friends, and his typical adolescent ordeals, came another alien influence, secular literature. Although he was president of the Literary Club of Chicago Christian High School, where "the discussions held at the bi-weekly meetings afford great enjoyment and benefit to those interested in pursuits along literary lines,"[25] the benefits De Vries enjoyed were not necessarily those intended by the school administration. In a 1959 *Newsweek* interview, De Vries "recalled that his own first great literary enthusiasm, acquired in high school, was Thomas De Quincey's stylistically elegant 'The Confessions of an English Opium Eater.'"[26] In 1962 De Vries reaffirmed his enthusiasm for De Quincey, averring "I can quote him by the yard—maybe his Biblical cadences have something to do with it."[27] Joost De Vries would have been shocked if Peter ever embellished the dinner hour with

> O just, subtle, and all-conquering opium! that, to the hearts of rich and poor alike, for the wounds that will never heal, and for the pangs of grief that "tempt the spirit to rebel," bringest an assuaging balm;—eloquent opium! that with thy potent rhetoric stealest away the purposes of wrath, pleadest effectually for relenting pity, and through one night's heavenly sleep callest back to the guilty man the visions of his infancy, and hands washed pure from blood;—O just and righteous opium! that to the chancery of dreams summonest, for the triumphs of despairing innocence, false witnesses; and confoundest perjury; and dost reverse the sentences of unrighteous judges;—thou buildest upon the bosom of darkness, out of the fantastic imagery of the brain, cities and temples, beyond the art of Phidias and Praxiteles—beyond the splendours of Babylon and Hekatompylos; and, "from the anarchy of dreaming sleep," callest into sunny light the faces of long-buried beauties, and the blessed household countenances, cleansed from the "dishonours of the grave."

> Thou only givest these gifts to man; and thou hast the keys of Paradise,
> O just, subtle, and mighty opium![28]

De Quincey's memoir was appealing on other than stylistic grounds. The *Confessions* recounts a youth's impatience with, pity for, and ultimate revulsion from his guardians; the physical and emotional bondage they impose on him; his escape, not unattended with inconvenience and anguish, into the great world; and exotic, "biblical" dreams of ecstasy and torment. The work is often very funny. De Vries was communing with a writer obviously unsuited in tone, subject, and character for the admiration of devout young Calvinists. The choice must be regarded as a gesture of rebellion, a fantasy revolt that helped De Vries survive. He began to see in literature a way of reckoning with an unsatisfactory and intransigent reality.

In declaring allegiance to De Quincey, De Vries joins those who "delight in the very combination of qualities that seems to unsettle other readers—a character at once shy and persistent, urbane and childlike; . . . the brilliant interplay of fact and fancy, of learning and impressionism . . . and an almost businesslike professional competence unpredictably graced by a rakish and Bohemian cast."[29] The same qualities were present, in different proportions, in Chicago Renaissance writers like Hecht, Dreiser, Masters, Sandburg, and Anderson, and De Vries recalls having an enthusiasm for them, too.[30] He was probably aware of the presence a few miles up Halsted Street, in Hull House, of Little Theater activities; of the "studio society" on Stony Island Avenue a few miles east, which "opposed genteelism, romanticism and realism with the new concept of 'arts [*sic*] for art's sake,' practiced what some called 'pagan love,' others simply 'free love,' . . . taunted Chicago with . . . radicalism, . . . anarchism, . . . socialism, . . . and espoused new philosophies of art—cubism, imagism, dadism [*sic*]"; and of Harriet Monroe's *Poetry: A Magazine of Verse*, whose first issue appeared on 23 September 1912, and which inspired undergraduates at the nearby University of Chicago including Yvor Winters, Elder Olson, and two of De Vries's future *Poetry* colleagues, George Dillon and Jessica Nelson North.[31]

De Quincey did not lack for allies in legitimizing De Vries's restlessness, but it was evidently De Quincey who confirmed the young Calvinist as a "catholic":

> a philosopher should not see with the eyes of the poor limitary creature calling himself a man of the world, filled with narrow and self-regarding prejudices of birth and education, but should look upon himself as a catholic creature, and as standing in an equal relation to high and low, to educated and uneducated, to the guilty and the innocent.[32]

De Vries went away to college with a spirit of De Quincean unworld-liness and insouciance.

* * *

He was about as inconspicuous as a flamingo.—John Timmerman

In 1927 Peter De Vries "was sent to" Calvin College, Grand Rapids, Michigan, where he "disappointed his parents by not training for the ministry."[33] He chose instead to major in English.[34] An institution of the Christian Reformed Church, Calvin was then a "small . . . but vigorous" college.[35] The students numbered 315 in 1931; De Vries's graduating class consisted of "about 50 persons" and included nine future Ph.D.'s and eleven future clergymen.[36] The campus and school regimen have been described by De Vries's classmate John Timmerman:

> There were but three buildings on the campus; no coffee shop, and a tiny gymnasium. Chapel was held every day, and there were regularly held classes at 7:10 in the morning. . . . There was then so much history to learn that every student had to take two courses in it, so much English that every student had to take four, and so much Bible that every student had to take five courses in the subject. Clubs abounded, oratory and debate were major school activities.[37]

The requirements included more "French or German" than "Bible," however. De Vries took French.[38] He certainly had "a chance to explore, extend, and refine" his "Calvinist moorings" but "made his mark as a prize-winning extemporaneous speaker, a clever writer, and a boisterous editor."[39]

De Vries was on the Calvin debating team all four of his college years and represented Calvin in the Michigan Oratorical League during his junior and senior years. In 1930 he won the Broodman Contest with a speech titled "Bolshevism or Vaccinate," advocating adoption of socialist policies. In 1931 he won the Michigan Intercollegiate extemporaneous speaking championship.[40] His forensics skill was applauded: state oratorical contests were "massively attended and cheered by the students," and the 1931 college yearbook accorded him the tribute "his Alma Mater feels honored to have had him as her outstanding forensic representative of the past two years" and reprinted his Broodman speech.[41] De Vries's later recollection of himself as a speaker was laconic and self-deprecatory. In 1959 he told Allen B. Borden: "Possible psychological explanation: stuttered in childhood. Determined to show 'em. Showed 'em. Quit. . . . Now wouldn't go near lecture platform for $10,000 fee."[42]

In his senior year, De Vries edited the monthly *Calvin College Chimes*, "writing brilliant, breezy editorials and introducing the newspaper format."[43] Roderick Jellema gives a good account of the sort of editor De Vries was:

> Surely I am not the only *Calvin Chimes* editor of a later era who has stood in awe of the sharp-tongued predecessor who could refer to the college's Board of Trustees (clergymen all, at that time) as "this, the 1930 vest-pocket edition of the Sanhedrin," the members of which can claim fame only for their "ability to circumnavigate about the hole of a doughnut." Fortunately, De Vries found other tones to displace the bombastic style, the Carlylese, the Menckenese.[44]

De Vries did not moderate his tone soon enough. Although Timmerman records that De Vries "retired after the first semester, presumably from nervous exhaustion,"[45] it seems equally likely that official pressure forced him out. Another classmate, Henry Stob, recalled that De Vries "worked great changes in" the *Chimes* but "also parodied the faculty and trustees . . . and failed to last out the year."[46]

That De Vries left a distinct "mark" on Calvin College is evident from reports of him there: "Peter De Vries is familiar by name and by somewhat apocryphal reputation to many Christian Reformed folk."[47] "There is a considerable amount of De Vries folklore at Calvin College recalled by those who studied there with him, who taught him, who dated or dated with him." De Vries may have appeared as much athlete as aesthete, continuing to play basketball as he had in high school. His classmate Henry Stob avers "everyone liked him, he was not arrogant, not stand-offish, but was friendly, gracious, would quip a lot."[48] This image is indicative of easily worn conventionality and poise, and it gains in perspective from comparison with the behavior of three other Calvin students of the era who would gain prominence as writers, David De Jong ("rather unknowable"), his brother Meindert ("inscrutable" and "rather disdainful"), and another basketball player and future novelist, Frederick Feikema Manfred ("everything else [but writing] was secondary").[49] De Vries was, then, neither aloof nor scholarly. Of two "loose associations of undergraduates," named Conblow and Friggers, De Vries belonged to Conblow, "a collection known mainly for monkey-shining and drinking; the other was more academic." "On dates he was quiet and gentlemanly, but in a crowd might become zany—help direct traffic, say."[50]

In several accounts the zaniness predominates. De Vries reportedly lived in his apartment "in some disarray, throwing dirty socks, banana peels, and the like into one corner."[51] De Vries's wits, however, were advantageously arrayed, and he did stand out, according to Frederick

Manfred: "Peter De Vries was there [at Calvin], a senior when I was a freshman. De Vries was interesting. He was a rebel and a strange one; they didn't know how to handle him because he was so terribly bright. He was so witty that he would devastate people. The profs left him alone pretty much."[52] The bohemian collegian is memorably captured by Timmerman:

> He was about as inconspicuous as a flamingo. Suave and sophisticated in looks, chic and natty in dress, with a walk full of bounce and a vocabulary fully adequate to all occasions, he burst upon the campus like a meteor. He never did much for class, and I once saw him ordered out of one. He was sharing his wit too loudly. He was an extremely gifted orator whether competing in a state oratorical contest . . . or mounting the counter of the De Luxe Cafe and giving a spontaneous oration on Buffalo Bill. He was an amiable and likeable person. . . . I once visited his apartment on Wealthy Street next to the old Wealthy Theater. In the course of the conversation he engaged in a heated diatribe against a print he had hanging on the wall. He then opened the refrigerator, took out an egg, and hurled it on the middle of the print. We all watched the egg dribble to the floor. Later it struck me as a prophetically symbolic act. . . . If someone had asked me in our senior year at Calvin, "Is Peter De Vries going to be somebody?" I would have said, "Most certainly." If he had asked me "What?", I would have said, "Mayor of Chicago."[53]

But De Vries recalls a young Whitman, rather than a young Illinois politician, in Manfred's recollection:

> He visited me once when I was a senior. Suddenly here's this immaculate fellow, wearing gray spats, a gray hat, and a cane, super dressed. He walks in the room without knocking, starts looking around to see if my bed's made, goes over to touch the sill with a gray glove to see if it's clean, looks at the books I got there, looks down at what I'm writing, checks the closet, doesn't say a word, and then he goes to the door, and just as he steps out, he turns around and says, "You'll do." And walks out.[54]

Manfred's letters to De Vries of a few years later suggest both the intellectual vitality of Calvin College and De Vries's independence of mind:

> My dear Peter:
>   I'm glad to hear that you and Tip [Youngsma] are still the irrepressible and mentally curious men you were in college. I've always regretted the fact that I wasn't awakened enough from my Calvinistic, farmyardish torpor to have joined you then. You Chicago boys were awakened before

you started school. Despite the I.Q. faddists (and in affirmation of the recent Iowa studies in mental growth) I'm convinced it takes years to unearth a brain if the selfsame brain has been buried beneath prejudice, religion and has been deprived of words, ideas, theories, books and vital experiences in its early years.[55]

Peter De Vries received his B.A. in English from Calvin College in the spring of 1931. The Northwestern University summer session he attended that year concluded his formal education.[56]

* * *

To turn stumbling blocks into stepping stones—*pick up your feet.*—"Pepigram" by Chick Swallow in *Comfort Me With Apples*

De Vries's literary apprenticeship was served in Chicago during the Great Depression. While "by 1930 Renaissance was past,"[57] the Chicago literary scene was vital, and De Vries sought a place there. His first efforts were modest. In 1931 Peter apparently lived in the family apartment on Halsted Street, and his first job, which lasted for "a year or so," was "editing a community newspaper at a salary of twelve dollars a week."[58] The paper was the Auburn Park *Spotlight.*[59] De Vries said in 1962 "I wrote only a little [in college]. My first regular writing was for a community newspaper, a weekly, in Chicago. I wrote everything in it, but fell on evil days when I described some guy as being both a Mason and a Knight of Columbus."[60] This gaffe was received with neither levity nor mercy. The "guy" was "a local businessman" De Vries described "in one of my 'Personality of the Week' sketches,"[61] and the editor's dismissal or his resignation swiftly followed this offense.

A year or so as a journalist puts De Vries in the tradition of American novelists whose training grounds were newspapers, but De Vries's novels did not come quickly. He followed Poor Richard's path: "The result [of his newspaper work]: I truly enjoy local, homespun philosophers. Right on top of that I actually did write Pepigrams, for use as wall mottos and such. I got two bucks a Pepigram, and they got in my blood."[62] Pepigrams, an example of which heads this section, are "homespun" aphorisms. De Vries later sprinkled them throughout *Comfort Me With Apples,* a novel whose narrator is appalled at his own facility in confecting these pastilles of Main Street "pep."

In 1932 De Vries spent several months as a patient in a church-run tuberculosis sanatorium in Denver, Colorado.[63] On his return to Chicago, or soon thereafter, he regained ambition and energy. He wrote, "mostly poetry at first" and some stories, "went to work operating a candy-vending machine route," and contemplated a political career:

> I planned first to be a lawyer and politician. In college I'd won the Michigan intercollegiate extemporaneous speaking championship in 1931. It's a kindred impulse, oratory, to politics. In the mid-1930s I worked in a reform movement, the People's Political Alliance. We ran Paul Douglas for Mayor of Chicago against the Kelly-Nash machine. I was a sort of barnstormer to lure church people out, getting individual choirs into a mass choir, to sing Handel's Messiah, all for Paul Douglas. Is that funny or sad? I almost ran for alderman. I've often wondered what would have happened to me if. . . .[64]

Two writers say that the reform party offered De Vries the opportunity to run for alderman in 1936 but that he declined.[65] De Vries is quoted in 1959 to the effect that he actually had run for alderman: "It was in '36. A reform group asked me to run. We tried to organize under the auspices of the churches. No go. Then we tried to get at the churches by way of their choirs. At one meeting—Paul Douglas was to speak—all that turned up was a double quartet with one bass missing. The machine polled the largest vote ever."[66] In fact the Chicago mayoral primary and aldermanic elections were held on a snowy Tuesday, 26 February 1935. Democratic incumbent Mayor Edward J. ("Big Ed") Kelly, who had not bothered to campaign, won a record vote of 479,825 and the largest plurality to that time.[67] The "fusion party" of future U.S. Senator Paul Douglas, which had pledged "militant honesty in city affairs,"[68] fared ill: "While the Democrats were rolling up the votes in the snowdrifts and the Republicans were sticking in the igloos, the petition for the 'fusion party' faded in the blizzard."[69] The fate of the fusion party could have been expected; the *Chicago Tribune*, for example, ignored it except to report its failure. No Peter De Vries appears in the returns for the City Council election,[70] and it appears that by declining to run he avoided a pummeling. In any case, De Vries's political ambitions ended in 1935. His liberal Democratic allegiance never wavered, but his reformist fervor was redirected, much as the disappointed political hopes of the Romantics were converted into poetry.[71]

While Peter was challenging the Chicago Democratic machine from the progressive side, Joost De Vries was going conservative. Joost had voted for Franklin Delano Roosevelt in 1932 but "became a Roosevelt and New Deal-hater," perhaps, his son thinks, because of Henry Wallace's agricultural policies, which included the destruction of livestock to control prices: "Imagine what that economic measure did to people who emigrated because of hunger and poverty, from

European farm and fishing villages." Around the same time, 1936, Joost began to suffer bouts of melancholia and hypochondria; from 1937 until his death at eighty-five in 1959, he was in and out of a church-run sanatorium in Grand Rapids.[72] The onset of his father's condition, and the added responsibility, justified lamentation. But during and after his political foray, Peter directed his energy toward writing.

Between circuits of the candy-vending route and political meetings, De Vries was sizing up the opportunities for freelance writing: "In those days I would scour *Writer's Digest* for the 'little magazines' that had names like *Manuscript*. The first stories I sold—'sold' in quotes—I got nothing for them. Of course what I did then was aim for *Story* magazine. If you sold to *Story*, you could take the verb out of quotes. I can remember the ecstasy of pulling out of the mailbox the envelope and it obviously not containing my manuscript."[73] His first recorded publications came in 1934 in a little magazine titled *The Calithump* published in Austin, Texas, which brought out one story in May and another in July, and a magazine called *Bozart and Contemporary Verse*, published at Oglethorpe University in Georgia, which printed a poem in its November-December issue.[74] Although De Vries was not paid for this work, it appeared nicely typeset in attractive formats, albeit surrounded by mediocre material. The next year, in March, *Story* magazine brought forth a De Vries short story— half a year before the nonpaying *Manuscript* ran a De Vries piece. But 1935 was a bigger year than even the *Story* breakthrough would indicate.

In the autumn of 1933, the first issue of *Esquire* magazine had appeared and met with success. David Smart, its founder, had set up headquarters in Chicago, in the penthouse of the Palmolive (later the Playboy) building on Michigan Avenue's "Magnificent Mile." "Up in an overheated roost beneath the Lindbergh Beacon, editor Arnold Gingrich sat stoking his pipe and scribbling notes to 'Hem' and 'Dos' in Europe. Dreiser and Hemingway might drop in. Sexy cartoons, chic Varga girls, and ritzy cars, clothes, and cosmetics filled out *Esquire*'s pages. In 1935, Peter De Vries telephoned Gingrich and got an appointment to meet with him. De Vries "identified himself" with the line "I do nothing and writing." The savvy editor saw the humor in the twenty-five-year-old newcomer's work and accepted a story, which came out in the issue of February 1936.[75] Another De Vries piece ran in December, and in all, *Esquire* would print six De Vries prose pieces and eight poems during the thirties and forties. These early and sustained successes with the worldly *Esquire* are clear signs that it did not take transplantation to New York to sophisticate De Vries.

According to Ben Yagoda, De Vries "took up with the proletarian literary crowd, led by Nelson Algren and Jack Conroy, that was then in sway."[76] "The poems of a young West Sider named Nelson Algren" were also appearing in *Esquire*.[77] This was the decade of James Farrell's *Studs Lonigan* trilogy and of Algren's and Richard Wright's work for the Federal Writers' Project office in Chicago.[78] Several of De Vries's sketches suggest involvement in the leftward movement.[79] By publishing chic radicalism in *Esquire*, he turned his political sympathies to account.

De Vries continued to publish stories and poems throughout the thirties in little magazines, in *Story, Esquire*, and *Coronet*. No doubt much to De Vries's regret, "to his Dutch Calvinist parents, writing was not a proper endeavor. 'When I began to write,' De Vries says, 'it was almost by mutual consent—my parents never read anything I wrote.'"[80] Indeed, after witnessing his son "increasingly alienated from the fold partly as the result of schooling the family had made sacrifices to provide,"[81] Joost De Vries now had to "endure" Peter's success outside the Dutch community. In a weak moment Peter might have been tempted to dwell on his inability to share his "ecstasy" with his parents and on the ineffectualness of his success to relieve his father's gloom, but his temperament was against yielding to the temptation, and he had no time to brood.

Apparently in early 1938, De Vries "took or sent some poems to the magazine [*Poetry*], and became an editor."[82] He first appeared in *Poetry* with a lyric in the January 1938 issue, and his editorship seems the result of good fortune and pluck, neither of which was unusual in Chicago publishing at the time. Bernard Geis joined the *Esquire* staff "by walking in, hanging up his hat, and refusing to leave."[83] A News Note in the June 1938 issue of *Poetry* announces: "Because of the increasing quantity of manuscript, Jessica North no longer finds it possible to shoulder the full duties of associate editor. She has asked to be relieved of some of the work, in order to devote more time to her novel writing. Peter De Vries, who has been acting as first reader since April, has kindly consented to remain, and now joins the staff permanently as an associate editor."[84] De Vries now had real literary power.

De Vries's power did not, however, pay. Perhaps owing to his father's illness, his need for income seems to have increased, for his labors soon multiplied:

After a few years of [the candy-vending machine route] I sold some poems to poetry magazines (if you can call nothing-to [*sic*] twenty-five cents a line "selling") and I simultaneously became part-time associate editor of *Poetry,* without relinquishing the precarious living afforded by my two days a week on the candy route.

Without relinquishing either of these two jobs (listen carefully; this is where the going gets tricky), I took on a taffy apple route from a man who was going into another line of work. That added a few more days a week, making six in all (the editorship also took two days). In those years I also picked up money as a free-lance radio actor, lectured to women's clubs, and worked as a furniture-mover on one of my father's trucks. . . . I also tucked in a few dollars writing a rhymed table of contents for an advertising magazine. The editor of that periodical telephoned the editor of *Poetry* one day, asking if he could recommend a poet for this job. I said yes, I'd send one right over, and hot-footed it down there myself.

N[ewquist]. With all this going on, how did you manage to get any writing done?

De Vries: Your guess is as good as mine, but I did get it done. As a matter of fact, I finished a novel [i.e., *But Who Wakes the Bugler?*].[85]

Another recollection evokes the same frenetic activity:

Politics behind him, Mr. De Vries regards his big year as '38. Here is how he occupied his time:

"Wrote Pepigrams; was an editor of 'Poetry'; radio actor; wrote rhymed table of contents for an advertising digest; worked as a moving man fall and spring; lectured to women's clubs (I was reciting Dylan Thomas 'way back there); ran a candy machine service; had a taffy apple route in the suburbs starting from Cicero; ran an employment agency for a church. I never got anyone a job there, but had nine of them myself.

"On radio I did mugg parts, gangsters and, oddly enough, business-men heavies. At 'Poetry' we'd get a call from a station saying they had a part of a business man of the sort who'd have a son who read poetry. They'd ask what we would suggest, and I'd run right over.

I sold real good candy apples, caramel apples. They came twelve to a box, but I never dared open a box to eat one. Never a taffy apple to comfort me."[86]

De Vries turned this kaleidoscope of banality and elevation for sev-eral years; its variety, if not its pace, did not wind down until 1942 when he assumed the coeditorship of *Poetry.*

* * *

Undoubtedly [other literary periodicals'] specialization accounts for the short-livedness of many, a fact which confirms again the importance of what has always been one of POETRY's cardinal principles: catholicity.—Peter De Vries on *Poetry*'s thirtieth anniversary[87]

Upholding the "cardinal principle" of catholicity would be De Vries's pleasure and shared responsibility from April 1938 through September 1947: fully nineteen volumes of *Poetry*. He is on the masthead of volumes 52 through 60 (April 1938 through September 1942) as George Dillon's associate editor. According to "An Announcement" in the September 1942 issue, Dillon had been inducted into the armed forces 14 July, and "the magazine is now being edited by Peter De Vries, who served as associate editor for four years of Mr. Dillon's five, and Jessica Nelson North, whose association with *Poetry* dates back to 1927. Marion Strobel, also long familiar to our readers, returns to active service as associate editor" (348). De Vries and Jessica Nelson North, *de facto* coeditors in September 1942, are so listed in volume 61 (October 1942 through March 1943). Volumes 62 through 67 (April 1943 through March 1946) show De Vries and Marion Strobel as coeditors. At this point, Dillon returned from the service and resumed the editorship. Volumes 68 through 70 (April 1946 through September 1947) list De Vries as one of the contributing editors, and there the formal relationship ends. Only one interruption is noted: in March 1943 readers learned the U.S. Army had claimed another *Poetry* editor. "The induction of Peter De Vries deprives us of a first-rate editorial and creative talent" (699). In June 1943 the News Notes announce "Peter De Vries, having been given a medical discharge from the Army, returns to POETRY in his former capacity" (175).

At no time was Peter De Vries titular editor of *Poetry*, but he may have been a dominant coeditor: the News Note of March 1943 announcing his departure for the army acknowledges that "during the months since George Dillon's departure he has headed the editorial staff" (699), and the roster in *The Poetry Anthology* listing "The Editors of *Poetry* and the dates of their tenure" lists De Vries as "Peter De Vries, September 1942—April 1946 (with Jessica Nelson North, Marion Strobel, John Frederick Nims, and others),"[88] a signal that the *Poetry* archives accord De Vries the "head" chair at a round table. In sum De Vries understudied Dillon from April 1938 through August 1942, played the lead from September 1942 through March 1946, and had a supporting part until fall 1947. ("Understudy" may be taken literally; among De Vries's first duties was "at a banquet at the University of Chicago, . . . crawling around on my hands and knees under the speakers' table looking for Ford Madox Ford's glasses."[89])

The main questions are what De Vries did for *Poetry* and what *Poetry* did for De Vries, and it is instructive in both regards to consider his colleagues. George Dillon had attended the University of Chicago. At twenty-one, in 1927, he became associate editor of *Poetry*. His second collection of verse, *The Flowering Stone*, was awarded the Pulitzer Prize for Poetry in 1932, when he won a Guggenheim Award that "enabled him to spend two years in France."[90] He took over as *Poetry* editor in 1937 from Morton Dauwen Zabel, who had succeeded Harriet Monroe in 1936.[91] Dillon's catholic taste and his exuberant News Notes about new and sometimes outré developments in poetry indicate that he shared Harriet Monroe's willingness to nettle and to shock. On the page facing the announcement of De Vries's addition to the staff in the June 1938 number, for example, a News Note recommends a new quarterly, dedicated to the memory of D. H. Lawrence, called *The Phoenix*, which promises "'intimations of and clues to a renascent, joyous deliverance from the blight of Christianity and Christianity's murderous progeny—Fascism, Marxian Communism, and Democracy.' We like the thoroughgoing spirit of this, though when all the above are disposed of there will apparently be nothing left but the work of D. H. Lawrence, 'the phallos and the womb.'"[92]

Jessica Nelson North, another Chicago graduate, who joined the *Poetry* staff about the same time as Dillon, wrote poetry and a gritty 1935 novel, *Arden Acres*, which "shows 'the backwash of the depression' over a settlement of families living . . . southwest of Chicago." Her husband, Sterling North (Chicago class of 1926), worked for Henry Justin Smith at the *Chicago Daily News* (Smith also had hired Hecht, Sandburg, John T. McCutcheon, Meyer Levin, and Vincent Starrett), edited a little magazine called *The Forge* in the twenties, and published in 1939 the novel *Seven Against the Years*, which shows clear union and socialist sympathies.[93]

Marion Strobel (Mrs. James Herbert Mitchell), a friend of Harriet Monroe's and a visitor of the literary salons on Stony Island Avenue, was associated with *Poetry* from the midtwenties. She published verse in magazines ranging from *Poetry* and *The Saturday Review of Literature* to *Good Housekeeping*. Her 1930 novel *Saturday Afternoon* is a parodic treatment of the Chicago Renaissance; *A Woman of Fashion* (1931) is a "smartly facile" "study in narcissism" set on Chicago's North Shore, which Strobel knew firsthand; and *Sylvia's in Town* (1933) recounts how the arrival of Sylvia Fix among a set of wealthy Chicago suburbanites sets "everything off like firecrackers." Her *Fellow Mortals* of 1935 is the epic of a family that loses everything in the Depression. In the years of collaboration with De Vries on *Poetry*, she turned to mystery novels. *Ice Before Killing* (1943) is set among "the affluent and decadent people of the Near North Side"; its "interest lies in its portrayal of a society with too much money for its needs, too much leisure time, and a rather generous icing of snobbery, hate, jealousy and lack of morals." *Kiss and Kill,* tapping a similar vein, was published in 1946.[94]

Against the view that Peter De Vries did not meet the sophisticated world until he moved in 1944 to New York,[95] it bears emphasis that his colleagues in the *Poetry* office at 232 East Erie Street were a leftist cosmopolitan with a taste for antibourgeois art who had spent two years in Paris, a leftward-leaning chronicler of the oppressed with a close connection to the fraternity of the *Daily News,* and a Chicago Renaissance socialite with a talent for ice-cold portraiture and caricature. There would, moreover, be contributors to the magazine dropping into De Vries's office. Except for the grub-street gags about snatching rhymester jobs, De Vries said next to nothing in interviews about his years at *Poetry.* There is one odd aside in a *Time* mini-interview in 1959: "[De Vries] is happy that he is too old and his children too young to be beatniks. Says he: 'The beats just sit around contemplating each other's navels. In the '20s [*sic*] we had people like—well, I'll go no further than Maxwell Bodenheim. He once walked into the office and accused me of having a face unmarked by sorrow. I didn't know what to do. I just took the day off and went home.'"[96] De Vries's remark suggests that the *Poetry* office, located an easy stroll south from the *Esquire* office, a healthy walk north from Printer's Row where the journalists gathered, and a shade east of the fashionable near-north-side spots, saw noteworthy visitors.

The "authorized" annals of *Poetry, The Poetry Anthology 1912–1977: Sixty-Five Years of America's Most Distinguished Verse Magazine,* express no enthusiasm about what De Vries did for *Poetry.* Although the editors, Daryl Hine and Joseph Parisi, do include one of De Vries's lyrics in their selection, Hine's introduction treats De Vries's tenure as merely a custodianship:

After [Zabel's editorship], except for service in the Second World War, George Dillon remained as editor, sometimes single-handed, sometimes with varying combinations of others on the editorial board, until his resignation in 1949. This is a dark and vexed period, for the historian as well as for the anthologist, and the only time at which *Poetry* has not borne the imprint of one absolute and responsible editor and of one man's or woman's taste. Some of Dillon's associates, who occasionally replaced him on the masthead, included figures not always associated with Chicago, or with poetry: Thornton Wilder, S. I. Hayakawa, and Peter De Vries. Despite some extraordinary issues, such as the British one just mentioned and St.-John Perse's introductory appearance with *Exil* in 1941, the general literary picture of *Poetry* at this period is not distinguished. Whole volumes, such as LXV (1944) offer little one could really want to read now. Chicago writers, such as Helen Carus, Marion Castleman, Marie Boroff, Jeremy Ingalls, Paul B. Newman, and Ellen Borden Stevenson—also a trustee of the magazine—abound: not even Nelson Algren's "Man with the Golden Arm" can dispel the gloom. At the same time *Poetry* remained a mirror, if not always a bright one, for the wider literature of the period, publishing, among the better known names, Dannie Abse, Elizabeth Bishop, John Malcolm Brinnin, John Ciardi, Oliver St. John Gogarty, Leslie Fiedler, John Howard Griffin, William Meredith, Nicolas Morre, George Barker, Henry Treece, Horace Gregory, and Marya Zaturenska. There was a special issue on postwar Romanticism in England, and a Canadian issue edited by E. K. Brown. Canadians figure in other issues and among the recipients of *Poetry*'s annual prizes: P. K. Page, A. M. Klein, F. R. Scott, and—a temporary Canadian—Patrick Anderson. *Poetry* continued to fulfill an essentially catholic and passive role. George Dillon himself nursed a desire to "express the city in writing"—an ambition that reminds us of Harriet Monroe at her most self-consciously modern, as well as of Theodore Dreiser and Ben Hecht; but his romantic and lyric gift could not cope with such material.[97]

This account proclaims a bias against the catholicity De Vries took as axiomatic and judges the Dillon–De Vries years by values those editors did not share. Insistence upon a "distinguished" role for *Poetry* conceals their magazine's democratic energies.

Despite its being "a dark and vexed period," the ten years beginning with 1938 are represented, in an anthology of which the "object is to choose the best,"[98] by seventy-seven pages of poetry: an average of 7.7 pages per year, as compared with 7.1 per year for 1912–37 and 8.3 per year for 1947–77. Among the poets included by Hine and Parisi for 1938 through 1947 (to fill out their list, quoted above) are Delmore Schwartz, Yvor Winters, Dylan Thomas, Theodore Roethke, E. E. Cummings, Stephen Spender, Edna St. Vincent Millay, Brewster Ghiselin, W. H. Auden, Wallace Stevens, Randall Jarrell, Paul Engle, Gertrude Stein, William Empson, Louis MacNeice, Peter Vierick, Walter De La Mare, John Frederick Nims, Edwin Muir, Karl Shapiro, William Carlos Williams, Robinson Jeffers, David Daiches, Robert Penn Warren, Babette Deutsch, Langston Hughes, Basil Bunting, Weldon Kees, Robert Duncan, Louis Zukofsky, Howard Nemerov, Howard Moss, William Jay Smith, Gwendolyn Brooks, Kenneth Koch, James Merrill, Robert Lowell, Ezra Pound, Muriel Rukeyser, and Paul Goodman—many of these poets making their first appearances in *Poetry* during these years. Wallace Stevens, Edgar Lee Masters, Loren Eiseley, Conrad Aiken, Witter Bynner, and Vincent Starrett also were published, though their works from these years do not appear in the anthology. Dillon and De Vries were not stinting on poems for the cultivated taste. But their notion of *Poetry* included other voices, each of which could furnish a separate anthology: the politically engaged, the avant-garde, and the homespun.

Immediately preceding the June 1938 announcement of De Vries's addition to the staff, *Poetry* declares "We have the honor to announce that our July verse section will be devoted to the work of poets employed on the Federal Writers' Project throughout America. This special number, which has been made possible through the generous co-operation of Willard Maas, will offer a striking variety of style and subject-matter" (169). The "Federal Poets' Number" is notable for poems of social protest and poems of experiment. The two trends they represent, political and avant-garde, are prominent in the years of De Vries's involvement with *Poetry*. The *Poetry* of these years contains less news of grants, awards, and soirées than polemics about poetry and politics, announcements of upcoming issues of *New Masses*, recommendations of surrealist journals, and bulletins deploring fascist activities and, later, recounting the fortunes of poets in the military. The July 1938 issue contains black social protest, Sterling A. Brown's "The Young Ones"; international political protest, S. Funaroff's "To Federico Garcia Lorca"; stylistically daring works by Kenneth Fearing and William Pillin; and poems by Dorothy Van Ghent, Kenneth Rexroth, and Harold Rosenberg that contain unmistakably surrealist imagery. Archibald MacLeish proclaims "poetry becomes once again the one deliverer of the people," Alfred Kreymborg writes on "Bread and Poetry," and Malcolm Cowley describes the federal "Poetry Project." De Vries, in his first review in *Poetry*, acknowledges surrealist poet Charles Henri Ford's "splendid virtuosity," while wishing Ford less "vague" and more focused on "social consciousness" poems. Although the poems here do not jibe with the criteria for inclusion in *The Poetry Anthology*, and the concerns of the magazine at that time escape notice in the introduction to that volume, the contents of the Federal Poets' number are lively, engaged, and "vexed" in constructive ways.

The proletarian poet Thomas McGrath appeared often in *Poetry*, beginning with volume 54. Maxwell Bodenheim was another frequent contributor; his "Sonnet" deploring police brutality to picketers appeared in February 1940 (245). Nelson Algren, Langston Hughes (in militant, well-wrought poems excluded from *The Poetry Anthology*), Muriel Rukeyser, and many less renowned writers, such as Richard Leekley in his raised-fist salute "Remembrance of Karl Lockner" in February 1939 (235), contributed to the political voice of *Poetry*, a voice too genteel for the *Daily Worker* but more strident than was comfortable for plenty of readers.[99] De Vries himself bluntly asked, "How clean a bill of health, for instance, can we give ourselves on the count of race prejudice?" and answered that while Americans had not approached "the drunken ethnology of Fascism, the prejudice is nevertheless painfully evident here."[100] In 1939 the magazine looked so radical to one would-be contributor, who "could not help being puzzled by the consistent stream of material entering the magazine on no other discernible grounds than that it dealt with the class struggle," that he fudged a "hurried scrap with a social message," submitted it under a pseudonym, and got it accepted and published. Dillon dryly replied, to the author's confessional letter, that "we still think the poem . . . the best we have seen" by that author.[101] The May 1943 Latin American issue included the Marxist and avant-garde poets Pablo Neruda of Chile and Nicolas Guillén of Cuba.

While *Poetry* provided a forum for expressions of solidarity with the political left, it was also an outlet for writers of the "verbal left," in the sense given that phrase in 1940 by James Laughlin: "By 'verbal left' I mean that they have been influenced by Surrealism—especially by the indigenous variety developed by Dylan Thomas—and are working with association and the free imagery of the dream."[102] When Dylan Thomas first appeared in *Poetry*, in August 1938, his contributor's note called him "perhaps the best known of the surrealist poets writing in English" (304). Harold Rosenberg was referred to in a review as "an eclectic, stemming largely from Stevens and William Carlos Williams with the enlargement of surrealist relaxation."[103] *Poetry* frequently contained poems and articles by Eugene Jolas and by Edouard Roditi, who had direct connections with the Paris surrealists, as did the frequently published poet Charles Henri Ford. When Jolas first appeared in *Poetry*, in July 1939, the note read "Eugene Jolas, though he has not contributed previously to POETRY, is well known to our readers as the editor of *Transition*, the magazine of experimental art and literature which has outlasted all others of its kind. . . . He is at present living in Paris" (233). Ford, listed on the same page, is also "now living in Paris." Roditi, who was "doing research work at the University of Chicago" in 1939 and whom De Vries once met in the *Poetry* office,[104] was, like Jolas and Ford, identified with the international surrealist movement. *Poetry* was also friendly toward the work of George Barker and Oscar Williams—who were thought of as surrealists[105]—and of Eve Merriam and Garrett Oppenheim, whose contributions use surrealist imagery. When, in August 1943, De Vries published Rolfe Humphries's translation of Louis Aragon's "Petite Suite Sans Fil," the apostate surrealist's lines bore markings of the original impulses of automatic writing: "Monday to Sunday, the idiot radio / Spits crabs on Mozart, dedicates to you / Its endless O be still insulting brew" (247–48). *Poetry* at this time also published William Pillin and Stephen Stepanchev, stalwarts in the 1960s and 1970s of George Hitchcock's surrealist magazine, *kayak*. Other avant-garde contributors were Kenneth Fearing and Kenneth Patchen.

Poetry was indeed catholic throughout the period. It published a "farmhand poet" and gave space to a notice of a mimeographed magazine put out by some students in Virginia.[106] It published elite poets and street poets, celebrators and malcontents. It published, in quantity in 1943 and 1944, traditional verse of varying degrees of sophistication, right down to some "homespun rhymes" in May 1944 that remind one of De Vries's genuine fondness for "homespun philosophers." But De Vries was doing nothing else than, as he had vowed, carrying forward Harriet Monroe's policy of inclusiveness. The founder's own catholicity had comprised "plasmodial delerium," as Yvor Winters referred to Carl Sandburg's later poetry, and "a certain amount of 'primitive' verse, cowboy ballads and Indian chants of varying degrees of inauthenticity."[107]

Yet not much was simple, least of all the feat of keeping the magazine going. *Poetry*'s solvency was in doubt, as frequent blandishments and benefits attest. De Vries became a mendicant, debtor, and extortionist: "Editorial toils . . . regularly alternated with time-outs to beg, borrow or bludgeon our tiny salaries out of civic-minded patrons. I say civic-minded because Chicago has always been proud of *Poetry*'s deficit. The magazine's annual critical financial illness was always reported in the newspapers somewhere near the obituary page."[108] Prominent magazines all over were in narrow straits.[109] Like other editors, De Vries had to be something of an impresario. In August 1939 he was scheduled to "conduct a poetry round-table" at a vacation school in the Hiawatha National Forest near the resort town of Escanaba, Michigan.[110] On another occasion, he tried to organize, with the help of Al Monroe, the theater editor of the *Chicago Defender*, "A Midsummer Night's Jam," hoping to include Count Basie, Dorothy Donegan, and some Chicago boogie woogie pianists of whom De Vries and S. I. Hayakawa were fans.[111] Guest speakers, including Frank Lloyd Wright, Rudolph Ganz, Robert Penn Warren, and James Thurber, were invited to give benefit lectures; Warren and Thurber became lifelong friends of De Vries.[112] And De Vries scrimped (to save paper a letter to Paul Engle about the jam session is typed on both sides of the *Poetry* stationery). Thanks to his efforts, the magazine managed.

* * *

It will be observed that in all of the instances in which I felt like a
Thurber drawing there were women around.—Peter De Vries in "James
Thurber: The Comic Prufrock"

De Vries, operating under the Keystone Kops conditions earlier
described, managed to publish his first novel, *But Who Wakes the Bugler?* with Houghton Mifflin on 19 September 1940.[113] *The New Republic* dismissed it in two sentences, and *The New Yorker*'s note, despite
Houghton's taking out a nice display ad on the facing page, would
not encourage purchase.[114] But other reviewers welcomed De Vries's
words, and the pictures by the cartoonist Charles Addams, with enthusiasm.[115] The novel, retailing for two dollars and fifty cents, did
not sell out its first printing of four thousand copies.[116] Critical praise
followed by relatively modest (though larger) sales would be the typical reception of De Vries's novels. The exceptions were De Vries's
second and third novels, *The Handsome Heart* (1943) and the political
satire *Angels Can't Do Better* (1944), whose modest sales followed
choruses of negative reviews, and several later novels that became
best-sellers.[117]

On 16 October 1943 De Vries married Katinka Loeser, and "everything fell into place after that."[118] Loeser was a young woman from
Ottumwa, Iowa, and 1936 graduate of the University of Chicago who
had published poems in *Poetry* in January 1941 and April 1942.[119]
The latter group of four poems was awarded the Jeannette Sewell
Davis Prize for a young poet, bearing an award of one hundred dollars, in November 1942, and De Vries had the pleasure of conferring
the prize.[120] According to a 1981 *Publishers Weekly* interview with De
Vries and Loeser, the honoree "had left her native Iowa to teach at
a girls' school in Chicago and to 'hang around' at the magazine, until,
she recalls, she was given the job of writing obits for its morgue."[121]
The contributor's note of January 1941 indicates that she was then
already living in Chicago. In the March 1943 *Poetry* she was named
an associate editor (699), and she continued as associate editor and
then contributing editor for the duration of her husband's tenure. As
De Vries told Ben Yagoda, "Getting married on $25 a week was an
act of faith. But my bread fell butter-side-up."[122] To supplement his
income, De Vries wrote book reviews for the *Chicago Sun Book Week*,
including a favorable review of Saul Bellow's first novel, *Dangling
Man*. Although the two men never met, De Vries and Bellow had
common friends in Chicago.[123]

James Thurber was one of De Vries's heroes in those days,[124] and
De Vries wrote an appreciative essay titled "James Thurber: The
Comic Prufrock" for the December 1943 *Poetry*. He asserts not only

that Thurber has more in common, especially in such sketches as "The Black Magic of Barney Haller," with modern poets than with modern humorists, but that "the middle-aged man on the flying trapeze"—the archetypal Thurber protagonist referred to in the title of Thurber's 1935 collection—is the "comic counterpart" of Eliot's antihero. The article is embellished with Thurber's winsome sketch of Pegasus (later the *Poetry* logo).[125] In mid-November 1943 De Vries sent Thurber an advance copy of the article. "Thurber was instantly taken with the piece . . . struck not only by the editor's flattering analysis but by a critic taking him seriously, the bugbear of his middle age."[126] De Vries had, in fact, "established Thurber criticism" with "the first serious discussion of Thurber in the United States," "the first and perhaps still the best."[127] Even De Vries's choice of "Barney Haller" was felicitous: Thurber had declared in a 1935 letter to friends that of all the stories in *The Middle-Aged Man on the Flying Trapeze* it was his "special favorite."[128] By the following spring, James Thurber had decided to make Peter De Vries his protege.[129]

Thurber, fifty years of age, a *New Yorker* staff member since 1927 when the magazine was two years old and now the dean of American humorists, lost no time in replying to his Chicago admirer. His warm return letter of 19 November 1943 noted "with pardonable pride" that Eliot himself had praised *My Life and Hard Times*.[130] It occurred to De Vries to invite Thurber to deliver a benefit lecture for *Poetry*, and, "at the urging of his wife,"[131] he made the effort. Thurber and De Vries exchanged some "oblique, tentative correspondence on the subject" and agreed to meet in New York to discuss the plan. Accordingly the De Vrieses took a "postponed honeymoon" in the winter of 1944, were welcomed by Thurber at his East Side apartment, and made arrangements for an 8 April lecture.[132] This was a coup, for Thurber regarded the lecture platform with extreme aversion. As the date drew near, he wrote De Vries complaining that "last night I got to fussing so profoundly about my coming ordeal that I developed a sharp pain in my stomach." Fortunately Helen Thurber assisted him by getting pencil and paper in the middle of the night and jotting down some ideas.[133] But in Thurber's Ambassador East hotel room on the eve of the lecture, Thurber and De Vries thought up "a rather shabby little stratagem," as De Vries put it, to "lighten the miseries of public speech":

> Thurber had declined to give a formal lecture but would not mind answering questions. To make it even more foolproof, I myself made up the questions the audience would ask: questions for which the remarks he was smoothly and eloquently getting off in the relaxation of the hotel

room—about men, women, dogs—would serve beautifully as answers. It would be as simple as putting nickels in a jukebox, and as painless for him. It was a quiz show in reverse. I scribbled down the queries, hastily tailoring them to fit the gems dropping from his lips. I wrote all these questions out in advance on slips of paper of different sizes, shapes and even colors, to bolster the fiction that they had just been jotted down by members of the audience.[134]

Concocting the ruse, "we had a pleasant evening together with our wives," De Vries recalled.[135]

When the Saturday morning crowd was gathered in the Arts Club "located in that pastry chef's dream, the Wrigley Building," Thurber took off with the first bogus question and proved himself "one of the great monologists of our time."[136] De Vries subsided backstage, discarding his prompts, but he had "provided an introduction so full of wit and outrageous puns (he described Thurber as an artist who 'hits the male on the head') that many in the audience thought that he was Thurber."[137] Thurber later told De Vries it was that introduction that convinced him De Vries really ought to join *The New Yorker*.[138]

There was an obstacle, in Harold Ross, founder and editor, to just anyone joining the *New Yorker* staff. However Thurber came to possess a selection of De Vries's manuscripts—the De Vries aficionado says his man took the initiative, the Thurber scholar says "Thurber asked De Vries for some samples of his work"[139]—Thurber had an inside track to Ross, and Thurber's account of his success is worth savoring:

Fifteen years ago I brought [Ross] a sheaf of some miscellaneous writings by Peter De Vries, whom I had met in Chicago, where he was then editor of *Poetry*, and told Ross I had found a perfect *New Yorker* writer. He stared at the material glumly, and said, "I'll read it, but it won't be funny and it won't be well written." Two hours later he called me into his office. Hope had risen like a full moon and shone in his face. "How can I get DeVree on the phone?" he demanded, his enthusiasm touched with excitement. Not many days after that Ross and I had lunch at the Algonquin with Peter DeVree—the name had become wedged in Ross's mind as French, not Dutch, and he was sure the sibilant should go unsounded, as in *debris*, and he never got it straightened out. I had warned Pete, since I was a veteran of such first meetings, that Ross's opening question might go off in any direction, like an unguided missile. "Hi, DeVree," said Ross as they shook hands. "Could you do the Race Track department?" This was the kind of irrelevancy I had in mind, and Pete was prepared for it. "No," he said, "but I can imitate a wounded gorilla." He had once imitated a wounded gorilla on a radio program in Chicago.

Ross glared at me, realizing I had briefed De Vries, and then his slow lasting grin spread over his face. "Well, don't imitate it around the office," he growled amiably. "The place is a zoo the way it is." Thirty years ago Ross would probably have opened up on De Vries with "Maybe you could run the magazine" or "Could you write the Talk department?"[140]

The gorilla performance actually took place just the week before, when De Vries "had played the parts of both a mad scientist and an ape that was terrorizing him."[141]

De Vries received the good news of his appointment in Thurber's oversized hand (the great cartoonist was already nearly blind) in a letter dated 14 June 1944:

> Dear Peter:
> By this time you have Ross's dazed and adoring letter—his first twisting into skyrockets in many years. And the fireworks are all deserved.
> I had handed the whole sheaf of your stuff to Ross who had said, sighing, "I'll read it, but it won't be any good." Half hour later [*sic*] he called me in and said, "Jesus Christ! It *is* good!"
> Thus in 1944 the advent of Peter De Vries.[142]

The letter went on in avuncular fashion, recommending a part-time appointment to reserve time for De Vries's own work, reassuring him that Thurber would be there to defend De Vries if necessary, expressing unbounded confidence in his talent, and even admonishing the new man to keep a carbon copy of his contributions.[143]

* * *

> So we moved to New York, and that was my introduction to the tents of wickedness.—Peter De Vries, interviewed by Ben Yagoda

Little of De Vries's life after he traded the green awnings of Division Street America for the striped canopies of Vanity Fair has received his chronicling. Although his "hermetically sealed" childhood has been opened by his own accounts and analyzed in the commentaries of others, the details of his life as a *New Yorker* staff member and celebrated author remain sketchy except to those researchers daring enough to read his biography in his imaginative works.[144] The available information, however, permits an episodic account that indicates how an extravagant imaginative life can coexist with domesticity and how a surrealist ticket may lead to as improbable a place as Westport. Peter De Vries and Katinka Loeser moved to New York on Labor Day 1944 and took an apartment at 32 West Eleventh Street in Greenwich Village.[145] De Vries assumed his *New Yorker* duties, which consisted of "two days as a poetry editor and two days on the 'rough basket,' where newly submitted cartoons were screened" each week. This was a "part-time" job with a vengeance, and because De Vries was also coediting *Poetry* until March 1946, he actually had little time for his own work. He published nothing in 1944 but what had already been written in Chicago and nothing at all in 1945.[146]

From 1947 on, De Vries's work at *The New Yorker* was in the art department.[147] For many years he dodged the question of what he did there. "Three days a week he comes to town for activities at the *New Yorker.* His work there he describes as 'utility man in the Art Department,' while others around the place describe him as a force in the Bull Pen" (1956 version). "Anybody who can clearly describe his functions on the New Yorker is regarded as a freak, so I'll content myself with saying simply that I go in a few days a week to finger pieces of paper having to do with comic art" (1964 version). It was *People Magazine* that elicited a bit more information in 1980: De Vries "helps out" in the art department twice a week. " 'If you can describe what you do accurately, you're regarded as a suspicious character there,' he says. But he admits to helping select cartoons and 'fiddling with captions.' " Finally, in 1983, Ben Yagoda overcame De Vries's diffidence:

> Further investigation reveals that the vagueness extends beyond De Vries himself. "I'm not sure what Peter does," says Whitney Darrow Jr., a veteran New Yorker cartoonist. "He's sort of a mystery man." Finally, the art editor, Lee Lorenz, reveals De Vries's precise duties: He is presented each week with a list of that issue's cartoon captions and is invited to suggest improvements.
>
> This might strike some people as the best single job in the world. De Vries's hesitancy to discuss it may spring from a desire to uphold the myth that cartoonists' works are never altered. In any case, when confronted at a subsequent meeting with Lorenz's testimony, De Vries comes clean. Yes, he works on the captions; in past years he often thought up gags for cartoons, the execution of which was farmed out to artists. He doesn't remember most of the cartoons. One of the few he does takes place in the loan department of a bank. A customer is saying to an officer, "Gee, thanks. I don't know how I'll ever repay you."[148]

Although he held conceivably "the best single job in the world," De Vries is mentioned neither in Brendan Gill's *Here at the New Yorker* nor E. J. Kahn, Jr.'s *About the New Yorker and Me*.[149] The omission would appear to fit the notion of *The New Yorker* as "traditionally . . . a rabbit warren of isolated writers, each of whom comes and goes to his office without speaking to his neighbors."[150] On the other hand, there is the testimony of Brendan Gill: "I omitted De Vries from my book only because I had little to say about him. A charming friend, a useful member of the 'New Yorker' family, but his main literary reputation has been gained by his books."[151] De Vries continued on the *New Yorker* staff until 1987, serving as a consultant for several years afterward.[152]

"In the early days of [the De Vrieses'] marriage his writing space was a corner of their small bedroom, further cluttered by a crib. 'My typewriter stand was always full of talcum powder,' he remembered. 'I am not an advocate of the principle that a writer should be tormented but not disturbed.'"[153] (The principle applies to books as well as authors; in a 1948 article for *Esquire*, De Vries recounts how his wife solved the space limitations of the postwar housing shortage by filing canned goods behind the classics on their bookshelves.[154]) The De Vrieses soon had four children: Jan, born 9 January 1945; Peter Jon, 26 March 1947; Emily, 26 October 1949; and Derek, 19 November 1952.[155] De Vries once said, discussing his style and his work habits, "The writer's problem . . . is how to make a living with four or five children."[156] He was solving this problem. In 1946 he won a thousand dollar award from the American Institute of Arts and Letters, "when I was safe in *The New Yorker* editorial offices and didn't need the money."[157] In 1948 the growing family moved to comfortable Westport, Connecticut, where they took the first of their three houses in the area.[158] De Vries turned out casuals, poems, and parodies for *The New Yorker*, with occasional pieces for *Harper's* and *Holiday*, during 1946–56. Thurber, meanwhile, was promoting De Vries right and left. He wrote his friends Herman and Dorothy Miller, "You will see pieces soon by Peter De Vries, whom I brought on from Chicago, where he was editor of *Poetry* magazine at $25 a week. Thurber, they say, is always right about talent." To Allen Churchill, Thurber wrote "This is Peter De Vries, who has since done excellent things for us."[159]

One cold night in late February 1950, John Malcolm Brinnin, who was now director of the Poetry Center of the YM-YWHA in New York and a Westport neighbor, dropped in on the De Vrieses with Dylan Thomas. By this first Sunday of Thomas's first American tour, Brinnin was beginning to realize what he had let himself in for by volunteering to be Thomas's American lecture agent, and he was nervous. He later recalled that "[De Vries] and his wife, Katinka, made good easy company and served us proper drinks until well after midnight."[160] Brinnin's tone is that of gratitude for so sedate an evening. De Vries's recollection is that "Dylan described the plot of a film he had seen, and then declaimed some *Lear*. He rather talked us into the ground. He made some remark to Katinka about talking a lot of bullshit, which she didn't contradict."[161] De Vries told Thomas that "I had lectured on him and publicly read his poems as early as 1938 in Chicago, but he didn't seem much interested. We had both been radio actors."[162] De Vries "felt sympathetic and friendly towards this strange man coming in out of the night. . . . But the Thomas legend was not constructed out of such ordinary occasions."[163] De Vries would give the "Thomas legend" its funniest and somberest rendition in his 1964 novel *Reuben, Reuben.*

In 1952 Little, Brown published *No But I Saw the Movie,* a collection of De Vries's *New Yorker* stories. The book was well received and inaugurated a thirty-three-year relationship between De Vries and the Boston publisher. Five novels followed swiftly: *The Tunnel of Love* (1954), *Comfort Me With Apples* (1956), *The Mackerel Plaza* (1958), *The Tents of Wickedness* (1959), and *Through the Fields of Clover* (1961). De Vries was typecast as the suburbs' comic laureate despite his prompt protestations.[164] It is true that these volumes take a mocking look at Westport:

> *Interviewer:* Do people around here think they recognize themselves in such books of yours as "The Tunnel of Love" and "Comfort Me With Apples"?
> *De Vries:* If they do, they don't say so. They would be lampooning themselves.[165]

But De Vries did not want to be read as merely a raconteur of middle-class follies. He saw his surroundings as a microcosm reflecting the universal.

The Tunnel of Love was De Vries's first major popular success. It was selected by the Atlantic Book Club and became a best-seller.[166] In 1956 De Vries collaborated with Joseph Fields on a stage version. The play premiered on Broadway on 13 February 1957, starring Tom Ewell, Nancy Olson, Darren McGavin, Elisabeth Fraser, Sylvia Daneel, and Elizabeth Wilson.[167] James Thurber almost spoiled the debut by monopolizing the Algonquin reception after the performance, and *The New Yorker* panned the play, but the show was a success.[168] A movie version starring Doris Day, Richard Widmark, and Gig Young followed. The *Wilson Library Bulletin* could report that De Vries's first novel since he moved East and joined *The New Yorker* "garnered fabulous riches as best seller, smash Broadway hit, and Hollywood film."[169] De Vries had attained celebrity status, and people wanted to interview him.

In his first recorded interview, with Lewis Nichols of the *New York*

Times, De Vries says he lives in Westport "in a state of hand-to-mouth luxury," collecting clichés to use in his work while riding the commuter train to and from New York City and attending cocktail parties. Readers of *Time* saw him at home at "the ten-room, one-acre De Vries place in Westport" and taking his four children out in winter to skate "like my father did on the frozen canals of Holland, with the kids strung out behind me like a bunch of Dutchmen." Readers of *Newsweek* saw him "49, tall and graying"; "his generously featured face suggests a battery of ill-concealed satiric weapons." The *New York Herald Tribune* recorded that "most of my spare time is spent these days playing with the children, whether they like it or not," and that De Vries's habit of requesting a Coke or Seven-Up from hostesses set up to serve scotch and bourbon "has prompted Jean Stafford to describe me as 'a problem drinker.'"[170]

The tenor of all these reports varies between cheerfulness and gaiety. With notoriety, though, came a controversy that made the pages of *Newsweek* on 28 September 1959. The Westport Parent-Teachers Association Council had determined it would help the local Community Theater produce four performances of *The Tunnel of Love* to raise funds. Several Catholic PTA members consulted their pastor, the Reverend Cornelius Looney, as to the advisability of this project, in view of the risqué content of the play. "Father Looney advised them that the Catholic Legion of Decency had labeled the movie version of 'Tunnel' immoral," whereupon one of the PTA groups, the Green Farms unit, withdrew its support from the play, and even the unit to which Peter De Vries belonged, the Burr Farms unit, wavered. De Vries attended none of the presumably tempestuous meetings but is quoted in *Newsweek* as calling the Green Farms PTA "invertebrate," denouncing the clergy for "meddling in secular affairs," and adding that in matters of sex "I'm not interested in the opinions of celebates [*sic*]."[171] The play went on as scheduled in October, but the surrounding spectacle was evidently repugnant, and De Vries apparently did no more interviews for several years.

It was at this time that the De Vrieses suffered the anguish of learning Emily De Vries had leukemia. The diagnosis was followed by a protracted illness whose characteristic rhythm of attack and remission ended when Emily died on 19 September 1960. *Through the Fields of Clover*, published 13 February 1961, is dedicated "To Emily with love." Peter De Vries's next novel, *The Blood of the Lamb*, which tells the story of a man whose little girl dies of leukemia, is dedicated "To Jan, Jonny, and Derek."

With the death of James Thurber on 4 November 1961, De Vries lost his mentor and an old friend. They had shared not only a midwestern background and an enthusiasm for elaborate word games but a keen appreciation for each other's work. It was a family friendship: Helen Thurber wrote the De Vrieses from European trips she and her husband took in 1955 and 1958 to recount happy times.[172] When James grew unhappy with the direction *The New Yorker* was taking in the early 1950s, he wrote candidly to "one of his few intimates left on the staff," Peter De Vries.[173] When Thurber's *Years with Ross* (1959) shook up the *New Yorker* inner circle, De Vries defended the book with a mollifying comment. Toward the end, Thurber was erratic and paranoid, but he seems never to have doubted De Vries. He wrote to Milt Greenstein on 26 April 1961, with reference to the *New Yorker* staff, "I shall always want to see you . . ., Pete De Vries, . . . and a few others." By 11 May he was writing a letter to De Vries claiming the "new world plague" was being spread by "mass mental telepathy." In late August, very ill and unmanageable but refusing treatment, he called De Vries:

> In his liberated wandering about the city like a helpless stray, Thurber sought out a few people he still trusted, trying to wring some direction and comfort from them. He telephoned Peter De Vries and asked to see him. "I went over to the Algonquin," De Vries said, "and just talked quietly to him. He swore he hadn't had a drink in four days. At that moment, he wanted some companionship, and there was still a trace of the old Thurber compassion shining through all that sick bitterness.[174]

When the Time Reading Program issued Thurber's *Lanterns & Lances* the following year, the special edition bore a "New Introduction by Peter De Vries" that concluded, "Thus his humor performed supremely the office of that precarious art, which is to keep ourselves in focus, in perspective and in balance. For all this, and so much more, we and our successors can be grateful to old Jim Thurber and his very keen vision."[175]

Critics saw a bleaker, blacker strain of humor in De Vries's novels of the 1960s. The author acknowledged it but seemed to wonder who thought that his levity had ever been unmixed with pain.[176] After *The Blood of the Lamb* (1962) came *Reuben, Reuben* (1964), *Let Me Count the Ways* (1965), *The Vale of Laughter* (1967), and *The Cat's Pajamas & Witch's Milk* (1968), each a dialectic of hope versus despair, rebellion versus resignation. A successful Broadway play, *Spofford* (1967), was adapted by Herman Shumlin from the first book of *Reuben, Reuben*. It starred Melvyn Douglas with Barbara Britton and prompted Walter Kerr to the uncharacteristic exclamation "hail De Vries." The movie *Reuben, Reuben* (1983), written by Julius J. Epstein and starring Tom Conti and Kelly McGillis, was based loosely on

Shumlin's play and the second book of the novel. *Let Me Count the Ways* was adapted by Everett Freeman and Karl Tunberg in the film *How Do I Love Thee?* (1970) with Jackie Gleason, Maureen O'Hara, and Shelley Winters. Critics regarded it as an exercise in miscasting, and it flopped. Epstein wrote and produced the film *Pete 'n' Tillie* (1972) based on *Witch's Milk*. This production, starring Walter Matthau, Carol Burnett, and Geraldine Page, was a critical and popular success and De Vries's favorite movie adaptation of any of his works.[177] De Vries occasionally appeared in periodicals during the decade, and he wrote two more introductions for the Time Reading Program.[178]

During the turbulent sixties, topical references enter De Vries's work, and he wrote for the record on the war in Vietnam. His statement appears in *Authors Take Sides on Vietnam* (1967), whose editors, imitating a 1937 questionnaire sent by W. H. Auden, Louis Aragon, Stephen Spender, and Nancy Cunard on the Spanish Civil War, asked: "Are you for, or against, the intervention of the United States in Vietnam? How, in your opinion, should the conflict in Vietnam be resolved?" De Vries voices a cogent, informed, and politically astute opinion:

The pedigree of errors is a long one. A decade ago we opposed the election prescribed by the Geneva Conference on the ground that it would result in a Communistic government, but it is interesting, in the light of recent events, to speculate on what that might in turn have led to. Given the strong nationalistic thrust of Vietnamese revolutionaries and the instinctive fear of being sucked into the Peking vacuum cleaner, a fresh young Marxist regime not dependent on China for support against a Western power might by now be contributing its bit toward the decentralization of world communism, along with North Korea, Yugoslavia, and, of course, China herself. The suspicion even begins to form in one's mind that the way to contain Red China might be with a ring of left-wing states. We for our part, at any rate, are doing our best to unify that squabbling family. With every bomb we drop in a war that apparently can never be won, we are driving Hanoi closer to Peking, and more Vietnamese nationalists into the National Liberation Front. Given time, we might even heal the breach between Peking and Moscow.

I think we should stop all bombing instantly (the lunacy of supposing it could destroy the will to fight should be clear to anyone able to imagine what bombs raining on American soil would do to ours) and limit any military activities to a defensive perimeter behind which to escalate the war against poverty and against social and political misery and inequality in that tormented land. This means rallying the basic nationalistic aspirations of the Vietnamese people behind somebody other than an avowed admirer of Hitler—that man shoulder-to-shoulder with whom the hawks fancy themselves as resisting a new Munich.[179]

This policy was advocated by, among others, the distinguished University of Chicago professor of political science Hans J. Morgenthau. Its reasoning is based on a principle, expressed here in the phrase "able to imagine," put forth by Shelley.

Despite his earlier animadversions about public speaking, during the sixties De Vries lectured at the University of Virginia (the Emily Clark Balch Lectures, 1962), Villanova (1966), and the University of Michigan (1968). In 1968 the University of Bridgeport made him a Doctor of Humane Letters. He was elected to the National Institute of Arts and Letters in 1969.[180] His modesty at the receipt of honors could take the form of facetiousness. When, in January 1969, the Princeton Theological Seminary invited De Vries to deliver the Stone lectures, he demurred saying "I have nightmares about accepting . . . I just can't believe theologians want to listen to me lecture. It's probably a clerical error."[181]

De Vries did give the most substantive interviews of his career: those with Roy Newquist in 1964, Douglas M. Davis in 1965, and Richard B. Sale in 1968, where he discussed his ideas about humor ("What is art, but a way of sharing experience. . . . As for the humorist, he does not laugh so much at mankind, as he invites mankind to laugh at itself"), his notions about himself ("like most humorists, I'm my own best butt. I don't think I have enough lemon in me to be a satirist"), and his working habits ("I like to get cuttin' early, like a surgeon, not too long after daybreak, after my characters have had another ghastly night's sleep in the hospital of my mind. . . . Morning is boss"). While De Vries sounds relaxed voicing his personal opinions, someone took considerable care in editing the transcripts of these interviews, for later statements repeat or improve upon earlier ones.[182]

Collecting scattered *New Yorker* and other pieces is the function of *Without a Stitch in Time* (1972), but inventing, not reprising, was De Vries's main activity during the 1970s and 1980s. Answering a 1978 *Writer's Digest* questionnaire, he owned to drinking "moderately to heavily" of "the masculine Montrachet and the feminine Musigny," noting, "Reality is impossible to take neat, we must dilute it with alcohol,"[183] but he neither sought inspiration nor suffered interference with his writing from that source. De Vries maintained a steady production of the urbane comic novels that portray, in Anthony Burgess's words, "an only slightly exaggerated picture of crazy America" in the "major style" he invented.[184] Their titles a litany of allusions—

Mrs. Wallop (1970), *Into Your Tent I'll Creep* (1971), *Forever Panting* (1973), *The Glory of the Hummingbird* (1974), *I Hear America Swinging* (1976), *Madder Music* (1977), *Consenting Adults, or The Duchess Will Be Furious* (1980), *Sauce for the Goose* (1981), *Slouching Towards Kalamazoo* (1983), *The Prick of Noon* (1985), and *Peckham's Marbles* (1986)—these novels are minority reports, records of civil disobedience to social and aesthetic conventions, filed by a man who could provide a peripheral view of our culture and a sharp focus on its center.

The novelist's wife, Katinka Loeser, died at the age of seventy-seven on 6 March 1991.[185] After a period of declining health, Peter De Vries suffered a series of strokes early in 1993 and died of pneumonia at Norwalk, Connecticut, Hospital on 28 September 1993, at the age of eighty-three. Eulogized in the days following in the diverse styles of *The New Yorker, Time,* the *Des Moines Register,* and many more, De Vries was perhaps most appreciatively remembered by Paul Theroux in a December reminiscence that celebrates De Vries's "many gifts," most especially his generosity.[186]

The culture had repaid De Vries generously, not only with material and symbolic success (*Consenting Adults,* for example, became a Book-of-the-Month Club "Christmas dividend"),[187] but also the distinction of election, in May 1983, to the American Academy of Arts and Letters.[188] Only Mark Twain, Joel Chandler Harris, and E. B. White, among American humorists, had previously been favored with election to the academy, which in De Vries's case was accompanied by a citation written by his old friend and Westport neighbor Robert Penn Warren.[189] Interview-articles of 1980 in *People* and 1983 in the *New York Times Magazine* portrayed a man with "an air of unshakable dignity," shy, "resolutely unjolly," but witty.[190] Although he always avoided promotional tours, his books did well, though not as well as friends like Calvin Trillin thought they should, and a publisher announced plans to issue all the books in paperback.[191] Pleasantly famous, De Vries was decorously amused by the very concept of fame: "My secret ambition is to sell a million copies of every book . . . and then also have a small, select cult of aficionados who look down on my mass audience."[192] The *People* piece, consonant with the theme and format of that magazine, includes a picture of De Vries dandling his grandson Gabriel, another snapshot of the author seated at his desk in his *New Yorker* office, and "the definitive photograph of the author, in a tuxedo, leaning on a lawn mower, with a look of killingly suave insouciance upon his face."[193] This last picture bears a touch of Daliesque incongruousness and recalls Mr. Shrubsole in *Sauce for the Goose,* who had "premises to keep and miles to mow before I sleep."

3

Peter De Vries and 1930s Surrealism

> The truth is that surrealism, or whatever other thing you want to call that
> magnificent obsessive journey the people who are really alive in this
> century have been taking, has barely started.—Caliban[1]

PETER De Vries belongs among those authors for whom the very
existence of the artwork poses some sort of problem. Such writers
tend to interrogate aesthetic forms and to apologize for them: Chaucer
recants his poems; Cervantes deplores fiction; both invent parables
about artistic representation, and their works call attention to their
own artifices, not unlike those of John Barth and other writers of
"metafiction." De Vries rejected his antiaesthetic upbringing before
he began to write, but he is aware of it over his shoulder. There is
always something renegade and often something contrite in his writing, which frequently reveals an effort to circumvent the art-versus-
life (or art-versus-dogma) dilemma by depicting the world as a work
of art and by making the writing a container of the world.

De Vries's first published story and poem share an image that
incorporates the phenomenal and art worlds: "a lead line of fowl
pencilled against the sky" and "a penciled line of fowl / Scrawling
farewell on this too northern sky."[2] The meditative poem and the
story, an exercise that brings the theme of *The Scarlet Letter* to the
Midwest, are gloomy. Soon, though, he was publishing light verse in
major magazines.[3] In these trifles, De Vries both draws inspiration
from and mocks the conventions of modernism. He is a writer in
spite of himself or, as in "The Reader Writes," not a writer at all but
a perplexed reader:

> What poets mean by what they mean
> Is tougher than it's ever been.
>
> Some swear that Ezra Pound's the ticket;
> I get lost in Ezra's thicket.

I'm stumped by what the lilacs bring
To T. S. Eliot in the spring.

I sit up late at night deciding
What goes on in Laura Riding.

Ah, never will the masses know
What Auden means, who loves them so. . . .

Such irreverence contrasts sharply with De Vries's first poem in *Poetry*, in which an old man expresses valedictory contempt for the world in language inherited from Donne and Eliot:

Beyond the world lies, hurrying and infirm;
The bracelets clatter on the arm, the typewriters
Clatter on the wall, the night is gashed with neon,
Splattered with pianos wheedling feet in alien rooms.[4]

De Vries's group of three poems in the March 1939 *Poetry* would have given fits to his "Reader." Each, like the sonnet "Mirror," which represents De Vries in *The Poetry Anthology*, could have easily monopolized an issue of *The Explicator.*

Mirror

Before this fever of the almost cold
Fierce things are gnawing on the sweated palm
And howl along taut sinews that behold
The awful tempest of the almost calm.
But not for long the paroxysmal hands
Like spiders writhing on the twisted sheet;
Time now abruptly cuts his flow of sands,
So simply deals him silence and defeat.
Now spent and vanquished in the bursting gloom
The limbs are quiet on the tortured bed;
The hands are rested in the raging room
And relaxation marks the fallen head
Whom peace has dealt his everlasting grace.
And when I turn they see death in my face.

Auden had reclaimed the sonnet for exercises of urbane wit. De Vries trumps the metaphysical game by crossing Donne with Poe, witty optical conceit with romantic agony. Intrigue arises from the poem's disruption of anaphoric relationships: Whose sweaty palms and taut sinews? At first we suppose the patient's, but the description seems more logically applicable to witnesses keeping vigil. The patient and the watchers reflect one another's suffering. Similarly, two catachreses mirror each other grammatically in "fever of the almost cold" versus "tempest of the almost calm," and rhymes create other mirroring relationships. The second quatrain refers unmistakably to the decedent. Time's "flow of sands" rescues a cliché by referring ingeniously to sand as an ingredient in mirror glass: the dead man is deprived of his powers of reflection. Time, in "cutting" his sand and "dealing" death, mirrors the other participants by doing something with his hands. The inanimate mirrors the animate: the gloom is "bursting," the bed is "tortured," the room is "raging." But whose hands are "rested"? The deceased's hands are ill described as "rested" in the "*room*" when they are lying inert upon the sheet, so the hands must be those of the watchers. "Peace" deals grace in this resolutely secular portrayal, and then comes the shock of the last line. Who is "I"? The reference is not crystal clear, the shift to first person is surprising. There seem to be two equally plausible possibilities. A hand mirror is used to determine whether breathing has ceased, and the watchers see clear glass, which, since its holder is turning it for inspection, gives back to them their own faces. Or the head, having fallen, at last turns passively to one side, and each beholder's face mirrors the death's head, with Poe-like anxiety that the dead are "everlastingly" trapped. The tableau mirrors the famous visual pun in which we see either a lady viewing herself in a mirror, or a skull. Ambiguity is posed against the fact of mortality by a subtle synthesis of metaphysical and Romantic means. Ultimately the "I" is the poem itself, which turns to the cold word *death* as it turns to face the reader at its own completion. The poem, scarcely quarantined from life and death, is a recording eye. In "Mirror," the transcript itself is a symbol that encompasses and is encompassed by life and death. Making an aesthetic object out of a household artifact and showing how aesthetic force waits in utilitarian objects, it is a masterly resolution of focus by an artist obligated to turn back the aspersion that art is nothing but a vanity mirror.[5]

While gaining respect as a poet's poet, De Vries also wrote verse for *Esquire*'s audience in a vernacular that looks forward to the pop surrealism of the Beatles' "A Day in the Life":

> A man sits on the corner curb,
> The inky menace of a headline stares—
>   the headline rumbles war.
> He turns the page, not quite awake.[6]

He could also produce a "Song for a Bride" for *Esquire*, whose audience may not have been alert to the poem's dialogue with Swinburne.[7] But De Vries may have thought that his poems were becoming overly ingenious, and he trained his agility as a writer toward prose. There is some lively light verse in the 1950s, but no poems after 1952 except as ornaments in novels.

The magazine stories De Vries wrote in the 1930s, not his early novels, are his apprentice works, and most of them hold up today. They range from courtship tales to studies of aesthetes to a naturalistic story about exploited workers to a spoof of man-in-the-street interviews.[8] As he had in poems, De Vries also considered in prose fiction the nature and role of art.

In his first outright comic piece, De Vries looks at the visual arts. "Art's a Funny Thing"[9] almost certainly was inspired by Grant Wood's *American Gothic*, which was first exhibited in 1930 in Chicago. Clem Dolliver is a sourpuss farmer who is sweet-talked into letting a group of art students depict his barn. One student gets permission to do a candid portrait of Clem himself. When Clem reads in his morning paper that one of the barn paintings has won first prize in an Art Institute contest, he assumes the fifty dollar prize belongs to him, because, after all, it's his barn. He drives into the city and calls at the Art Institute to claim his winnings. After a Mr. Gilmore regretfully informs him that the prize was awarded to the artist, Clem prowls around the exhibit room and comes face to face with his portrait: *The Grouch*. Gilmore has no success in mollifying Clem, who in primitive rage pulls out his pocketknife and slashes the picture to ribbons. On his way out, Clem commends the pigeons for defacing the institute's neoclassical façade. This story is not a work of snobbery that makes fun of rubes. Clem Dolliver is more Don Quixote than Clem Kadiddlehopper. The story's bipartisan satire mocks both Clem's pride and the vainglory of the official art world. The collision of worlds, the juxtaposition of rusticity and sophistication, energizes this piece, just as a Gothic window on a modest house in Eldon, Iowa, sparked *American Gothic*. That Grant Wood has been written of in relation to Salvador Dali[10] scarcely makes Wood a surrealist, and "Art's a Funny Thing" is not "Soluble Fish." Yet De Vries is seeking something beyond comedy.

In his last published story before his first novel, De Vries again examines the role of art. In "It Goes Like This,"[11] Rudy Hoffman, a truck driver, calls on a Miss Cieciel, "Teacher of Piano" in some western Chicago suburb, with an unusual request: "I don't want to learn to play the whole piano. . . . All I want is I want to learn how to play one certain piece." He hums a few bars, which she identifies

as Chopin's "Waltz in C Sharp Minor." Rudy learns to play the opening in a single lesson. He enjoys the waltz because it reminds him
of his girlfriend. His landlady, Nettie, has her sights set on Rudy, so
when he next sets out from Chicago for the long haul to Los Angeles,
she goes downtown to purchase a record of the waltz to remind her
of him. She hums the melody to the store clerk, as Rudy had
hummed to Miss Cieciel.

This little study fits in between Sherwood Anderson's and Saul
Bellow's pictures of the midcentury Middle West. In her suburban
"white cottage," "tall slender red-haired young" Miss Cieciel is a
midwestern muse. The normally taciturn Mr. Hoffman expatiates on
his travels in her presence: "It's like in the olden days they went on
ships and the sea got in their blood," he says, reciting with Whitmanesque fervor the names of the cities through which he circulates.
Miss Cieciel's ethereal name signifies her elevation as a cultural ves-
tal. She regards Hoffman as "a child." When he leaves, she watches
him through the window until he vanishes: "She felt the insidious
melancholy stealing in . . . and it was lonely—with an engulfing emptiness." Maternally kind, she must watch him go, admirable but incomplete, into the confused world of activity from which she,
alienated by her enculturation, is isolated. The desolating effect of
a deep engagement with art is rendered here with particular force
because the emotional needs of both muse and suppliant are clearly
and respectfully exposed to reveal seemingly irreconcilable differ-
ences; the hierophant will be lonely because her petitioners will apply
their knowledge toward private ends. Chopin's waltz becomes a talis-
man for Rudy and Nettie; it ceases to be Chopin. The "It" in "It
Goes Like This" stands for any aesthetic object. Again, De Vries, in
exploring relationships between high culture and popular culture,
and between artworks and their makers, audiences, and subjects,
indicates a desire to go beyond the available norms.

"It Goes Like This" was the only story De Vries published in
1938, and he published none in 1939. He was working on his first
novel. In his short stories, he had already experimented with a range
of narrators and points of view. He had not yet developed a style but
was a resourceful borrower of techniques and was developing an ear
for distinguishing diverse voices. His array of character types was
growing. He had chosen two main subject areas: courtship and the
relations between socioeconomic and cultural classes. He had a tendency to satirize and a countervailing tendency to empathize; thus,
even his most wayward characters enjoy the compassion of familiarity,
and even contemptible behavior is more likely to receive tolerance
than wrathful judgment. His keen sense of the incongruous and

comic invention steered him toward comedy; his depth of feeling steered him the other way. Still wrestling with the relationship of art to life, and his Calvinist father's conviction that art was vain, he was drawn into using devices of metafiction to bring his artwork under the scrutiny of real life and to include as much of the world in his works as possible. In the same campaign, he set up aesthetes as straw men who had gone too far in exalting art; by this gambit he snared especially brightly plumed birds in his net. De Vries was primed for a major fictional effort.

De Vries was also a poet, editor, candy deliveryman, and radio actor. Daunting practical and aesthetic problems hampered his progress as a novelist. His time and attention were divided. He had a living to make—what he wrote would have to sell. And how could he write marketable fiction when he had imbibed distrust of the marketplace, impatience with its values, and elitist, formalist standards? T. S. Eliot's grandfather had founded a university; Eliot could work patiently in the bank. De Vries's ancestors were unlikely to rest quietly while Peter worked his dreams through alembics over refining fires. Impatient and ambitious, he wanted not only to make it new but to make it now. His family would not praise his literary conquests, but they would welcome material success. What De Vries needed was a way of harnessing all his horses to the same wagon, as his father had done. He found a method ready-made in the surrealist collage.

*   *   *

The imagination is perhaps on the point of reasserting itself, of reclaiming its rights.—André Breton[12]

Poetry magazine published a good amount of surrealist poetry in the De Vries years, and *Poetry*'s commentators were alert to the influence of surrealism. In January 1939, Edouard Roditi wrote approvingly of the "august tradition" of "irrational philosophies" moving from antiquity through Romanticism to surrealism.[13] In July of that year, *Poetry* ran H. R. Hays's cogent discussion of "Surrealist Influence in Contemporary English and American Poetry."[14] Hays welcomes the work of the American poets Harold Rosenberg and Charles Henri Ford and the English poets Dylan Thomas and George Gascoigne. Hays's article would have held particular interest for Peter De Vries.

Hays notes that, by 1938, surrealism "has had its schisms and burnt its heretics." The surrealists had become notorious for internecine flare-ups, and their banishings and apostasies were far from over. As a hereditary "product of schism," De Vries must have felt a tug of kinship toward these spectacles of feuding artists and antiartists. Drawn by their spirit of controversy, he would have been swept by the tempests, amused at their alleged ferocity when compared with the disputations among which he grew up, and annoyed by the futility of their factionalism. Hays acknowledges that, indeed, surrealism "has been sentenced to death a number of times by the critics." The most avant-garde European movement of the 1920s had arrived in England and America a decade later suffering signs of disintegration and decadence not especially encouraging to young mavericks interested in new directions.

Hays also remarked that surrealism as a protest movement depended on its "power to shock the bourgeoisie" but that "the power to shock exists no longer." As his political record shows, De Vries was not averse to protest, but he already had seen proofs of the inability of American citizens to be deeply shocked either by poetic incitements or prosaic evidence of flagrantly corrupt politics. Surrealist protest tactics were not viable in the United States, where its provocations were more likely than in Europe to be treated by the public as tantrums or criminal acts rather than as threats to the state. Moreover, Hays's opinion that surrealism could in any case "never appeal to a wide audience" could only have troubled a young writer seeking to solve the aesthetic problem of avoiding solipsism and hopeful of living by writing. What, then, did surrealism offer?

For Hays, the "something [that] still remains alive" in surrealism was its stimulus to the creative imagination, its fundamental character as "a reassertion of the poetic process." "Indeed," he says, "much of the best poetry in any period is surrealist," agreeing that Poe and Coleridge belong among the surrealist "ancestors" claimed in the first manifesto. Surrealism had walked through the door Freudian psychoanalysis had opened on the subconscious, seeking there "what keeps poetry alive . . . the sense of magic." The allure of this maneuver for an author whose first literary enthusiasm was *The Confessions of an English Opium-Eater,* and whose early works express impatience with convention and realism, is clear. It is equally clear that his skeptical nature would incline him to share Hays's criticism: "Magic alone is not enough. Civilized man is not a creature of pure emotion and fancy. Ingrained in the tissue of his spiritual emotional life is the necessity for making judgments." The word *judgment* evokes the eighteenth-century arguments about wit and judgment,[15] and Hays invokes a stalwart Enlightenment concept to help him sustain his selective admiration for surrealism: taste. Eluard and Cocteau, "the best products of French surrealism," have it, and it rescued them from the "complete irresponsibility" of "many others of the move-ment." At this juncture, Hays sounds reactionary to anyone familiar with André Breton's insistence that surrealism must never be reduced to an aesthetic category and his anathema for "taste." Hays deliber-ately presses his attack: "As with many other movements, it is the orthodox practitioners who tend to recede into the background while the effect of the literary impulse continues to have significance in moulding the course of poetry."[16] Fighting orthodoxy was a De Vries specialty. Fighting the orthodoxy of Calvin, he had used cool logic; fighting the orthodoxy of Breton, a more carefree exercise, he would use surrealist wildness. He could feel confident in both his wit and judgment: he knew he had imagination, and when he was appointed an editor of *Poetry*, his taste had been certified.

De Vries would have had little occasion to dispute with Calvinists had he not been raised one, and he could not have interestingly done so without absorbing Calvin's teachings. Similarly, De Vries could not have contested with surrealists had he not read and thought about their ideas and actions. Certainly their methods appear in his works as often as do the Calvinist themes most of his critics have focused on. In the course of discussing his four chosen poets, Hays enumer-ates "the association method," "the pure principle of amazement," "a sort of nightmare cinema," "a kind of relaxed playfulness, a surrealist humor which differs entirely from traditional forms of wit," "a tech-nique akin to painting, the blending of overtones, indirect implica-tions, incongruous humor, and emotional ambiguities which juxtaposed images create," and "incongruity of style . . . from the colloquial to the decorative to allusion to the grand manner."[17] That list is a fair, if incomplete, characterization of De Vries's work. Surre-alism is more than a congeries of methods, however. Among De Vries's difficulties were the fundamental ones of situating the work of art and of overcoming a sense of transgression in writing at all. Surrealism, as Hays, no longer sounding quite so reactionary, con-cluded, could help De Vries out by "toughening" him up:

> In these times, when the pressure of immediate events is never re-laxed, poetry, jostled by the melodrama of the headlines, often becomes a meaningless twitter, or relapses into non-poetry. It is only the stoutest imagination which can ride the contemporary earthquake. The exercise of surrealism has toughened the muscles of the poets we have just been considering. No writer who has submitted to its influence will ever be content with inherited imagery. Nor will he be dismayed as the world becomes increasingly surrealist.[18]

Whether the world since 1938 has become more surrealist is a question for future historians and surrealists to ponder. The world was already surrealist for Peter De Vries, as the products of his editorship and authorship proclaim.

References to surrealism are common in *Poetry* commentaries of 1938 through 1946. In December 1939, Delmore Schwartz, writing on "Rimbaud in Our Time," says, "The Symbolists, the Dadaists, and the Surrealists . . . resume in their own way different moments of Rimbaud's efforts. It is in this sense that Rimbaud can be said to have *tried out* the whole century to come *in advance*."[19] Such references will strike resonant chords in readers of De Vries. Surrealism is a special case of the already seen and the "cultural level" phenomena often explored by De Vries. Schwartz's emphasis alludes to one of the themes in Rimbaud most celebrated by the surrealists: the poet as seer. De Vries has investigated that idea, too.[20]

Surrealist enthusiasm for the extravagant and the uncanny, ridiculed elsewhere, was not abused in *Poetry*. The writers published by Dillon and De Vries did not patronize surrealism but treated it as a solid, if obstreperous, contender for readers' allegiance. Eugene Jolas wrote for the August 1940 *Poetry* an obituary for the movement in France:

> Surrealism was dying. The movement that had given its name to the collective nostalgia for the fabulous and the oneiromantic tendencies between the two wars was drifting towards politics. It no longer had anything to say to the new generation. It had done its duty and had liberated the imagination. After fifteen years of heroic battles, it conquered the Anglo-American and Latin-American youth, but in France it was no longer of any importance. It did not correspond to the vital needs of the generation that was living under the incessant threat of totalitarian aggression and that was now beginning to rebuild the bridge with the Gothic tradition of France. Surrealism refused to face the problem of ontology and thus ended in macabre impotence.[21]

In an October 1940 review of Amos N. Wilder's *The Spiritual Aspects of the New Poetry,* however, Jolas sounds sardonic when he reports that "surrealist irrationalism leads us to perdition, asserts Mr. Wilder." Jolas, who by this time was promulgating his own program, "verticalism," nevertheless defends surrealism. Jolas had no sooner declared French surrealism dead than he encountered surrealism alive and well as a threat to the modern soul—a slur Jolas could not leave unchallenged.

Jolas upbraids Wilder for being unaware "that the romantic movement, historically speaking, had two currents to which Goerres once gave the name of 'descending and ascending mysticism.'"[22] Surrealism follows those currents, and they are illustrated in a review in the May 1944 *Poetry*. In the April issue, David Daiches had praised the surrealist poetry of George Barker.[23] In the May *Poetry*, Kimon Friar praises Oscar Williams's surrealism, preferring it to Barker's: "The poetry of Oscar Williams shows to some extent this complex of romantic and surrealist persuasion in a more coherent compositional line." Friar invokes the agonistic side of surrealism: "Man and society are to Williams a surrealist nightmare of mechanical evils." However, surrealism can contribute to a reconstruction of man and society; Friar emphasizes this aspiring side in his summation on current American and English verse as represented in three anthologies edited by the indefatigable Williams:

> Perhaps it is not unreasonable to hope that out of this fecundity will come a poetry classical in line and composition without much loss of romantic and almost surrealist dislocation of image. Such a poetry would impose on the eclecticism of our age an ideological pattern (primarily political and historical) to replace our lost mythological and religious beliefs.[24]

The quest for a myth is characteristic of our century, exemplified by no one better than André Breton, studied by no one more assiduously than Claude Lévi-Strauss (who was a Voice of America colleague and friend of Breton's in New York during the Second World War),[25] and mused over by none with more gusto than Peter De Vries (who suspected it was a part of the new myth that we were searching for a new myth). If Calvinism had been a mystery play for De Vries, then surrealism was a current drama.

The editorial policy of *Poetry*, though friendly toward surrealists, did not protect them from criticism. In April 1942, Charles Henri Ford's book *The Overturned Lake* (the title poem had appeared in *Poetry* in 1940) was blasted in a review by Howard Blake.[26] Ford is again treated harshly in a September 1945 review of *Poems for Painters*, in which Francis C. Golffing sneers at "devotees of surrealism" and Ford's "still" using "the orthodox surrealist technique of joining the incongruous and reconciling the disparate." Golffing acknowledges Ford's imaginativeness and verbal power, but he ends his review by condemning Ford for wasting his passion and perception on "imaginative toys." Golffing has little use for surrealism, referring to Ford's adaptation of "the iconography of Chirico, Tchelichew, and Dali" as having "neuropathic rather than esthetic" interest.[27] In contrast, Edouard Roditi, reviewing books by Philippe Soupault and Jules Roy in April 1946, upbraids both authors, à la Breton, for selling out.[28]

Surrealistic latecomers were treated uncharitably in *Poetry*'s pages by the early 1940s. Oscar Williams deals swiftly with a hapless surrealist epigone: "The nine surreal poems by Hugh Argraves convince me that the real world has it all over surrealism."[29] Howard Moss, reviewing a 1943 anthology of English art and writing, is irritated by surreal inertia: "As a last gun shot, there is the inevitable surrealist section, which, sadly enough, seems as academic now as the art it once attacked seemed twenty years ago. It would seem wise at this point to issue a new manifesto stating that the purpose of surrealism was to extend the consciousness, not smother it."[30]

Poetry's treatment of surrealism was hardly brief, superficial, or one-sided. Surrealism was perceived as an important development and came to be regarded as an integral part of intellectual life. Its trends and events were chronicled, and various opinions and shades of opinion had an airing. Peter De Vries himself wrote perceptively about surrealism. His remarks, while not unqualified, are friendly and appreciative.

* * *

Ford probably senses the shortcomings, as he certainly senses the hazards of his idiom. "Imagination's cloak makes us invisible," he says in the title poem. And "dilute the sadistic monopoly's whirlpool that twisted the artist out of all recognition"—a proposition to which the reader, lost in a thicket of private associations, is quite ready to assent.—Peter De Vries[31]

De Vries's first review article in *Poetry,* "Fusion and Confusion," in July 1938, revolves around a central problem of surrealism: how to reconcile the poetic use of emanations of the unconscious with the need to communicate. Of Charles Henri Ford's *Garden of Disorder and Other Poems,* De Vries begins:

It is regrettable to have to report of Ford's splendid virtuosity that it does nothing so well as seal him hermetically in Ford. "When the trees ride bicycles" is an intelligible enough line (and a representative example of this poet's method of rendering phenomena directly as experience); but others—"if the hunchback hinders the corn's turning yellow" or "Perfume the clock and the cricket will take care of Aunt Bess"—wrench things a bit too violently out of their dimension. The angle of refraction intelligibility will allow a poet in personalizing experience is debatable. Here, at any rate, it has been exceeded.

These are all excerpts from the title poem, a kind of phantasmagoria where the impressions of a profuse and chaotic material world are presented in a dynamic succession of images, and "things" are rendered as psychic impacts. Ford's technique is thus, in intention, direct—yet the total effect is devious. The poems are often brilliant in disjointed passages, but do not jell. Ford is difficult even to an ear trained to receive images as he uses them—not to "evoke"; not "representationally"; but as subtly connotative elements in a context where tonal and pictorial values are carefully blended. Here is the first part of *Left Instantly Designs:*

> describe the circles
> first; terror
> will stay and
> the moon displace
>
> them and control
> the rain;
> then walk away
> in the rain's disgrace;
>
> the blood's obedience
> will follow
> instantly designs
> left in the sky's hollow;
>
> once fearful often
> each ear then
> accepts its
> rightful coffin . . .

Images shuffled into such arbitrary juxtapositions as often as not miss the highly specialized responses at which they aim. This kind of thing is too vague for good surrealism; it recalls the Objectivists' exquisite weddings of image and cadence, their anxious polishing of "particulars."[32]

As one who had described himself as emerging from a "hermetically sealed" community, De Vries sees little difference between hermeticism and plain inarticulateness. His desire to overcome solipsism is strong, his conviction that the effort is necessary is firm, and his fascination with the difficulty and often desperation of the struggle is keen enough to make the theme a fixture in his work. "Brilliant in disjointed passages" may be ideal for orthodox surrealist poets and audiences, but to De Vries the sacrifice of sense is too great for "good surrealism": "To communicate the insanely delicate tones of awareness that offer themselves to the poetic impulse, it is hardly enough to set forth the associations and images that supply them in the personal experience, and then to polish these particular effects over and over."[33] De Vries's use of the word *insanely* is revealing, signaling as it does his ironic perception that "bizarre" surrealism is sometimes not insane *enough*.

What kind of surrealism, then, does De Vries think "good surrealism"? "Metaphor, to function, must be predicated on some reasonably clear referent in mutual experience." De Vries praises those poems in Ford's book that "*sustain* heightened imagery" (emphasis mine), producing "many rich and intense effects," and, especially, those in which "he is most communicative, probably because a larger consciousness, a social consciousness, supervenes. Here there is less attempt to dissolve the world in private vision, and more to evaluate it." For De Vries, good surrealism is not that of poets writing for other poets but of people writing for other people—a Wordsworthian surrealism, if you will, that can produce a poem like "the excellent *Plaint*, . . . subtitled *Before a Mob of Ten Thousand at Owensboro, Ky.*," protesting against racial violence:[34]

> I, Rainey Betha, [22,]
> from the top-branch of race-hatred look at you[.]
> My limbs are bound, though boundless the bright sun
> like my bright blood which had to run
> into the orchard that excluded me:
> now I climb death's tree.
> The pruning-hooks of many mouths
> cut the black-leaved boughs.
> The robins of my eyes hover where
> sixteen leaves fall that were a prayer:
> sixteen mouths are open wide;
> the minutes like black cherries
> drop from my shady side.
> Oh who is the forester must tend such a tree, Lord?
> Do angels pick the cherry-blood of folk like me, Lord?[35]

Here, Ford avoids the great pitfall of surrealism, solipsism. De Vries's friend John Malcolm Brinnin described the problem well in his discussion in *Poetry* of "Muriel Rukeyser: The Social Poet and the Problem of Communication." He commends Rukeyser for breaking free of "the contemporary equivalent of the ivory tower, refurbished, perhaps, with surrealist and Freudian furniture, but a familiar landmark in its isolation, its detachment from the political flow of masses and men." She does not abandon surrealist methods but channels them: "In [her] latter work," says Brinnin, "images become those of the psychologist, or of the surrealist, charged with meaning."[36] De Vries concludes his review of Ford with the fillip "Ford's further development will be interesting to note." Ford might have preferred *Poetry* had taken no interest in view of the later salvos cited above. Because he had, in fact, shown increasing social awareness in his work, Ford may have wondered why less sympathetic reviewers than De Vries kept panning him.[37] In general, though it is plain that surrealism had an impact on *Poetry*, *Poetry* probably had little influence on surrealists.

The other book De Vries reviewed in "Fusion and Confusion" is Sydney Salt's *Christopher Columbus and Other Poems*. He admires Salt's use of "a kind of picture writing, wherein a play of thought [is] suggested by images always adroitly in the service of concept" and praises Salt's "sure touch" in lines like "Now my forest of desire is the leaf of your smile" and "that wild knot in the bosom—the lives of men to stain the silk cloth of my d[r]eam," lines reminiscent of Eluard.[38]

Even in *Poetry* articles that do not mention surrealism, De Vries is on that wavelength. In "Voice in Babel," his appreciation of the French socialist poet Charles Péguy, De Vries makes laconic reference to Péguy as a representative of "the modern revolutionary ending in the arms of the church":

> He died a believer indeed; yet his life itself rather makes one feel again that the church needs its saints more than the saints need the church. All in all *Basic Verities*, a new collection of his prose and poetry translated and prepared by Ann and Julian Green, proved unexpectedly rewarding to one reader who, though some of his best friends are converts, picked it up with something of an indisposition, pressed as he has been to the conclusion that the church is like a woman—you cannot fall into her arms without falling into her hands.

De Vries imagines Sidney Hook and Jacques Maritain, representing, respectively, "naturalist" and "supernaturalist" viewpoints, "contending briskly for [Péguy's] soul" in a burlesque that contemporary surrealists would have enjoyed for showing that both sides miss the point. What interests De Vries in Péguy's work is that it "radiates a comprehensive and simple rapport with mankind, a goodwill which was the wellspring of his socialism." Péguy apparently "just sat down and wrote, never cutting out a line because that would be disingenuous, would be second-thinking," and the cumulative effect is "a steady mesmeric kind of expansion, like listening to one note growing louder and louder, stop by stop, or like staring into a dome"—a populist mantra, in the manner of Jack Kerouac and other "automatic" writers. Péguy's faith in man, not God, is what interests De Vries, and it offers an antidote to racial rivalries and antagonisms: "It means breaking prejudices like bones." Péguy's faith, internationalist and progressive, as De Vries sees it, "is dear. Without his being the great poet some of his admirers make him out to be, he was that 'priest of a continually developing religion of life' for which Stephen

Spender, writing in the current issue of *Horizon*, calls." The phrase "religion of life" brings to mind Picasso's naming his villa "Our Lady of Life." While seeking to avoid the broil between the Hooks and the Maritains, De Vries sides with the Spenders and Picassos seeking a "'literature to save humanity.'"[39]

The Spender article from which De Vries quotes regrets the "hardening of each [modern] poet into a final attitude which he has decided to be his intellectual sphere. A poet's traditionalism or symbolism or surrealism is not just his particular 'line' within a defined intellectual activity called poetry, it is his justification for poetic activity altogether." It is to that sort of dogmatism, as well as to the "harnessing" of poetry to "the traditional orthodoxy of the Churches" that Spender opposes the "religion of life" to which De Vries was drawn.[40] In the same issue of *Horizon*, Spender swipes at surrealism, "which exists really on the level of sensational headlines in the press," but he also commends the "inhuman-human faces of a passionate, suffering, unconscious humanity 'waiting to be born' . . . present in the recent works of Picasso, and in the drawings of Henry Moore" as images capable of inspiring a humanist faith that would sustain morality independent of belief in God.[41] Amid spirited debates, there were deep affinities between the surrealists and nonsurrealists like Spender.[42] For example, De Vries's attitude toward Charles Péguy is similar to André Breton's. Breton admired Péguy but became disillusioned by Péguy's application of his art to patriotic ends during World War I: "Nationalism had never been my forte," Breton observed. De Vries emphasizes that Péguy was not only a "staunch patriot" but also "a critical one" who prophesied nationalism's end.[43]

In his last *Poetry* review, De Vries took up a poet in whom surrealist concerns are prominent: E. E. Cummings. Discussing Cummings's *One Times One*, De Vries begins by acknowledging his discomfort at analyzing a poet who is against interpretation. Cummings, "you are sure, would much rather you just set your glass down and said Thanks, that was good," says De Vries, anticipating his own statements about how readers should take his novels. Yet "it has been in sophisticated criticism that [Cummings's] poetry has encountered its fullest appreciation"; De Vries notes that "wide numbers suppose his significance lies at a not exactly determined point somewhere between the Elizabethan lyric and bubble gum." To help properly locate Cummings, De Vries brings up items of interest to surrealists: folk speech, the approach to a realer reality through exertions of language, the primacy of love, the power of derision, and an ambivalence toward reason and science. De Vries takes exception to Cummings's "distaste for 'reason'" and science, asking "with or without the scalpel, may not 'only the impossible happen' still. . . ?" but he concedes that Cummings's cautions about the hegemony of science "ought to be brought home to all those who regard the war as an interruption after which we can once more pursue the vision of Progress through Prosperity, our destinies turned over, once again, to Congressmen purring like refrigerators."[44]

* * *

Stephen Spender, giving surrealism its due, noted that when it fell to someone to express "an anticipation of the complete breakdown and disorder of existing social systems . . . The surrealists have certainly expressed this."[45] Perhaps still thinking of Spender's barb, De Vries wrote in the August 1943 *Poetry:* "Who will deny for instance that the horrors of the last war played a part in producing the drunken illuminations of surrealism, with its air of delirium and fragmentation. But the conceptions and stated principles of surrealism have ostensibly nothing to do with the subject." De Vries felt he knew "the stated principles of surrealism." He portrays surrealism as a means resorted to in desperation; and desperation, as many commentators have shown, is a staple of De Vries's novels. His statement appears in an acerbic article De Vries wrote in response to the question "'What of poets and the war?' a question which we sometimes feel more inclined to reprimand than to answer." What De Vries reprimands the askers for is their implication that poets should be writing patriotic poems. "Only the naive would expect any such flamboyant idealism as that of Rupert Brooke, now." De Vries shares the poets' knowledge that "to retain the least chance to live the Axis must be defeated" and avers that "we publish this number" of servicemen's poetry "out of that affectionate interest all of us continue to have for those who are working and fighting for us, wherever they are, here and abroad"; but his loyalty does not blind him to the "horrors" of the war or prevent him from mentioning that both world wars are "often viewed as successive cataclysms of a capitalist order."[46]

De Vries's most extensive remarks on surrealism are in an article he wrote in 1943 on "Poetry and the War" for *College English.* As in the *Poetry* piece, he inveighs against the "tenaciously glamorous conception" of war and deplores, in terms reminiscent of Freud's, "modern war, which at bottom we recognize for what it really is—a pure, anthropoid horror." He points out that poets such as Auden and Spender had anticipated the war, "Seismographically sensitive, as poets are, to disturbances collecting in the world." He commends Karl Shapiro's sardonic treatments of "contemporary disaster," his being "too intensely aware of those social ills and inequalities" to produce the paeans to democracy "expectant patriots" await. De Vries then turns to surrealism:

> Side by side with the astringent Auden-Shapiro sort of idiom, there has flourished a looser, freer diction, a more expressionistic style often brightly dyed with surrealism. It is exemplified in the work of the young Welshman Dylan Thomas, in that of George Barker, David Gascoyne, Henry Treece, and Randall Jarrell, most of whom are in the Army. In many cases, even where the intention is not strictly that of surrealism, or is perhaps even far from it, as in the poetry of Oscar Williams, the surrealist technique is there: the riot of imagery, the phantasmal cast, a luxuriance of free association, the flotsam and jetsam of the oppressed psyche, all useful for the re-creation of the anxiety, tension, and horrors of the modern world.

> > Where formerly he saw birds in bushes, now
> > The cyclist resting from his uphill labours
> > Observes the skull of Cromwell on a bough
> > Admonishing his half heart, and he shoulders
> > His way upward against the wind to the brow.
> >
> > The political cartoonist in his bed
> > Hears voices break his sleep he does not know:
> > The morning papers show what the people said.
> > Librarians in their studies, the lights low,
> > Sense Milton breathing in his marble head.

writes George Barker in lines typical of this combination of pictorial extravagance and bold diction, this suggestion of dense and buried emotions tossing and smoldering in a general *Weltschmertz*. The consciousness of war and the general devastations of the machine age of which war is part and parcel permeate the most obscure emotions, invade everything from the meditations of an old man at evening to the rapture of lovers in the park. War is "total" in the human spirit also and was so for the poets, too, a long time before it was declared by statesmen.

The surrealist touch is now familiar, even to people who have probably never heard the word, being visible on book jackets, billboards, phonograph-record albums, and even in the movies—Don Ameche having been clearly seen striding among amorphous and eerie fragments of landscape in a sequence surely aided and abetted by Salvador Dali. But with few exceptions the poets have not done as well with it as have the painters, perhaps because it is suited only to the canvas and not to the printed word. At any rate, all the skulls and keys and other surrealist bric-a-brac with which verse has become cluttered have grown tedious. Repetition has long ago anesthetized us against their shock value. Nevertheless, their appeal to artists bent on expressing a world's chaos and fragmentation in terms of an overwrought and premonitory consciousness is easily understood.

Dylan Thomas practices the technique with success. His imagery—lush, centrifugal, fused at astonishing high speed—is the work of a rich imagination:

> How shall my animal
> Whose wizard shape I trace in the cavernous skull,
> Vessel of abscesses and exultation's shell,
> Endure burial under the spelling wall,
> The invoked, shrouding veil at the cap of the face,
> Who should be furious,
> Drunk as a vineyard snail. . . .

[De Vries here discusses Thomas's mixture of Christian with pagan symbols and his alleged obscurity.]

Dylan Thomas represents at its best a new strain noticeable among the young British poets which David Daiches has recently accounted as an open revolt away from the thin-lipped intellectualism of Eliot and Auden and toward a more spontaneous, personal expression—a romantic reaction, in other words. How far it will go no one can predict, or whether the current will emerge in any poet of importance. It is also impossible to foretell how the future inclinations of artists will be affected by world events as they culminate—those world events which both the surrealist immersed in Freud and the Marxist occupied with politics have already been reflecting, each in his own way. Between the astringency of Shapiro and the lush expressionism of Thomas is a wide gulf; but, opposites though they be, they are equally contemporary results. It is conceivable that the war (and its outcome in the peace) may keep the young artists as aware as ever they were in the thirties of the truth of Thomas Mann's statement: "In our day the destiny of man presents itself in political terms." It is just as possible that the weight of it all may make them turn, as even so socially minded a poet as Spender did, to a more personal form of expression. We can only wait to see how time and events will influence the concerns of artists, pledged once again to Our Lady of Social Significance, brooding above the world-ash, or seeking the green tree. Or, it may be, expressing the new sense of humanity which we like to think this war is generating among us. Who knows but that this may be the burden of someone of great size as yet unheard from, who, with the night of grief still dark about us, prepares his *aubade* for the coming sun.[47]

De Vries, unlike Spender, sees surrealism as neither moribund nor superficial. Although formulas have grown tedious, and there is uncertainty about who is a surrealist, imagination will find its way among the new poets. Dylan Thomas's difficult relationship with surrealism need not be examined here.[48] It will be necessary, though, to expand on what ideas De Vries bore in mind when he applied the term *surrealism*, where he got them, and what the situation of surrealism in America was in the mid and late 1930s.

* * *

This magazine is most unusual and stimulating, and will be indispensable to all "connoisseurrealists."—*Poetry*

Edmund Wilson's *Axel's Castle*, to which De Vries alludes in "The Comic Prufrock" in order to establish symbolism as a context for James Thurber's work, mentions "Surrealisme" as the outgrowth of "Dadaism," which, in turn, Wilson sees as "a queer special development of symbolism." Wilson refers to dada as "systematic comic nonsense" and reprints Tristan Tzara's "entertaining history of the Dadaist movement," "Memoirs of Dadaism," from *Vanity Fair*. Wilson's treatment is interesting for its emphasis on the ludic element in dada and its vivid description of "the patron saint of Dadaism," Isidore Ducasse, the "Comte de Lautréamont." Wilson remarks that *Les Chants de Maldoror*, while "full of the familiar ferocities and blasphemies" of extreme Romanticism, and "immature," was nonetheless "not unpromising," and that "the images of [its] nightmares and tirades have that peculiar phantasmagoric quality which was to be characteristic of symbolism." Wilson's portrayal of the continuity of dada and surrealism with symbolism, the movement he celebrates as having "revealed to the imagination a new flexibility and freedom" and as having wakened us "to the hope and exaltation of the untried, unsuspected possibilities of human thought and art," was certainly read with interest by adventurous young writers.[49]

A News Note in the September 1939 *Poetry* announced the founding of the International Workshop in Rochester, New York: "Its manifesto is a plea for the expressionistic, the exploration of the unconscious—'the "I" in its many dimensions.' . . . Those pledged to engage in the rescue work include Richard Eberhart, Anais Nin, Dylan Thomas, Man Ray, Parker Tyler, Salvador Dali, Henry Miller, and others. Everyone interested is invited to write to the director."[50] Such notes, with their varied cast of characters, suggest the fluidity of the avant-garde and the openness of the *Poetry* of that time to it. In April 1939, *Poetry* was exceptionally cordial to one new magazine:

London Bulletin, 28 Cork Street, London, W.1, is one of the most beautiful and enjoyable publications which have appeared in recent years. Originally intended merely as a guide and catalogue to exhibitions of the London Gallery, it has greatly widened its range to include, besides reproductions of modern art, poems, essays, and stories by such writers as André Breton, Paul Eluard, Georges Hugnet, Herbert Read, and Djuna Barnes. Numbers have been published on the work of Magritte, Delvaux, and Max Ernst, also a special number on the recent London exhibition of Picasso's mural painting, "Guernica." This magazine is most unusual and stimulating, and will be indispensable to all "connoisseurrealists." We are happy to learn that its rapid growth has warranted the appointment of representatives in Paris, Brussels, Amsterdam, and New York.[51]

It is further noted that Charles Henri Ford is the New York representative. The *London Bulletin*, which existed for only two years (April 1938 through June 1940), was one of the principal surrealist magazines in English during that short time. Not dogmatically Bretonian, its twenty numbers contained work by Samuel Beckett, William Carlos Williams, Henry Miller, Henry Moore, Giorgio de Chirico, Yves Tanguy, Marcel Duchamp, and many others besides those mentioned in *Poetry*'s note; Dylan Thomas is listed among those who have "offered collaboration." The *London Bulletin*s in the *Poetry* office were a surrealist archive.[52]

If De Vries cared to read more about surrealism, he would have found it easy to do so. Indeed, it was hard to avoid, for American magazines were filled with news of surrealism. It had arrived in America with the first American exhibit of surrealist art at the Wadsworth Atheneum in 1931; the show moved to the Julien Levy Gallery New York in 1932. In 1934, Salvador Dali made his first trip to America for a show at the Levy Gallery. In 1936 the surrealist show at the Museum of Modern Art was attended by rousing controversy; the London show that year was internationally notorious, as was the big Paris show in 1938. In 1939 Dali (whom an exasperated Breton would finally expel from orthodox surrealism for good with the acronymic epithet "Avida Dollars" in 1941) created a sensation with his decoration of two Manhattan Bonwit-Teller's display windows, and his *Dream of Venus* created a sensation at the World's Fair.[53] The press thrived on surrealism, and some surrealists cheerfully manipulated the publicity. Most of the public scandal and entertainment attached to surrealist visual art, but literature was not overlooked. A glance through the welter of articles suggests their variety.

The Living Age in August 1936 ran a witty treatise on surrealism that contained a brief and accurate history of the movement. In December 1936 *Time* and *Newsweek* ran feature stories on surrealism. *Newsweek* gave it a crude sideshow treatment, while *Time*, managing a more urbane smile, conferred the distinction of appearing on its cover to "Surrealist Salvador Dali," who peers Svengali-like from the almost holographic depths of a photo portrait by Man Ray. In July 1937 *The*

Commonweal fought surrealism by declaring it a passing threat that would soon be laughed into oblivion (some hope is held out for Eugene Jolas). In the same month, *Harper's* ran a tirade against dada and surrealism that railed against "these dadaists and the frightful imps who slavishly follow their lack of pattern." In September 1937 *The Nation* printed a scathing review by Meyer Schapiro of Herbert Read's *Surrealism*, which, in the course of lambasting the surrealists for rankness and destructiveness (some hope is held out for Eluard and Picasso), gives a fair précis of several surrealist ideas. In February 1938 *Time* sank to the circus sideshow style in its notice of the Paris exhibition. That April *The American Scholar* printed an imperious essay by Jean Charlot that mixes disdain, and insinuations of shrewd dealing by art promoters, with the recognition that surrealism had in fact rescued the spiritual element in art and freed the artist from the ivory tower. (On 1 April, *The Commonweal*, having apparently overcome its resistance, printed a rather foolish appreciation of the formerly despised Dali and various other surrealists.) The October 1938 *Canadian Forum* contained an article by Northrop Frye welcoming "the first Canadian showing of representative surrealist pictures" with genuine interest. One year later, *The Reader's Digest* condensed from *The New Yorker* a beguiling piece on Salvador Dali, who comes across as the prototypical "Most Unforgettable Character." In the same month in which De Vries's first novel was published, *The Living Age* ran an article by the redoubtable Eugene Jolas entitled "Beyond Surrealism," proclaiming that "surrealism has really conquered America" and inviting "American poets to continue the work." By September 1940 surrealism had reached the crest of its wave in American popular culture.[54]

Surrealism's wave in literary culture could be tracked in James Laughlin's annual volumes of *New Directions in Prose & Poetry*. The first volume, when it appeared in 1936, was dedicated "To / the editors / the contributors / and the readers / of / *transition* / *who have begun successfully* / THE REVOLUTION OF THE WORD," that is, to Eugene Jolas and his collaborators. Laughlin noted in the 1937 volume that the contributor "Henry Miller . . . uses Surrealism as part of his repertoire," and the 1938, 1939, and 1940 volumes all contain work by Charles Henri Ford and news of him (e.g., in 1939, "he is in constant touch with the Paris surrealists"). The 1940 volume is a special surrealist number that includes a "Surrealist Anthology" edited by Nicolas Calas, an interview with Calas and a "Surrealist Pocket Dictionary" by him, a selection of surrealist "Chainpoems" edited by Charles Henri Ford (Ford's project had been announced in the April 1939 *Poetry*), and critical appraisals of the movement by Laughlin, H. J. Muller, and Kenneth Burke.[55]

Contributing to the rise of interest in surrealism were a number of 1930s English-language books by and about surrealists. Among the most noteworthy were David Gascoyne's *Short Survey of Surrealism*, which includes a précis of Breton's manifestos; Gascoyne's translations of various of Breton's writings collected as *What Is Surrealism?*; Herbert Read's lavishly illustrated *Surrealism*, containing a polemical introduction by Read, credos by Breton, Hugh Sykes Davies, and Paul Eluard, and a survey of French surrealist poetry by Georges Hugnet; and gallery owner Julien Levy's *Surrealism*, containing Levy's informed but scarcely disinterested appreciation of the movement, a farrago of surrealist statements, many translated from French by Eugene Jolas and Samuel Beckett, and an index and bibliography.[56]

Whatever his sources on surrealism, De Vries stood well informed. He was aware of surrealism's fundamental ideas and attitudes, its celebrities, its historical position, and its entanglements, and he would exploit the whole spectacle in absurdist and surrealist comedy. The fundamental ideas of surrealism are tidily set forth in Gascoyne's *Short Survey:*

> After an account of certain early surrealist experiments, Breton makes "once and for all" the following definition, which is by no means so well known in England that I need not quote it here:
>
> "SURREALISM, n. Pure psychic automatism, by which it is intended to express, verbally, in writing, or by other means, the real process of thought. Thought's dictation, in the absence of all control exercised by the reason and outside all aesthetic or moral preoccupations."
> "ENCYCL. *Philos.* Surrealism rests in the belief in the superior reality of certain forms of association neglected heretofore; in the omnipotence of the dream and in the disinterested play of thought. It tends definitely to do away with all other psychic mechanisms and to substitute itself for them in the solution of the principal problems of life."
>
> There you have the essentials of surrealism in a few words.[57]

To this certainly should be added Breton's statement in the first manifesto that "I believe in the future resolution of these two states, dream and reality, which are seemingly so contradictory, into a kind of absolute reality, a *surreality*, if one may so speak."[58] The goal of surrealism is, then, the merger of poetry and life, of interior and exterior reality. As Gascoyne put it in his introduction,

It is the avowed aim of the Surrealist movement to reduce and finally to dispose altogether of the flagrant contradictions that exist between dream and waking life, the "unreal" and the "real," the unconscious and the conscious, and thus to make of what has hitherto been regarded as the special domain of poets the acknowledged common property of all. This is what was meant by Lautréamont, a poet who had tremendous influence on Surrealism, when he spoke of "Poetry done by all."[59]

Some of the more prominent supporting ideas invoked by Breton were Reverdy's notion of the poetic image as a "fusion of two mutually distant realities" presented in juxtaposition, as in dreams; the amusing corollary to Lautréamont's dictum "Poetry should be made by all. Not one" that "We have no talents"; and the idea that automatism was not the only form of poetic composition but was to "canalize" the forces of the depths of the mind "in order to submit them later, if necessary, to the control of the reason."[60] Surrealist enthusiasms included word games, investigations and imitations of "morbid mental conditions," and Gothic novels like *The Monk* and *The Castle of Otranto*.[61] Contrary to appearances, this program did not prevent surrealists like Read from making value judgments akin to De Vries's phrase "good surrealism": "The Surrealist, therefore, by no means denies or ridicules aesthetic values as such. To him, no less than to any other sensitive creature, there is good art and bad art, good painting and bad painting, *good Surrealism and bad Surrealism*."[62] Read's standard is "the success with which [the artist] conveys the sensations or ideas," though many surrealists held the opposite value, hermeticism.

In his chapter on "Surrealism To-day and To-morrow," Gascoyne gives the following résumé:

It might be as well before concluding to summarise briefly the chief preoccupations of surrealist research during the last ten years. These fall roughly into two categories: firstly, passive or subjective; secondly, active or objective.

To the first category belong automatism, spontaneous and "pure" poetry, and the idea of the synonymity of poetry and dream. Parallel with these features, in the realm of art, may be placed *collage* and *frottage*, and the development of the idea of the element of anonymity and chance in artistic creation. From this idea of chance, or hazard (which really began in the days of Dada, with the production of poems by extracting words at random from a hat) to the paranoiac system introduced by Dali, the development is much the same as that followed by Freud from his *Interpretation of Dreams* to *The Psycho-pathology of Everyday Life*, in which he advances the theory that accidents are very largely predetermined by psychic necessity. Objective hazard as the pivot of the surrealist conception of life, is the subject to which Breton is at present devoting his attention; and Dali has always contended that surrealist objects "take the form of desire." No longer does a surrealist await the message or the image to arise from the vast unconscious residue of experience; he actively imposes the image of his desires and obsessions upon the concrete, daylight world of objective reality; he actively takes part in "accidents" that reveal the true nature of the mechanism that is life far more clearly than "pure psychic automatism" could.

In addition to all this we must take into consideration the unchanging political position of the surrealists in opposing bourgeois society, attacking religion, patriotism and the idea of family, and in declaring their belief in the principles of Communism and their solidarity with the proletariat of all countries.[63]

Surrealism had an artistic program that took its point of departure from Freud and a political program based on Marx—though Breton declared that surrealism should not be restricted by an affiliation with any party.[64] Surrealism confronted two *problems:* the "relations between the conscious and the unconscious" and "the social action we should pursue."[65] Anyone who read a fraction of the literature about surrealism witnessed contradictions, hurried modifications, and squabbling that gave unintended resonance to Breton's statement "Surrealism, as I envisage it, displays our complete *nonconformity.* . . . [I]t can but testify to the complete state of distraction to which we hope to attain here below."[66] Fortunately the surrealists were not without humor, even had a doctrine of "objective humor" corresponding to "objective chance."[67] They had, also, faith: "a new affirmation . . . of the *omnipotence of desire,* which has remained, since the beginnings, surrealism's sole act of faith," a faith fulfilled in surrealist works. "The contradictions of the personality are resolved in the work of art: that is one of the first principles of Surrealism."[68]

All these surrealist "fundamentals" are touched on in De Vries's work, and it is unnecessary to seek further to define a coherent surrealist "theory" that De Vries might have adapted: surrealists and nonsurrealists alike drew attention to the diffuseness of the movement. Breton, despite his attempts to impose orthodoxy and his tyrannical reputation, could also be expansive. In his 1934 address "What Is Surrealism?" which moderated many of the positions taken in the manifestos, Breton says that the word *surrealism* "expresses—and always has expressed for us—a desire to deepen the foundations of the real, to bring about an ever clearer and at the same time ever more passionate consciousness of the world perceived by the senses"; that "surrealism has not been drawn up as an abstract system, that is to say, safeguarded against all contradictions"; and that surrealism is a living movement in a "constant process of becoming." As Gascoyne had remarked, "it should be clear that surrealism is by no means simply a recipe, or 'specific method of creation.' Rather is it a starting-point for works of the most striking diversity, capable of almost infinite variation and development." Herbert Read stood by the formulation "superrealism in general is the romantic principle in art." Eluard was capable of the blithe assertion in a single essay that "Surrealism is a state of mind" and "an instrument of knowledge." Georges Hugnet followed Breton in saying that surrealism's "faith is that it always has existed, and always will," and perhaps went further than Breton in asserting that "Surrealism puts the emphasis on the experimental power of poetry . . . so any number of forms of expression find their place within the surrealist system." Julien Levy put the case in the most salesmanly terms:

> *SURREALISM* is not a rational, dogmatic, and consequently static theory of art. *SURREALISM* is a point of view. . . . *SURREALISM* attempts to intensify experience . . . hence for the surrealist point of view, there can be no accurate definition or explanation. The point of view is essentially anti-definitive and anti-explanatory. . . . Surrealism should not be difficult to understand. It is not a specialized monopoly of a few mysterious initiates. . . . Every one shares the subconscious. Every one can enjoy poetry and every one can make it.

As Dali had proclaimed at the Museum of Modern Art in 1934, "For Surrealism the only requisite is a receptive and intuitive human being." As a literary man, De Vries might have been distressed at the ease with which one could be a surrealist artist, were he not impatient with the high tradition and capable of being amused by Hugh Davies's sally at "Mr. Eliot" as "the last (surely the last?) of the Jacobites."[69]

As a writer seeking a large audience, as a student of American culture, and even as a radio actor, De Vries would have been interested by the surrealists' opening the movement to popular culture. Breton admired "the Mac Sennett Comedies." The apocalyptic 1920 Paris "Dada Festival" was heralded by the (false) advertisement "Personal appearance of Charlie Chaplin." The first number of the review *The Surrealist Revolution* contains a "'still' from a Buster Keaton film." Levy's *Surrealism*, which declared cinema "the perfect medium" for surrealism, shows the Marx brothers in *Animal Crackers*.[70] Journalists, critics, and curators perceived the popular culture connections. *Time*'s review of the 1936 Museum of Modern Art show notes that the "fantastic art" segment included "comic cartoons of Rube Goldberg and the frustrated drawings of James Thurber." When Barry Byrne refers

to the vogue for surrealism in New York as an "art circus," it is hard
not to be reminded of P. T. Barnum's American Museum. Northrop
Frye observed that "Max Ernst's 'Burning Woman' is not far from
the comic strip Olive Oyle," but was outdone by Alex McGavick,
who mentions Cab Calloway, Mickey Mouse, Popeye, and Ripley (of
"Believe It or Not") in his earnestness to share his enthusiasm for
surrealism by analogies all can understand.[71]

De Vries may have been sensitized to such popular-culture connections by a book written in Grand Rapids, Michigan, while he was a
college student there. Constance Rourke insists in *American Humor:
A Study of the National Character* that "humor is a matter of fantasy,"
that "humor has been a fashioning instrument in America," and that
"a characteristic humor has emerged, quiet, explosive, competitive,
often grounded in good humor, still theatrical at bottom and full of
large fantasy." Her book offers abundant evidence that American
popular culture and high culture are inextricably related, nowhere
more so than in the realm of humor. In discussing the folk culture
that underlies canonical American literature, she employs the term
"supernatural" as in "the true tall tale with its stress upon the supernatural."[72] The phenomena described, however, are not ghosts or
spirits, but exaggerations, prodigies, twists, incongruities, dreams,
and surprises; they are, like Popeye cartoons, "full of large fantasy."
They might just as well be called surreal. When Rourke traces the
evolution of the emblematic figure Uncle Sam, she follows Emerson's
observation that "the schools of poets, and philosophers, are not more
intoxicated with their symbols, than the populace with theirs. . . .
The people fancy they hate poetry, and they are all poets and mys-
tics!"[73] She writes, in fact, that "the poetic sense of life and of character has prevailed."[74]

The decade following publication of Rourke's *American Humor* confirmed her views. Adversity bred a great decade of American humor.
The New Yorker thrived. Thurber and Perelman, Benchley and White,
did much of their best work. So did the Marx brothers, W. C. Fields,
the Three Stooges, in film, and Elzie Segar (*Popeye*), Chester Gould
(*Dick Tracy*), and Bill Holman (*Smokey Stover*) in cartoons. It was the
great age of radio: "In some adventure and mystery programs of
radio's so-called 'Golden Age' (I was listening, intensively, as a child
between 1934 and 1942) radioland was peopled by figures, images
and mythic concepts which served as formidable initiators of poetry
and enchantment," wrote the surrealist poet Philip Lamantia. His
article appears in *Surrealism & Its Popular Accomplices*, which makes a
spirited case that the "qualities of the best in popular culture are no
less qualities of surrealism." Adversaries of surrealism are repelled by

such appropriations; surely many surrealist "accomplices" (Chester Gould leaps to mind) are unwitting accessories. Yet there is no denying that the surrealists have identified a common ground. It is hard to dispute the assertion that "W. C. Fields is surrealist in everything," or to gainsay Antonin Artaud's pronouncement that "if there is a definite characteristic, a distinct poetic state of mind that can be called surrealism, *Animal Crackers* participated in that state altogether."[75]

*   *   *

Sometimes it is difficult to extract, whole, the nut of an author's meaning from the intricate shell of his style.—Peter De Vries, "Poetry and the War," 119

In 1940, then, the year of Fields's *The Bank Dick*, of Breton's *Anthologie de l'humour noir,* in the same month as the first issue of Charles Henri Ford's *View* magazine, De Vries published *But Who Wakes the Bugler?*—a first novel that includes an incompetent detective, De Quinceian black humor, and a parody-before-the-fact of *View*.

4

A Reading of *But Who Wakes the Bugler?*

In 1932 in *Les Vases Communicants* André Breton wrote, "*The poet has come into being to overcome the depressing idea of an irreparable divorce between action and dream*"; and Salvador Dali states that, "*Realism, practical-rational, includes all the sordid mechanisms of logic and all mental prisons. Pleasure includes our world of subconscious desires, dreams, irrationality and imagination.*"—Julian Levy[1]

*B*UT *Who Wakes the Bugler?* is a burlesque of both the comedy of manners and the mystery.[2] Its plot is a courtship, its subplot the investigation of a death. Each, and the numerous subsidiary plots, is treated as farce. Written under a hectic schedule that made De Vries feel he was living in a Mack Sennett reel, the novel took an unusual form.

De Vries was a radio actor, and his episodic novel sounds like a radio serial. An emblematic Charles Addams cartoon heads each of its thirty-five chapters. As the action unwinds and the plots ravel, the insouciant third-person narrator who mediates the hero's thoughts employs allusions and parodies that keep the reader's literary synapses jumping. This variety show resembles a surrealist collage, creating unstable ironies in which disquieting improbabilities become possible.[3] When the irony does stabilize, *Bugler* satirizes, with equal enthusiasm, both surrealist and bourgeois. The setting is Chicago in the springtime and summer. Much of the action takes place in a rooming house whose landlord is Mr. George Thwing (whose name, according to one reviewer, is "the only bit of corny humor in the volume").[4] Mr. Thwing is a cranky, timid bachelor in early middle age, a scion of the Thurber antihero. Like Thurber's men, he is victimized by a woman: he allows himself to become engaged to Hermina, a youngish, middle-class woman of Margaret Dumont proportions. Mr. Thwing (the narrator invariably uses the title *Mr.*) is in a state of continual irritation because he fervently wants and does not want to marry. The violent death of a guest at Mr. Thwing's rooming house provides a secondary plot; Mr. Thwing engages in the investigation out of Mitty-like aspirations and nervousness and to obstruct the marriage.

There you have the recipes for several Thurber confections, complete with dinner at Schrafft's (here, sandwiches and stiff drinks at Rago's bar), but De Vries does not spend 297 pages imitating. De Vries stretches a single scenario further than Thurber ever attempted. He does so largely by resorting to "the riot of imagery, the phantasmal cast, a luxuriance of free association, the flotsam and jetsam of the oppressed psyche, all useful for the re-creation of the anxiety, tension, and horrors of the modern world," the "combination of pictorial extravagance and bold diction, [the] suggestion of dense and buried emotions tossing in a general *Weltschmertz*," the expression of "a world's chaos and fragmentation in terms of an overwrought and premonitory consciousness"—by resorting to what are in his own words poetically surrealist means.[5] De Vries made a new thing: surrealist farce. The key to this new kingdom is Mr. Thwing, the "overwrought and premonitory consciousness" who, *Bugler*'s reader is told, "often felt on the verge of something," whose "world was, take it all in all, luminous" (6)—and who is a surrealist without knowing it.

* * *

In the surrealist novel the principal personages have a function similar to that of a lightning conductor.—J. H. Matthews[6]

Each morning, as we learn first thing, Mr. Thwing does a getting-up exercise: automatic writing.

> Mr. Thwing was neither asleep nor awake, but in that subaqueous twilight he had become singularly skilled at prolonging, for sometimes as much as hours after the stupidly punctual jangle of the alarm clock. Mr. Thwing loved sleep in all its degrees—from the briefly fluttered veil of a thirty-second doze in somebody's waiting room to the obliterating curtainfall of night. But what he fancied most was this lush middle-point at which he could so handily arrest his awaking, a faint and luxurious appeasement still swimming with the green-refracted sea-girls, but curiously sensed, and hence stranger for it, from the returning level of daylight consciousness.
> This night there had been many voices in his dreams, calling strange things. They were still there. . . .
> Then turning over he dozed back into the delicious languor shot with the receding jabberwocky of sleep.
> He lay there for about ten minutes. Then he got up, promptly and

with no preliminary stirring and stretching, walked to his desk, drew a sheet from the drawer and, standing up, wrote swiftly the following:

All the birds whimper and my bed goodbye, the engines beat and the wind blows rain, rain rain in vain on the clanking man whose tall candles bleed and the bushes laugh on the whanged scarlet of my sullen shore and the heaved melons burst on the hissing sea.

He wrote this down with no hesitation and as fast as he could make the pen go, underneath about a half-page of other writing. (2–4)

Unlike Saint-Pol-Roux, Mr. Thwing does not have a notice posted on his door every evening before he goes to sleep reading THE POET IS WORKING.[7] He is a truly clandestine poet, diffident as the Prufrock his revery recalls. Yet he does have inklings that his dreams, like his occasional drinking binges, make him "tributary of something illimitable and resurgent," and he feels "within himself a force, an *élan*" (6). He is also a seer: he dreamed of the murder victim, Captain Jehoiachim, before the latter arrived at the rooming house. But Hermina "pooh-poohed" the dream; "everybody always pooh-poohed his belief that there were more things Horatio than are dreamt of in your philosophy" (35). Bourgeois complacency rejects everything magical.

De Vries's conceit is to arm a Thurberesque *homme moyen sensuel* with surrealist artillery only to install him as the ineffectual landlord of a Chicago rooming house. Instead of juxtaposing images, De Vries juxtaposes worlds. When his surrealist-in-spite-of-himself opens his eyes while kissing Hermina and sees "a Cubistic sketch" (34), "a Picasso" (92), he finds heightened reality unsettling.

Yet Mr. Thwing shares with the narrator (and with such poets as Charles Henri Ford[8]) a metamorphic, allusive imagination:

The effect of the man, tall and bristling yet with a quality of cloudy remoteness about him, seen through smoke from a vile black pipe, was hallucinative. He had a beard about the texture of a street-sweeper's broom. Looking at him you felt he might be not altogether man but part cactus.

He seemed a facsimile of several things at once. Mr. Thwing's mind began to sort out these impressions. Frankenstein, a Chicago *Tribune* bolshevik. (20)

Mr. Thwing collects his leaves of automatic writing, fiddles them into free verse, and muses "Author. The idea made him pause. Well—why not?" (47). Undeterred by his inability to understand his own poems—"none of it made any sense to him, ever,"—he sends them off to a magazine chosen at random (47). He receives a rejection note that suggests "Might try *New Age*," published in Connecticut by George Henri Brezon (61), and has the good fortune to have the poems accepted there. Mr. Thwing is flustered by Brezon's acceptance letter, though, for it is as "bewildering" as Mr. Thwing's poems: "How vividly you retain the hegemony of the Unconscious. . . . And the phallic substance will make them go well with an article I'm doing," Brezon breezes on, sending Mr. Thwing in search of a dictionary (62).

When Mr. Thwing receives *New Age,* he finds, among works as unintelligible to him as his own, the promised article:

> There was an article by the editor Brezon on the latest trends in Surrealism, in which he made reference to Mr. Thwing's group, and their "preservation of the pure *élan*," and the sense of "leashed hysteria" he found in them, thus giving first publication to what was an "unmistakably authentic and startling talent."
>
> Mr. Thwing thought he would like to go out and take a walk. (145–46)

Mr. Thwing is discomfited to see his *élan* characterized in just that way. Brezon compounds the foolishness of his blithe assumption that only another avowed surrealist could write such poems with the pretentious fraud of inventing a whole "group" to which Mr. Thwing can belong. It is worth noticing that in promoting "talent," Brezon departs from the surrealist doctrine of talentlessness, of poetry made by all. "Very well, then, I contradict myself," might be Brezon's defense. In making his surrealist impresario a poetic P. T. Barnum, De Vries lampoons surrealist opportunism. He also lampoons surrealist elitism and obscurantism. When Brezon arrives in Chicago, Mr. Thwing hurriedly attempts to grasp some of the meanings of the magazine with the help of a dime-store dictionary, but he fails again (223). Hoping to gain insight into his own work, Mr. Thwing asks Brezon to explain the poems to his acquaintances but, for *their* sake, to "put things as simply as possible" (228).

* * *

> How much of all our emotions, our longing, our impulses, our motives, are sexual, and we don't know it!—George Henri Brezon

Brezon is an intriguing creation. De Vries denies satirizing any individual—"Brezon wasn't based on anybody"[9]—so it seems he is to be taken as a sort of surrealist straw man. His stuffing comes from various sources. Brezon's location of *New Age* in Connecticut alludes to Charles Henri Ford's having set up there, as announced in *London*

Bulletin number 7 (December 1938–January 1939).[10] The name
George Henri Brezon can only be an amalgam of *George* Dillon, the
editor of *Poetry;* Charles *Henri* Ford, the poet, whose own *View* magazine would appear simultaneously with *Bugler;* and André *Breton*,
whose surname De Vries tweaks into a gallic pronunciation of the
word *brazen*, as well as playing on "breeze on." Both Breton and
Brezon are, naturally, French. Brezon physically resembles Breton:
"Mr. Brezon was a short, energetic, dark man who came through the
door (and ever after that seemed to walk) as though a terrific wind
were blowing behind him" (223).[11] Suiting a flimflam artist, his pos-
ture and gait are also reminiscent of Groucho Marx: "He seemed to
arch forward slightly in the middle, like some of those people apparently bent on walking a little better than erect" (224); "Mr. Brezon
preceded him into the hall, offspring of a Spanish dancer and a sling-
shot" (234). Like Breton, Brezon fulminates against Salvador Dali:
"cheap, crass, sensational, obvious stuff to tickle the ribs of people
who think they are really *avant-garde*. Compare him to somebody
like di [*sic*] Chirico. Oh! . . . You see him for what he is—not quite
as important as Walt Disney" (226). Like Breton, Brezon is a friend
of Eluard (226). There is at least one in-joke alluding to Breton, in
an otherwise unmotivated paragraph:

> Mr. Brezon, sunk in deep thought, had been reminded of a cousin of
> his. He told Mr. Thwing about him. Alapert his name was, and Mr.
> Brezon wondered what had ever become of him. He was an employee of
> a large publishing house who had gone insane proofreading Proust. (233)

Breton himself once had a contretemps with Proust:

> Fortunately he had rich companions who could come to his aid; fortu-
> nately also, through his connections with Paul Valéry and Apollinaire, he
> made contacts with the publishing world and got occasional editing jobs.
> But his mind was not on copy reading and he made a poor editor as Proust
> in a letter to Soupault pointed out ever so delicately and discreetly: "I
> see that my next book, though copy-read by M. Breton, contained so
> many mistakes that if I did not list an erratum I would be dishonored."
> It had taken the disgruntled Proust eight days to find two hundred mis-
> takes in twenty-three galley pages, which comprised half the book. He
> reached the height of politeness not unmarked by benign innuendoes
> when he added: "But by no means let M. Breton take this for a
> reproach."[12]

How De Vries learned this story remains an open question; the *Poetry*
network must have carried interesting bulletins. De Vries never met

Breton, though he was later to live on the same street in Greenwich Village as the surrealist in exile.[13] Unlike Brezon, Breton spoke no English. Another send-up, "young Carpenter," who publishes the annual *Trends* and Mr. Thwing's first book (224, 277), appears to be a caricature of New Directions founder James Laughlin.[14]

In one aspect, Brezon is a caricature surrealist given to damaging admissions: "'This country's only just now becoming aware of us, now that it's about done in France,' he smiled wryly. 'But of course the poetry didn't make its own way in,' he went on sarcastically. 'It rode in on the coat-tails of the painters. It had to be semi-ridiculous before the Americans would pay any attention to it" (225–26). He declaims like Falstaff while stuffing himself with bread and butter. Brezon also refers to a "Mrs. Frethney-Budd," apparently a wealthy patron (62), no doubt the result of De Vries's sniping at the reliance of surrealists on patronage while preaching revolution. These insults would have stung the Breton who denied the death of French surrealism and proclaimed the priority of verbal over visual surrealism; as in his light-verse sallies at Eliot, Auden, and company, De Vries knew where to aim.

Brezon has, however, a more sympathetic side. When he reads Mr. Thwing's poems at a cocktail party at Hermina's, the bourgeois are lost: "Nobody understood them. 'It's modern poetry,' the librarian was heard, in the suddenly quieting crowd, to whisper. 'You're not supposed to understand it'" (236):

> Mr. Brezon lit a cigarette. "Well," he plunged, "with Thwing the poem is a kind of fantasia on a chosen theme. As with most of us writing in his vein. Spiritually he is best considered an heir of D. H. Lawrence—one of those exploring what he discovered. His poetry is eruptive, vital, automatic—to an extent—a release of the deepmost springs. The *élan vital*. Of course the phallic symbolism is clear," he said, and now Mr. Thwing lit a cigarette himself. "The bellowing plow, for instance; you could not ask for a more vital, savagely vital, if you please, expression of the male principle. There is the immemorial kinship," he went on more or less routinely, "between the female and the field." Mr. Thwing looked at Hermina, who was looking down at the floor. "The One upsurge, the fierce and phallic asseverations, grape and maypole." And then Mr. Brezon went on, shifting in his chair, and speaking now more deliberately and less glibly, frowning at the floor: "There is another element in him—the negative, which is of course, in all of us, warring with this positive. Fear, denial . . . fear. The regressive tendency, the longing to go back to the womb rather than prevail over it, the . . . fear. The nightmares of the dissolving candles and the loss in the obliterating sea . . ."

"What on earth does he mean by 'my gouged mansion'?" the former missionary asked. . . . (236–37)

Mr. Thwing's lighting up a cigarette is part of the novel's phallic humor, imbedded in what might be taken ostensibly as a send-up of Freudian criticism; what Brezon describes in Mr. Thwing's poems is true of De Vries's novel: phallic symbolism is one of the languages spoken here. Brezon's apologetics for George Thwing sound, in fact, like a sexier version of De Vries's for Dylan Thomas in his *College English* article.[15]

Brezon doesn't get very far with his program of enlightenment: "What does phallic mean?" finally asks one of the ladies, possibly echoing one of the women De Vries addressed in his benefit lectures for *Poetry*. As the group breaks up for refreshments, Brezon, nettled, disparages "sentimental bourgeois songster" Jessica Dragonette,[16] then extols Mr. Thwing as the grandson of Mallarmé and the great-grandson of Coleridge—certainly news to Mr. Thwing. Like the Breton of the second manifesto, Brezon asks "After all . . . what is surrealism but another, further, liberation of the imaginative and the spontaneous and the individual—the aim of the Romantics from Wordsworth down" (243).[17] Brezon challenges his hearers by exclaiming, "How much of all our emotions, our longing, our impulses, our motives, are sexual and we don't know it!"—an assertion supported by many proofs throughout the novel. Finally he confides to Mr. Thwing "the more I think of it, . . . the more I am convinced there's absolutely no use of our worrying about the *bourgeoisie*—in any way at all," to which Mr. Thwing replies "Nah" (245). This exchange caps the comical colloquy between the two, Brezon sublimely confident in his own views and the loyalty of Mr. Thwing and Mr. Thwing agonizedly attempting to conceal his own befuddlement. Brezon's rejection of the bourgeoisie is his way of masking the ineffectuality of his ambiguous efforts to assault and educate them.

Brezon is a poseur and a victim of his own romantic enthusiasm. He is made credulous by his supposed sophistication, which leads him to wildly overvalue Mr. Thwing's poems—parodies of Charles Henri Ford's. (It is characteristic of De Vries's world to have a caricature judge a parody.) But Brezon is perceptive about the sexual element in discourse, while their willful ignorance renders the social intercourse of his bourgeois companions ludicrous. As for Brezon's being in effect the goat of a hoax, Dillon and De Vries had just suffered that indignity themselves.[18] If Brezon were ever to realize that Mr. Thwing is a fake, he would no doubt handle it as blithely.

In Brezon, De Vries ridiculed surrealism's self-promotion, made merry with the tenets of orthodox surrealism, and dabbled in the *roman à clef,* while acknowledging the surrealists' vigor and the accuracy of their critique—if not necessarily their final judgment—of the middle class. For, as the abject Mr. Thwing illustrates, middle-class life is a waking nightmare and the bourgeois worldview nothing other than a complete fiasco.

* * *

> When that I was and a little tiny boy,
>   With hey, ho, the wind and the rain,
> A foolish thing was but a toy,
>   For the rain it raineth every day.
> —*Twelfth Night* 5.1.398–401

Mr. Thwing is a lightning rod for the forces of clashing cultures—or culture and counterculture—a "thing" meant for the conduction of ideas. As Joseph De Roller has observed, the name *Thwing* combines the words *swing* (for indecisiveness) and *thing* (for phallus),[19] marking its bearer as both a live wire and a short circuit. In the dramatic action, Mr. Thwing is "a little man of many sides, most of them regrettable."[20] According to one view, Mr. Thwing "seems clearly to be drawn from Thurber's Walter Mitty," but this is an oversimplification.[21] Mr. Thwing does lapse into heroic daydreams, but daydreaming is among his milder eccentricities. Of "The Secret Life of Walter Mitty," De Vries wrote in 1961: "What is more universal after all than the private daydream? What have we more in common than the urge delusively to set ourselves apart? It is no accident that [Thurber's] most famous and widely enjoyed story is one that distills the very essence of this human weakness—if that is what it is."[22] De Vries's qualification signals that there may be mitigating circumstances—that daydreaming may even be a strength. In any case Mr. Thwing's problems run deeper.

All the emphasis in "Walter Mitty" is on waking dreams. *Bugler* emphasizes Mr. Thwing's sleep dreams and the leakage of their hallucinatory quality into waking reality, the dreams' portentous content, and the use to which Mr. Thwing puts his dreams in his writing. In Mr. Thwing's poems De Vries parodies Ford, as he would later parody Cummings and other poets he admired,[23] but Mr. Thwing is nevertheless an artist, actually a purer, more disinterested artist than Brezon. Mr. Thwing's status as an imaginative man relates him much more closely to the heroes of Thurber's *Middle-Aged Man on the Flying Trapeze* (1935) and the Thurber of *Let Your Mind Alone!* (1937)—the sources of the pieces De Vries discusses in "James Thurber: The

Comic Prufrock"—than to "Walter Mitty" (1939). In particular Mr. Thwing is beset by the conflict of his inner visions with outward restraints in ways familiar from "The Private Life of Mr. Bidwell," whose hero ends up walking down a country road with his eyes closed; "The Curb in the Sky," whose hero's invented dreams land him in an asylum; and "The Remarkable Case of Mr. Bruhl," whose hero's paranoid fantasy of being mistaken for a gangster leads to the schizoid belief that he is the gangster.[24]

De Vries's use of a Thurburesque hero leads to the question of what surrealism might mean for American writers. Thurber rejected Freud's "theory of the unconscious origins of art,"[25] and he spoofed popular psychology's vulgar Freudianism with such sallies as *Let Your Mind Alone!* In "The Secret Life of James Thurber," he disparages the antics Dali had celebrated in his *Secret Life of Salvador Dali* (1942).[26] Nevertheless, a kinship between Thurber and Dali has been established by several critics:

> Thurber found that he could not arouse much sympathetic admiration for the behavior of Salvador Dali, who as an *enfant terrible* attempted to escape from the commonplace by biting bats, kissing dead horses, kicking tiny playmates off bridges, [etc.]. . . . Thurber did not join with the townspeople of Figueras in worshiping Dali; instead he objected to Dali's conduct as a "desperate little rebellion against the clean, the conventional, and the comfortable." . . .
>
> Thurber dismissed the conceited exhibitionism of artiness (as distinct from art) as precious affectation. He recalled that the adult world in which he was brought up consisted mainly of "eleven maternal great-aunts, all Methodists, who were staunch believers in physic, mustard plasters, and Scripture, and it was part of their dogma that artistic tendencies should be treated in the same way as hiccups or hysterics. . . . It never occurred to me to bite a bat in my aunt's presence or to throw stones at them."
>
> Of course conformity is not the answer either. Thurber himself was an artist; and, though he washed his hair with Ivory soap and owned a bull terrier, he shared with Dali the imagination of a surrealist. Though objecting to the irresponsible extremes of Dali's youthful conduct, he could hardly be in complete sympathy with his great-aunts, whose outlook requires a dull conformity to the norm—and a turn-of-the-century norm at that. He too had to escape, he explained, through his secret world of idiom; and the "Ah there, Salvador," with which he concluded his essay seems as much a greeting as a reproach. This conflict between romantic individuality and unimaginative conventionality is at the crux of much of Thurber's art.[27]

The conflict is also De Vries's and Mr. Thwing's. As Francis Hackett pointed out, Thurber develops fantasy "against the dead weight of the bourgeois community"; Thurber deflates deviations from the norm, yet "to be inflated, to be enchanted, to admit magic, to be carried away, is still native to him, and comes to him in blasts of fantasy that are touched with nightmare and fear and horror. He does not want to be differentiated lest he be too much so. He may be from Columbus, but he may also be brother to Salvador Dali under his skin."[28]

Thurber may have been brother to Dali subconsciously as well as subcutaneously: "The drawings which spring from the Unconscious (or 'Stream of Nervousness,' as Thurber called it in 'The Lady on the Bookcase') are those dealing with neurosis, hallucination, and other psychic disturbances. Some mix dream elements and reality so that we are never quite sure which is which, as with the seal in the bedroom. . . . Some drawings are 'Unconscious' in the sense that their meaning is obscure, like the images in dreams," observes Charles S. Holmes in *The Clocks of Columbus*. It is easy to imagine those Ohio clocks melting like Dali's limp watches. As Holmes points out,

> Disorder and confusion are anathema to the world at large, but for Thurber they are sources of possible liberation. They are at the heart of a set of closely related values which, until his very last years, he habitually champions in opposition to the dominant ideals of contemporary society. In a world committed to logic, organization, conformity, and efficiency, Thurber stands for fantasy, spontaneity, idiosyncrasy, and confusion. . . . The whole of *My Life and Hard Times* is a celebration of what might be called the Principle of Confusion, or the Fantasy Principle. Nearly every episode shows the disruption of the orderly pattern of everyday life by the idiosyncratic, the bizarre, the irrational.[29]

More recently, Catherine McGehee Kenney has shown that "both Thurber and Dali see the dream in the reality and vice versa":

> their work portrays the constant interchange of the real and unreal, the movement between the dream world and the actual world. Although Thurber protests too much that Dali has had a more lively and exotic life than he ("Let me be the first to admit that the naked truth about me is to the naked truth about Salvador Dali as an old ukelele in the attic is to a piano in a tree, and I mean a piano with breasts"), he gradually admits to a kind of kinship with the antic surrealist. As surrealism stresses the nonrational and subconscious significance of imagery and especially exploits unexpected juxtapositions, Dali and Thurber share a similar artistic vision of the ever-changing face of reality:

> Two years ago my wife and I, looking for a house to buy, called on a firm of real estate agents in New Milford. One of the members of the firm, scrabbling through a metal box containing many keys, looked up to say, "The key to the Roxbury house isn't here." His partner replied, "It's a common lock. A skeleton will let you in." I was suddenly once again five years old, with wide eyes and open mouth. I pictured the Roxbury house as I would have pictured it as a small boy, a house of such dark and nameless horrors as never crossed the mind of our little bat-biter.

> The "fantastic cosmos" that Thurber inhabits as a result of the ability of language to transmogrify experience is haunted by an infinite number of such images and visions, visions that are often only slightly reminiscent of the literal or factual reality to which the words relate. A skeleton key, in no way a horror in the actual world, becomes an image of indescribable horrors.[30]

In sum, Mr. Thwing's many ancestors in Thurber had more than just a few old coat hangers hanging around in their closets.

Among the stories in *The Middle-Aged Man on the Flying Trapeze*, "certainly the most disturbing piece, for Thurber's friends and readers," says Thurber's biographer Burton Bernstein, "was 'A Box to Hide In,' the tale of a miserably lonely man on the brink of insanity searching for a womblike box to call his home."[31] It is from this nameless protagonist that Mr. Thwing inherits his most strikingly regressive trait: hiding in his clothes closet. Thurber's pathetic man, unable to find a box big enough to hold him, hides in his darkened room, musing "I could have hid in a closet, I suppose, but people are always opening doors. Somebody would find you in a closet."[32] De Vries's Mr. Thwing is more confident:

> It was cool and dark in there. It was quite a while since he'd gone into the clothes closet, he mused, sitting there on the floor with his head against the clothes. He pushed away a slipper that got caught under his legs and settled himself comfortably. He heard dimly the sounds of the outside world, faraway voices and footsteps in the house, the dim, reiterant thrum of traffic, like dim surging sounds undersea. He thought back down time, how he used to do this, the old lost years; but it was not like playing grotto now; different.
>
> It was cool and dark in there. He wondered if they would ever find him. They would never think of looking here. Might as well get lost in the Canadian Northwest. (176)

He indulges in a daydream that commingles Jack London, Longfellow, and Thurber, and he airs his chief resentment:

> They all want you to settle down, marry and settle down, leaving them the car to go to the bridge club and the League of Women Voters, and

then they feed you soft salads, they make you chairman of women's clubs, they shear you, leaving you no Matterhorn. (177)

The matter with his Matterhorn, Mr. Thwing thinks, is that the humdrum world had deprived him of challenge, of a mountain to scale, but the reader sees that Mr. Thwing is afraid Hermina is castrating him. Mr. Thwing's day-long revery leads through questions about religious faith, couched in parody as part of the Jack London daydream;[33] a keen sense of "exquisite pleasure . . . in this close and pleasantly musty, secret-smelling darkness"; a recital of his neurotic symptoms (failing, in that, to leave his mind alone); and finally the bald admission "I was afraid of the poetry, which fascinated me, and [Hermina], who fascinated me too. I wanted to do two things. One was get married; the other was to stay single. But I tried to hold up in one piece" (177–81). He later mentally revisits this "cool and dark" sanctuary (235, 258), trying to hold together his aspirations and his reality by shutting out the world.

Being driven into close quarters puts Mr. Thwing in the company of de Chirico's hero in the 1929 novel *Hebdomeros:*

> Hebdomeros does not take long to succumb to a sense of estrangement, which instills the feeling that any gesture, however heroic it may be, is useless. . . . At the same time his state of mind produces in him a preference for rooms in which one can shut oneself up behind locked doors, with curtains drawn. "But he breathed not a word of all these preferences which he had, fearing not to be understood and fearing above all to be taken for insane and brought to the attention of the medical authorities. . . ."[34]

For another surrealist novelist, Julien Gracq, the most crucial question in literature is, "'Can one get out of a room hermetically sealed?' . . . Subconsciously, he believes, the reader raises in his own mind the even more intriguing question: 'Can one get out of this room we all live in?'"[35] Mr. Thwing, finding no exit from the room of social intercourse, retreats within, to Prufrock's "grotto."

In his remarks on Thurber as comic Prufrock, De Vries notes:

> It is hard to think of anyone who more closely resembles the Prufrock of Eliot than the middle-aged man on the flying trapeze. This preoccupied figure is Prufrock's comic counterpart, not in intensity of course, but in detail. There is, for instance, the same dominating sense of Predicament. The same painful and fastidious self-inventory, the same detailed anxiety; the same immersion in weary minutiae, the same self-disparagement, the same wariness of the evening's company. And the

same fear, in summary, that someone—in Thurber's case a brash halfback or maybe even a woman—will "drop a question on his plate."[36]

The question for Mr. Thwing is "to wed or not to wed," which is bound up for him with the questions to bed or not to bed, to be read or not to be read. Inability to cope with a woman, De Vries says, is a "landmark" in Eliot's early poetry: "There is a 'sensation of being ill at ease.' Is there a sensation of which Thurber has given more repeated illustration? . . . What contemporary disquiet has he caught here? . . . The male is on the wane, corroded with introspection, deflated by all his own inefficient efficiency, without 'strength to force the moment to its crisis,' his love lyric in desuetude" (153–54). Mr. Thwing joins Prufrock and the middle-aged man on the flying trapeze as an icon of sexual repression, but he differs in taking the step of becoming a surrealist artist. De Vries in effect discusses the surreal in his piece on Thurber:

> The contempt of the man with both feet on the ground for the artist with one of them in fantasy, is familiar. See how you end up? You get farther and farther from reality, till you finally get simply in a state of whatayamacallit—schizophrenia. That's what modern artists are, high class schizophrenics. The answer is of course, simply, what do you mean by reality; and the point is an important one. I referred, with rather loose whimsicality I suppose, to Thurber as jester in Axel's Castle, and his work may be a rivulet running "individual sensibility" off into a kind of *reductio ad absurdum*—not that some of the serious exponents of Symbolism haven't already done so. But whatever the excesses of Symbolism may have been, it has not only made a notable contribution to modern literature but by its emphasis on subjective experience has helped us to a richer idea of what "reality" is. Just as poetry and profit are where you find them, reality is what you make it. The angle of refraction according to the perceiving psyche is *always* there, and the individual's extracting from the world round about him constitutes an experience that is itself a reality; a point which modern artists have been trying to make for over a generation. (158)

Mr. Thwing's artistic strength is that he does have an open window on the unconscious; his flaw is that he cannot grasp the message that "is itself a reality." He tacitly accepts the contemptuous diagnosis of the man with both feet on the ground—schizophrenia—and remains indecisive: "Thus it was all the time. The tide of paranoia going in and out" (143).

A reviewer once glibly wrote that "Peter De Vries does for schizophrenia what the late James Thurber did for paranoia," and more recently one encounters the view that "Thurber's tendencies were toward paranoia while De Vries's incline much more in the direction of schizophrenia."[37] De Vries's bantering of "whatayamacallit" psychiatric terms cautions against such simplistic formulations. Yet surrealists blithely adapted psychiatric jargon, revealingly for *Bugler* in one case, that is, Salvador Dali's famous *paranoiac-critical method*, which he expounded in an essay translated into English by J. Bronowski in 1932 and widely discussed in the surrealist literature of the 1930s.[38] As André Breton pointed out, Dali's paranoiac-critical activity was a way to discover "irrational knowledge"; "the secret of surrealism lies in the fact that we are persuaded that something is hidden behind [appearances]."[39] Mr. Thwing's always being "on the verge of something" recalls this secret. David Gascoyne spelled out that Dali's *paranoia* meant not "persecution complex" but the ability "to draw from the objective world a concrete proof, or illustration, of his obsessions, or even of his transitory ideas."[40] This Daliesque activity, which Mr. Thwing engages in constantly, resembles Eliot's objective correlative. Is it surprising that the champion of the metaphysical poets should share a doctrine of the image with Dali, who celebrated the yoking together of images by violence?

Dali emphasizes the double image: "The way in which it has been possible to obtain a double image is clearly paranoiac. By a double image is meant such a representation of an object that it is also, without the slightest physical or anatomical change, the representation of another entirely different object, the second representation being equally devoid of any deformation or abnormality betraying arrangement."[41] In a Dali canvas, a locust and a woman's face, for example, alternately may be visible. In *Bugler*, Mr. Thwing is such a double image. A shirker and ditherer as an Everyman, an *homme revolté* and vatic poet as a surrealist, he is himself a surreal object, a paranoid-critical image. He is both himself and his double. The doubling motif is sustained in doubled words like *Baden-Baden* and *hula-hula* (135–36), double-decker buses (211), and the doubled personae of "it seemed there were two of him" (213) and Mr. Thwing's disguise (198–205).

Dali liked to proclaim ignorance of his own intentions: "'That is why it is so amazing,' he will say innocently. 'Even *I* do not know what it means'"—but then he will go on to deliver elaborate pseudo-explanations.[42] Mr. Thwing's work is amazing because he actually *doesn't* know what it means; ergo, it is even more amazing work than Dali's. De Vries pries meaning loose not only from banal reality and from logic's straitjacket but also from surrealist reality and surrationalism. He dares to go the surrealists one better, offering to beat them at their own game. The point is, it is their game he is playing. Much of the humor in *Bugler* is surrealist in that it plays on controversies within surrealism. For example, Mr. Thwing tampers with his original dream transcriptions and soon "was beginning more and more to revise" (99). The nugatory effect of his rewriting pokes fun at the contest between "automatic" surrealists like Georges Hugnet—"this automatism which promises to fulfill the desire of Lautréamont. . . . The eternal revolt against mere existence in favor of profound life"— and surrealists like Paul Nougé, who demanded that dreams be whipped into shape: only a "poor beginner . . . under the pretext of Surrealism, devotes his attention solely to dream-worlds, the appearances of automatism."[43] That Mr. Thwing is a surrealist *primatif* to whom the word *automatism* would give the lexical bends is an irony best appreciated by readers acquainted with surrealism's enthusiasm for artistic *naïfs*. Similarly, the parodies of surrealist verse are funniest to those who have read the originals.

Similar ironies apply to other situations in *Bugler*. Mr. Thwing is generous and altruistic, and these qualities are emphasized by most of the critics. He also has a mean streak, though, and like many Thurber men, he is capable of outrageous malice. At one point, Mr. Thwing's revery is broken by the bleating of his neighbor's sheep. (Even in 1940 stockyards Chicago, this flock is as incongruous as those in Luis Buñuel's *Discreet Charm of the Bourgeoisie* or a Rauschenberg environment.)

> Phony. Phonily plaintive. . . . It was as though every time they opened their mouth they were trying to live up to a part—as symbols, by sentimental tradition, of defenseless pathos. Perfectly insipid! How I hate sheep, he thought. . . . Mr. Soller . . . was now fattening them up for butchering. Mr. Thwing lay back—who had few enough perversities in him—and contemplated their soon extinction with a faintly sadistic relish. (71–72)

A few pages later, he is enjoying a fine restaurant dinner of lamb chops (84). Not long after that, he is grinding his teeth and telling Hermina "I'd like to kill that guy. . . . I'd like to slaughter him and his darned old sheep both" (93). "Few enough perversities" turn out to be enough for anybody, as Mr. Thwing's sadism finds other outlets. He is rough on suspects, for example (151, 201–5). Mr. Thwing's most striking display of wickedness, however, is drunken brutality.

Mr. Thwing, sitting in Rago's bar, has just been hearing the worst from a veteran of twenty-eight years of marriage when a women's-club dinner meeting convenes in the next room. Mr. Thwing, observing with "a jaunty disdain," watches the chairwoman arrive: "She was large and imposing and swept up to the table with a kind of burly majesty. You could say that she docked" (98). In that he has recently visualized his fiancée as "a crushed blimp" (81), it is plain that Mr. Thwing connects the chairwoman with his marital fate: "That woman had had it completely," thinks Mr. Thwing while chivalrously hanging up the chairwoman's coat, "that gowned potency presiding in there among all that trussed mammalian meat" (98). By the time the ladies have generously dined, Mr. Thwing is three sheets to the wind. Fascinated by the spectacle, he drifts to the door and observes the huge desserts being served. He focuses on the chairwoman:

> She reminded him of the scene in some sea story where they cut the whale blubber. He had a terrific yen to go up to her and just knead her, knead her all over savagely. She was, they were, the Principle, the Which-will-not-let-you-be of the season which had, now, gotten him, the accomplice of the warm-blowing and progenitive month. . . .
> "Will you please not annoy us?" the chairman asked.
> Mr. Thwing went up to her. Grabbing her fleshy arm he began to knead it, digging his fingers into the muscles, baring his clenched teeth in a weird pleasure. Then, spinning her smartly around, in a vertigo at once delicious and delirious in which faces and arms and voices and conspiring hair went whirling in butterscotch fluff off to the ends of space and time, lifted his foot, poised it, and, with one more grimace, kicked her in the soft spring earth.
> There was a gasp. The chairman pushed him away. He took her by the shoulders and smacked her down in her seat. "Sit down and behave yourself," he said.
> "Why, you—!" a woman at the end of the table said. She was a tall, slim, severe-looking woman, and stood there with her hand on her hip with that menace women can get into their breathing.
> "Get out or we'll call the police," said the chairman.
> "Ah, shut up, Mrs. Moby Dick," Mr. Thwing said, and, sending a leer along the table, walked out. (101–2)

T. Jeff Evans reads this remarkable scene as a parody of "the scene in *Moby Dick* [*sic*] where Ishmael, drunk with the Life Principle and the heady draughts of a romantic idealism, squeezes the whale sperm in a joyous fellowship of brotherhood. . . . Although Thwing here, as Mitty is never able to do, accomplishes a full frontal attack on the opposite sex, the final effect of the scene is self-parodic and deprecatory." Evans uses the scene as an example of how "De Vries' parodic style can be seen as a means by which he alerts the reader that the character's conscious actions are distortions of or deviations from the true self."[44] Mr. Thwing's actions here, however, are not conscious, but semiconscious, and the "true self" is just as often revealed by delirium as distorted by it. "What evil lurks in the hearts of men," as the Shadow (whom Mr. Thwing imitates in his amateur sleuthing) knows, is not a deviation but a constant. It is hard to see here a parody of the "joyous fellowship of brotherhood" or a "full frontal attack" in a lusty kick in the buttocks. Rather than depicting Mr. Thwing as a basically nice fellow deflected from virtue by what Evans calls a "typically romantic attempt" at escape, the parody amplifies Melville's mordancy toward romantic optimism about human nature. Mr. Thwing really enjoyed digging, baring, kneading, and kicking:

> "Whad you do that for?" his companion asked. . . .
> "I couldn't help it."
> "Something just snapped, eh?" he said, putting his arm around Mr. Thwing.
> "No," Mr. Thwing said, staring firmly ahead as they wove down the street. "Something got firm." (102)

It is this same delusion of power that induces Mr. Thwing to go home and stuporously write and post a letter proposing marriage to Hermina—a proposal whose acceptance will horrify Mr. Thwing after his alcoholic sense of mastery has faded. Mr. Thwing's "sweet" proposal of marriage, thus, is a product not of love and sociability but of a hostile fantasy and a will to dominate. When the bartender, no doubt protecting Mr. Thwing from arrest for assault out of concern for his own bar license, says, "He'll be okay. He comes in here now and then; mild guy. He just had too much" (102), we hear the voice of middle-class denial of human perfidiousness. Under the "mild" rind, Mr. Thwing is as misanthropic as Ishmael, as misogynist as a Father Mapple sermon.

As Constance Rourke pointed out in 1931, Melville turned "continually toward the illusive province of inner fantasy."[45] Kenneth Burke, writing in 1940, sheds light on De Vries's parody:

> Since Mr. Calas would claim Melville as a precursor of Surrealism (I think correctly), it might also be relevant to note in Melville also the great prominence of cannibalism as motive. Indeed, to my way of thinking, it can, as a pattern of thought, be discerned as perhaps even the essential motivation of Melville, a core about which many apparently disrelated aspects of the writer's style are clustered. I have collected a quite large list of such references in "Moby Dick," ranging from the explicit mention of cannibals, cannibalism, cannibalistic acts, etc. to many more outlying variants (i.e., variants on the theme of something-living-on-its-own substance, being used by itself, etc., somewhat as with the almost mystical

laughter that arises at one point, in Mann's *Death in Venice,* laughter that is without external cause in anything funny, but that grows from one man's laughing, and others laughing at his laughter, and then laughing more and more because they were already laughing).[46]

For Ishmael, the sperm he kneads is unctuous; for Mr. Thwing, the flesh he kneads and needs is alimentary. The whale may be for fellowship, but "Mrs. Moby Dick" is for consumption, as Mr. Thwing shows by baring his teeth and leering hysterically. The sequence deprecates Mr. Thwing, all right, but not as a middle-class regular guy run temporarily amok (always merely a prelude, in the literature of uplift, to a docile gathering into the fold). Mr. Thwing is a liquored-up, watered-down sufferer of romantic agony. Surrealists were fond of claiming kinship with surrealism for any depiction of extreme human experience. Discussing via Praz's *Romantic Agony* Charles Brockden Brown's dark fictions, Swinburne as the conduit into English of Sade, Blake's sexual imagery, and other literary events, Hugh Davies notes that much Romantic art is preoccupied with the taking of pleasure in cruelty and celebrates surrealism's "magnificent iconography of melancholia and algolagnia."[47] The tableau of Mr. Thwing and the chairman is somewhere between a Dali monstrosity and a Thurber vignette. The ridiculousness of De Vries's treatment deflates not romantic idealism but romantic-surrealist anguish and perversity. This does not mean that De Vries approves of romantic idealism or sneers at romantic agony; it means that the deflation of romantic idealism is a foregone conclusion, requiring no elaborate expounding by parody, and that romantic agony is real agony, worthy of treatment by humor. The novel's premises lie far beyond, in the course of romantic irony, the starting point its commentators have claimed. In keeping with his existence as an exercise in incongruity, Mr. Thwing's substance has been most attenuated, at least for readers unattuned to *Bugler*'s surrealism, when "something got firm."

* * *

One should always be in love; that is the reason one should never marry.—Oscar Wilde, *A Woman of No Importance*

Nothing could be more flaccid than Mr. Thwing's and Hermina's off-again, on-again wedding plans. It is sentimentalized romantic idealism, enshrined as middle-class virtue, that entrapped Mr. Thwing, and he knows it: "[Hermina's] mouth was full and warm, and she was, as all women in one's arms after weeping, sweetly and ineffably suffused with Emotion" (33)—he said "what was expected": he loved her. "That's all that matters," Hermina replies, adding in typically addlepated form, "After we're married nothing will matter." "This was precisely the qualm that had, at intervals, recently troubled Mr. Thwing—that, once at that stage, nothing *would* matter any more" (34). After much suffering, climaxed by witnessing a female spider consume her consort after mating, Mr. Thwing tells Hermina that "he didn't feel, after all, that he was a marrying man" (78). Hermina reacts to George's failings of heart by becoming "nervous" and getting a "peculiar sensation in her head" that makes her feel "she was on the second floor" (82), to start, ascending inexorably until, by his last bid for freedom, she has "the hallucination she was up in an airplane" (278). Mr. Thwing yields to this weapon when he drunkenly proposes (92).

Mr. Thwing is instantly regretful on learning what he has done. Fearful that Hermina might sue him for the breach of promise he fully hopes he will be man enough to achieve, on his next visit he goes "to her bedroom once while she was in the kitchen and [has] a frantic, hasty look around for his note, but couldn't see it" (121). When Hermina makes the public announcement, "Mr. Thwing— laughed. It was a soft, gentle, queer laugh" (136), and it is immediately followed by Mr. Thwing's renewed desire to procure his letter. He abruptly asks Hermina for "the key to your apartment," plainly so that he can recover the letter, but upon her smiling assent his physical desire revives (136–37). In a tranquil moment, though he still feels trapped, he fears "the mixtures of sentiment becoming the mortar of platitudes: saw himself floating till death did them part in the bourgeois gravy," and he seems reconciled to the inevitability of the marriage (164). At this stage, chance intervenes. On a date with Hermina, Mr. Thwing wears a shirt recently returned by a friend. Hermina, noticing a message penciled on its front, "Lola, Ashland 2098" (184), assumes Mr. Thwing has been seeing another woman. Sensing an opportunity to discredit himself, Mr. Thwing allows Hermina to believe that he was made up to by "a little chit" who "reminded me of a lynx" (186–87). He wouldn't mind at all, in other words, if his plump ermine was chased away by the rumor of a lynx. His stratagem fails. Hermina is delighted that another woman has found her George attractive, but she takes the precaution of rubbing out the phone number with an eraser. Mr. Thwing bids goodnight and then hurries down Hermina's stairs reciting "Ashland two-o-nine-eight" like a mantra out of *The Waste Land.*

Mr. Thwing calls Lola and goes to see her as soon as he can.

> Her walk was the apotheosis of insinuation. . . .
>   She was tall and dark, feline. She was one of those women who try to look exotic and succeed only in looking sleepy.
>   Mr. Thwing knew this, that it was the plucked and preened Holly-woodish facsimile of exotic, the eyebrows like strips of nerve, the whole business ready to twitch and no more; but knew it only with an outermost integument of his mind. For the rest, he ignored it, looked at her, smelled her, and gave up. (193–94)

Lola recalls the Lolah of Byron's *Don Juan* 6.41 and looks forward to the Lola of "Whatever Lola Wants, Lola Gets" in *Damn Yankees* (1955). Mr. Thwing yields to her charms at once and promises to get her a lynx coat for her birthday (195). Before long, he has given her a lavaliere as a prelude to dinner at the Pompeian Room and immolated himself by declaring his love, proposing marriage (Lola replies "Sure"), giving her Hermina's engagement ring (209–213), and leaving her Hermina's telephone number to provoke a confrontation (214–15).

When Lola calls Hermina, Mr. Thwing believes he is free (249, 256), only to learn that Hermina has gone over and blackened Lola's eye (256) and that "instead of being sent forever from [Hermina's] side, by a woman now only too eager to break it off, as Mr. Thwing had expected, he was now a Lothario doubly intriguing, doubly captivating, and doubly pursued" (262); this new tactic, too, has rebounded on him. Defeated but determined to go on fighting, Mr. Thwing claims "I'm diseased." "Mentally or physically?" comes the reply. "Both," says Mr. Thwing. "I've got paresis" (264). Caught in that lie, Mr. Thwing next turns himself in to the police, confessing he is guilty of stealing a vase from the Art Institute, when in fact he has confiscated it from a suspect and held it as evidence (147–52; 173; 267). "My mind is warped," he pleads. Hermina, equal to every reverse, forgives: "George, you don't think that I'd leave you *now!*" (270–71). Caught again in the lie of his confession, and released from jail, Mr. Thwing tries one last note to Hermina, calling the whole thing off (278).

While Hermina lies prostrate at home, a tremendous storm arises. In this tempest that pitches the rooming house like a ship at sea, Hermina's brother Brabant catechizes Mr. Thwing in "what makes it all hang together. . . . Love," and Mr. Thwing is reminded "Yes . . . all things both big and l—— All things both great and small!" (287). With the stumblingly recollected line from "The Rime of the Ancient Mariner," Mr. Thwing proves, in one small way, an heir of

Coleridge after all, and he agrees, at last, to marry Hermina (288). In the final chapter Mr. Thwing and Hermina are settling into their honeymoon suite, but the morrow is likely to find him a sadder man.

The romantic plot is a burlesque of the comedy of manners, with a vengeance. It captures the screwball tone of Dick Powell movies and other Hollywood fare, and the whimsicality of Wodehouse, but its critique of the middle-class ethos is as acerbic as *Main Street,* as calculatedly anarchic as *Duck Soup,* and as flamboyantly disgusted as *A Cool Million.* The final chapter presents not a comic fulfillment but a travesty.

> They went into the hotel, and there was an inexorableness in the way the bellboy took his bags, and the elevator operator whisked them upstairs, like strict, simple cogs, factors in a foreordination, involvement, and Mr. Thwing felt continuously that visceral slow leak. (292)

Mr. Thwing is not a resilient Charlie Chaplin threading through the gears of *Modern Times* but a punctured carcass moving up the packing-house line. When he has "an overwhelming sense of Process: at once incredibly elaborate and inescapably simple" (293), we recall not only the mating process but the beef-packing process evoked by "trussed mammalian meat" and "bourgeois gravy"; "the racket," we're reminded, "from what was tied to the limousine as you shot away was an intimation of kitchen clatter." The conversation does not sparkle: "Well, it's sure nice weather." "Well, here we are." "Yes, here we are" (294–95). Hermina orders champagne and burgundy, but George has a headache and excuses himself.

> Mr. Thwing went out for a walk. The city lay dark and secret under the mild wild night, his heart was beating, though he still had that visceral slow leak. He sensed something terrific in the universe that somewhat frightened him, something coming to focus now, in all of this there was in the world, in all that sang and thumped in him, all love's delicate and pollenous pantomime.
>
> Mr. Thwing was still quite on edge when he came back. Coming in the door he dropped his hat. "Hello," Hermina said, and put her face up to be kissed and he kissed it, just as he had when she held it up to be kissed when he went out, which, in that moment, gave him an intimation of the way it would, of course, become, after a while.
>
> "What'll it be?"
>
> "Just a reflex," Mr. Thwing murmured. (295–96)

Hermina offers Bacchus, but Mr. Thwing foresees Pavlov. They drink wine until they're "glowing," and Hermina retires to the bedroom. The bellboy had "buzzed and hovered like the delivering bees," and now Mr. Thwing starts to "hum faintly to himself" like a good drone. He muses, in a mood like Molly Bloom's,

> So it is, so will always be. Lola, Hermina. It makes no difference which of the after all more or less limited range of types she is, exotic or innocent; Snake or Clinging Vine. The end has ever been, is and ever will be, the same: your entwinement.
> "George."
> Mr. Thwing rose, opened the door, and went in. He felt that now he was on the verge of something.
> THE END   (296–97)

Despite the urging of some critics, that last sentence cannot be taken straight as an affirmation of Mr. Thwing's going in to his woman and joining the social order. Mr. Thwing has been "on the verge of something" before: on the day the murder victim arrives (6, 9), just before he sees the lady spider eat her mate (78), when he begins his Inspector Clouseau detective antics (124–25), and again when he felt "he was in some grotesque web, and on the verge of something" as he gathers misleading clues that will entangle him in even more trouble (128). The final "verge" is an additional catastrophe. Hermina's convenient spells of floating anxiety have elevated her to her goal, whereas Mr. Thwing is stumbling over the brink. Even etymology conspires against Mr. Thwing. The word *verge* refers in common usage to "something that borders, limits, or bounds . . . brink, threshold" but derives from the Latin *virga*, "rod, stripe" and refers also to "a rod or staff carried as an emblem of authority or symbol of office." Mr. Thwing thinks of himself not as a rod but as "a trellis" (294). *Verge* also has the meaning "the male intromittent organ of any of various invertebrates," a sense ratified by Mr. Thwing's malleability and his attitude:

> Mr. Thwing sat in a steady drizzle of conversation, wringing his hands with indifference. Why did Hermina have to insist on his coming tonight, to meet these people in whom he had not the slightest interest, and whose indifference to him was perhaps equally fathomless, people, just people, the anonymous jelly? (130)

The novel's conclusion is a naturalistic portrayal of hideous mechanisms, in images sharing the brio of Thurber and Dali and the verbal elasticity of Thurber and Duchamp. It is truly "objective humor" in the surrealist sense.[48]

If the "verge" argument seems far-fetched, there are stronger reasons for reading the novel's conclusion as farcical revulsion. One is Mr. Thwing's new family. Hermina is a Rhinemaiden who faints on cue but can pull herself together to punch Lola. After that episode, Lola refers to her resentfully and cruelly—but echoing Mr. Thwing himself—as "that Zeppelin" (257). As a character, she is introduced as "large and gusty," so bejewelled that she "glitter[s] like an opera-house chandelier, earrings, bracelets, rings, diamond pendants, a diamond belt clasp" (31), and never loses the Margaret Dumont shallowness. She has three brothers, more Marx than Wagnerian or Karamazov, whose antics make them fates and furies to Mr. Thwing. Brabant's name, like Peter De Vries's, refers to a Netherlands province. "De Vries" refers to the northern province of Friesland; Nord-Brabant is in the boggy south, and Brabant wears the air of the stage Boetian or Gomer. The previous year, he'd played shortstop for the Cincinnati Reds. In the world series, however, what would have been his winning home run in game seven hit a pigeon and was caught. Brabant refuses to go to spring training, feeling he is jinxed because as a child he robbed birds' nests (64–66). He neurotically blames every misfortune on birds, a quirk that detracts from his evangelism for universal love and guarantees he will be an albatross around Mr. Thwing's neck. Ludwig, whom De Vries seems to name after the mad king of Bavaria, is a "go-getter" out of Sinclair Lewis. "This is a honey of an idea, Mr. Thwing" is his prelude to a description of his grandiose business idea: a digest of digests, for those too busy to read digests (30). This seems an inspiration certain to lose Ludwig his shirt and confront Mr. Thwing with another improvident brother-in-law. The result is worse: the enterprise succeeds and Ludwig becomes a pompous ass. The horror of the digest itself is not lost on Mr. Thwing, who, on learning of its triumph, "saw American journalism like a colossal funnel" (133). But the worst of the three brothers is an academic, for which type De Vries often reserves the lowest circles of his hell. Odin is named for the Teutonic god of wisdom, poetry, war, and agriculture, any oath to whom it is infamous to break. Odin is doing "some research on moving pictures. We're making a study of the serial, and its effect, harmful or beneficial, on the child. The emotional reaction is on the whole unsalutary" (56). Odin's instrument of investigation is "the apparatus": a machine for measuring "respiration, circulation, skin sweating . . ." (57) that also can be used, as Mr. Thwing later points out, as a lie detector (138–39, 187). With a genius for self-annihilation, Mr. Thwing suggests to Odin, who has been casting about for a dissertation topic, that this research should qualify. Mr. Thwing thus unwittingly ensures that

Odin will acquire the instrument of Mr. Thwing's torture. Odin immediately "touches" Mr. Thwing for the price of the equipment (58).

Mr. Thwing may be the only practitioner of polygraphic onanism in literature. Determined to discover whether he loves Hermina, he lets himself into her apartment when no one is home, prepares the recorder, and straps on the apparatus: "Then he sat down, pulled up his pants leg and wound the sphygmomanometer cuff around his ankle. He took the rubber bulb and pumped the cuff up. Then he strapped the pneumograph around his chest" (251). Swathed in the rubber of the apparatus, he is cousin to Joyce's man-in-the-mackintosh as he asks himself questions and waits for the needles of the apparatus to prick out his desires. True to Dali's famous image, Mr. Thwing is a *Great Masturbator.* He says he loves Hermina: no reaction. Satisfied he has his answer, he unstraps and leaves. But on the front steps he realizes he hasn't tried the other side of the question. Apparently it came up heads when he would have preferred that it come up tails. He goes back (would he do so if he really loved her?) and says "I do not love Hermina": no response. He recites a number of his favorite power fantasies, claiming he has actually achieved them: no reaction, either. Mr. Thwing decides the apparatus doesn't work when you're alone, and leaves again. But wait. He goes back and lubricates his hand and tries once more:

> This time he got out the apparatus for recording electrical changes in the skin—the positive electrode heavily coated with kaolin paste and covered with a pad of absorbent cotton soaked with the solution of zinc sulphate, for the palm of his hand, and the negative electrode for the back of his hand—along with the other two, and, when everything was ready, he just sat back, closed his eyes and thought of Hermina. Rather, visualized her. He dreamed of her in various voluptuous attitudes, with him, without him. Thinking, this ought to do it, ought to tell—blood, pulse, respiration, skin . . . peeking at intervals at the indicator. Nothing seemed to happen, much. He went on, slow, savoring, garment by garment, till there was just Hermina. Just as he opened his eyes he saw the indicator convulsed, but there had been the sound of a door somewhere in the building and Mr. Thwing was leaping to his feet and tearing the apparatus off him. He got all tied up in a maze of straps, tubes, cuffs and electrodes, from which he finally extricated himself in a frenzy. Frantically he put things back, grabbed his coat and tore out of the house.
>
> The noise had been in another apartment. Relax, Mr. Thwing said to himself, and after a mile or two, he did. (253–54)

Mr. Thwing will never learn whether he loves Hermina, though evidently he supposes he might determine an answer by measuring his lust. Half of the double image here is the absurd flagrante delicto, a farce on the organism and on orgasm. The other half is a satire on faith in science and technology and offers another reason to read the novel's conclusion as farce.

The marriage won't work because love is in jeopardy when men try to calculate and calibrate human nature, as both Odin and Mr. Thwing try to do. Kenneth Burke, in his perceptive remarks on surrealism, notes that the elitist ideal of rationalism, which found its material realization in machines, resulted in a problem for the many (i.e., industrial exploitation, scientific social control). One reaction was "Maldorian defiance" and "an aesthetic of self-abuse." But, "we should also recall that, in the dialectics of cultural phenomena, the competitor will necessarily, though possibly in a transubstantiated form, employ the properties of the very agent against which he would compete."[49] Indeed, while surrealism as Breton envisaged it was anti-rational, surrealists, including Breton himself after a time, tried to recover lost ground. Herbert Read claimed that "surrealism is also superrationalism," reason being understood as "the sum total of awareness," and that "the surrealist is not a sentimental humanitarian; the superrealism of his art has its counterpart in the realism of his science," namely, the science of psychology.[50] De Vries was a friend of science, as his review of Cummings showed, but a skeptic about the power of science, rational or superrational, to measure the psyche. In *Bugler* the effort to apply measure to the illimitable proves fatuous in both Odin and Mr. Thwing. Their incorrigible desire to measure the heart by a needle bodes ill for Mr. Thwing's and Hermina's marriage; when Mr. Thwing is in his final redoubt, Odin uses the machine to extract from him the truth that he had promised to marry Hermina. Mr. Thwing exclaims "No!" and the needle jumps (266).

Mr. Thwing's life with Hermina's clan promises to be as comfortless as Tony Last's Brazilian exile in Waugh's *Handful of Dust*. At best he'll be the poet trotted out at cocktail parties. His situation travesties Paul Eluard's idea of "fraternisation": "Today the solitude of poets is breaking down. They are now men among other men, they have brothers."[51] Mr. Thwing has odious brothers-in-law. Married, as single, he will be pinned down under the guns of the "unassailable pill-boxes of convention" (265). For all their seeming impregnability, the bastions of middle-class culture are seen, in Brabant, Ludwig, and Odin, to be built every bit as much on fantasy as any surrealist dreamland. As René Magritte and Jean Scutenaire had put it, in the *London Bulletin*, "L'ordre bourgeois n'est qu'un désordre. Un désordre au paroxysm, privé de tout contact avec le monde de la nécéssité."[52] De Vries's portrait of the middle class trounces its sanctimonious claims and treats Mr. Thwing's absorption into it as a sorry spectacle. "The time has come for poets to proclaim their right and duty to maintain that they are deeply involved in the life of other men, in communal life," wrote Paul Eluard, soon to declare himself a communist. Mr. Thwing, to his chagrin, can scarcely *escape* from the capitalist commune of his rooming house, and there's slim chance that he will find anyone to commune with in life with Hermina. He is a seer manqué, sharing the austere vision Eluard attributes to the great spirits—"on the high peaks, as elsewhere, more than elsewhere, perhaps, for him who sees, for the visionary, misery undoes and remakes incessantly a world, drab, vulgar, unbearable, and impossible."[53] Because Mr. Thwing shrinks from this vision, he sticks in the bourgeois quagmire.

Mr. Thwing has a wandering eye. It narrows on every female in sight, from his nubile lodger Hecuba (10), to "slim girls . . . with their breasts like apartment-house doorbells" (118–19; though these slim, Daliesque creatures are not really to his taste), to Brabant's new wife, Julie, who, like Lola, floats "his senses in perfume. He was drowning" (246–47). Civilization's discontents are not supposed to matter in romantic comedy where mismatches pan out. But Mr. Thwing in effect has been lovelessly married all along; his misadventures are a preview of his married life. His laughter will always be "queer," spoiled by a conspiracy of convention and chance, as both his rebellious and submissive selves are flayed. Only through the temporary anodyne of a mixture "whose influence was greater than he'd thought" (296) of champagne and burgundy does he summon the strength to peel himself off his chair, rise, open the door, and go in to Hermina. Mr. Thwing does so as a technical virgin; even after "dissolving" with Lola (196), he is a "celibate Casanova" (207). Opening Hermina's door in his new house of matrimony, Mr. Thwing is sure to enter a gallery of frustrations. André Breton wrote,

> Today it is up to man unhesitatingly to deny everything that can enslave him, and if necessary, to die on a barricade of flowers, if only to give body to a chimera; to woman, and perhaps to her alone, to rescue both that which she brings with her and that which lifts her up—silence!— There is no solution outside love.[54]

The lukewarm affection in *Bugler* is a travesty of love. The novel is hardly a celebration of the Pauline injunction. That is "no solution." Anguish in the absence of love is the pain to which *But Who Wakes the Bugler?* ministers.

*   *   *

"Was I in here last night and did I spend a twenty-dollar bill?" "Yep!"
"Oh boy! What a load that is off my mind. I thought I'd lost it."—Egbert
Sousé and Joe the bartender in *The Bank Dick*[55]

Mr. Thwing's accomplishments as an amateur detective are on a
par with his amatory conquests. The old Dutch sea captain antago-
nizes Mr. Thwing's guests, and there are plenty of suspects when
"there was a noise like a gunshot in the rooming house, and then a
terrific thumping as Jehoiachim's body rolled downstairs" (121). De
Vries conflates the names of two kings of Judah, Jehoiakim and his
son Jehoiachin (2 Kgs 23–24, 2 Ch. 36, 38), in the victim's name.
Just as the wicked Jehoiakim's death gave rise to "conflicting Biblical
statements on this point,"[56] it is difficult to harmonize the roomers'
accounts of how the old captain died. He may have been killed by
a scorpion bite, a possible allusion to Dali and Buñuel's *L'Age d'or.*
Mr. Thwing is as coy as Vincent Price in doling out hints to the
police (200–210) and prowls hallways and peeps in at keyholes like
the Marx brothers in *Room Service* (146).

A prime suspect is a Chinese laundry deliveryman, whom Mr.
Thwing sees taking a vase from Captain Jehoiachim's sea chest (147).
When Mr. Thwing discovers that the vase, which he confiscates, is
a genuine Ming vase stolen from the Art Institute (173), he is thrilled
that "he alone knew what he knew; and so he kept his secret hermetically sealed to himself" (198)—although he drops a few hints when
the police get stuck. (The protectors of middle-class security do not
follow up on the clues Mr. Thwing lets fall and thus never get to the
bottom of anything.) When he is forced to play his trump card in
evading Hermina, Mr. Thwing withdraws the vase from his bureau
drawer, carries it in a bag down to the Art Institute, says "Here, . . .
I stole this" (267), and goes to jail determined to solve the murder
in stir, by ratiocination (268). He is released when a lie-detector test
proves his confession was false (272). Mr. Thwing learns from his
hired man, Jubal, that he *had* lifted the vase—had come home from
his binge on the night of the women's club meeting bearing the vase,
given it to Jubal, and forgotten it. Jubal had traded the vase to the
captain for a blue sash and some whips, kinkily enough, and the
captain had stashed it in his chest unaware of its value (289).

The vase has a plot of its own: Who stole it? Who knows what
about it? Will it save Mr. Thwing from matrimony? It is usually
hidden. Its most intriguing aspect is that it links Mr. Thwing's sleeping and waking states. It remains mysterious to the end: we never
learn how Mr. Thwing came into its possession. Surely he would not

have been admitted to the Art Institute in his condition, late at night, much less allowed to cart off a priceless treasure. Communing thing-to-thing, Mr. Thwing immediately recognizes the vase as "an exquisite thing" (147) when he first sees it while awake, but he came by it via delirium. Inscrutable, it becomes the toy of the journalists and the sower of confusion in the rooming house. When it is turned in to the authorities—the cultural curators at the Art Institute—Mr. Thwing goes to jail. The vase is a *vase communicant*, André Breton's archetypal surrealist object.

Breton first used the image in *Surrealism and Painting*, which he quotes in "What Is Surrealism?":

> All that I love, all that I think and feel inclines me towards a particular philosophy of immanence according to which surreality will reside in reality itself and will be neither superior nor exterior to it. And conversely, because the container shall be also the contained. One might almost say that it will be a communicating vessel placed between the container and the contained.[57]

He further elaborated the image in *The Communicating Vessels*, and it quickly became an icon in surrealist literature. Julien Levy quotes from *The Communicating Vessels* in *Surrealism*: *"The poet has come into being to overcome the depressing idea of an irreparable divorce between action and dream."* David Gascoyne discusses the essay and the image in his *Short Survey of Surrealism*, and so on.[58] In "Beauty Will Be Convulsive," Breton, in discussing the found object, could just as well be describing Mr. Thwing's vase: "It alone has the power to enlarge the universe, to do away with a part of its opacity, to discover in it for us an extraordinary capacity for receiving stolen goods"; everyday life is a *"forest of* [such] *signposts"* awaiting the "delirium of interpretation."[59] Mr. Thwing's interpretation goes awry, and he misuses the gift that has been delivered into his hands. He treats the vase merely as a commodity; surrendering the Ming surrenders the magical back to a sterile display case and lands Mr. Thwing in a cell. As surrealist as well as realist, Mr. Thwing fails to seize, or even see, his opportunities. That he will have a book of poems published (279) is a Pyrrhic victory, for he has missed his main chance to change his life.

*   *   *

What is Surrealism?
It is the Cuckoo's egg laid in the nest
(whose brood is lost) with the
complicity of René Magritte.
—André Breton in *London Bulletin*, no. 1 (April 1938).[60]

All the characters, actions, and images in *Bugler* help to blend fantasy with the quotidian, dream with waking reality. Mr. Thwing's black houseman, Jubal, named for the inventor of the lyre and flute, has a "grin like a piano keyboard" (11); his wife, Delia, bears the name of one of Virgil's shepherdesses but is more in the line of Pope's Delia. Caricatures are employed throughout, the minor figures constituting a gallery of oddities.[61]

Mr. Thwing is infatuated with the nubile Hecuba, who happens into his rooming house as naturally as Hecuba fell to Ulysses' lot. The narrator's descriptions of her (10, 14) are parodies of Joyce—parodies of parodies. Mr. Thwing finds a drinking partner in one Mr. Thwackhurst. Unlike Fielding's Thwackum, he is phlegmatic and resigned (94–97, 106). Among Mr. Thwing's lodgers is a "gnarled little man" who brews "Doctor Zoro's Elixir, The New Wonder Tonic That Renews Life" (110–11, 215–16). This failed Zarathustra parodies surrealism's interest in alchemy. Another roomer is a sly juvenile delinquent named Hank, for whom Mr. Thwing takes responsibility as his Big Brother (37). Yet another, Claude M. Darney, is a lazy and talentless reductio of William Claude Dukenfield (12). Among Hermina's "vaguely academic" friends are a "professor of correct English" and a "former missionary who could talk Choctaw"—a blend of Eric Erickson and Robert Bly (90–92). She also knows a bunch of strays from *The Great Gatsby*. De Vries deploys evident allusions (e.g., Eckles and Myrt for Fitzgerald's Dr. Eckleburg and Myrtle, 135) and obscure ones but always does something to the originals, the way Duchamp, Ernst, and Magritte "assisted" others' works.

The title *But Who Wakes the Bugler?* poses a chicken-and-egg problem, and birds and eggs are among the novel's guiding images (others include plants and a clarinet—no doubt a prophecy of Woody Allen). Though it does him little good, Brabant cares for canaries as part of his psychotherapy (65–66, 112–13, 127, 247, 284). "All the birds whimper" writes Mr. Thwing (4), who is likened to both a heron (5) and bird food: a worm (257). His mood swings are traced in his reactions to seeing pairs of birds billing on a bough (64, 84). The most persistent bird linked to Mr. Thwing is a robin (73, 77–78, 84), the harbinger of spring but also an omen of death.[62] The robin's death in the storm cuts Mr. Thwing's last tie to the wild. Eggs hatch gags. "Claude M. Darney had come to Chicago in a flutter of publicity as the son of the upper Michigan farmer whose hen had laid three eggs with distinct letters on them, C, M, and D, the initials of the son" (12). Mr. Thwing hears Hermina's voice as "rich and yolky" (64, 163); he finds the clubwomen's voices biliously "yolky" (97) and has "a hallucination that he was floundering in a sea of whipped yolks" (100). The next morning he remembers the chairman "sharply in that blathering and albuminous phalanx of the Who-get-you, the wives of the Rotarian hordes" (105). To name a thing can kill it, and Mr. Thwing puts an end to this motif by incantation. To divert his mind from the dilemma of whether to marry, he tries to "think of a good word for the sound frying eggs make" (165). Hermina offers him something to eat, and he asks for a fried-egg sandwich. He soon has his word: "squeligulating" (166). Misogyny, even cannibalism, may lurk there. But, as Constance Rourke said, American tall tales simply reveled in made-up words; one of those she cites is *absquatulate*.[63] De Vries's use of symbols in this first novel is, to use a term both Brezon and De Vries applied in their criticism, fantasia.

* * *

"Les mots font l'amour," as Breton said.—Georges Hugnet[64]

Bugler is the work in which the verbal and conceptual playfulness for which De Vries is celebrated first appears in full force. *Bugler* is a fantasia of language as well as of symbolism. De Vries peppers the chapters with jokes Freud would call "conceptual": "I was a homeless landlord. To add to the neurotic psychiatrist and the skin specialist with pimples" (178), laments Mr. Thwing; when Claude despairs, Mr. Thwing says he needs "less wishbone and more backbone" (170). A friend of Mr. Thwing's gets married, and "a whimsy that had once been the veins in the marble was now the fat in the ham" (134–35). Hank's family "were poor but dishonest" (38). But it is in more surreptitious verbal wit that the book vies with Ionesco:

> ["]Six-letter word for scabbard," said Ludwig, who was sitting with a folded newspaper and pencil beside Hermina's bed when Odin took him back.
> "Beetle," said Hermina.
> "Oh, George!" she said, sitting up. "How are you darling? Flowers!"
> "How are you? Ludwig tells me you've been having another spell." (86)

The gag closest to the surface is Hermina's malapropism in confusing *scabbard* with *scarab*, but that mix-up is just the pretext for the joke the reader must supply: both *sheath* and *vagina* have six letters. In this sexually charged scene, *sheath* carries the meaning Casanova would give it. As Brezon later asks a guest at Hermina's house-party, "Did your husband ever give you flowers? Or, more significant and concise, a flower? All right, what does it mean? Well, what *does* it?

What are flowers but the sexual organs of plants?" (244). Brezon is funny in his militancy, but right. The "spell" Mr. Thwing refers to is a fainting spell, but it is the play of meanings that is dizzying.

An isolated instance of such double entendres could be accidental, but they are prevalent. Brezon insists on the sexual interpretation of signs, and the text backs him up everywhere; De Vries, an observer of the saturation of everyday life in Freudian symbolism, assists his characters only slightly in doing and saying what comes naturally. He has things both ways, mocking psychology while his Punch-and-Judy characters enact Freud's psychopathology of everday life. And as we worry the truth out, we must accept responsibility for our knowledge of the text.

During the initial murder investigation, there is enough talk of guns, stage business with cigars, and fingering of books to furnish a treatise on the semiotics of phallic aggression (122–28). Ludwig holds forth on his digest of digests with a "freshly lit cigar poised between his two fingers, like a man who is looking into the future," obviously looking forward to engendering yet further new enterprises, whereas Mr. Thwing sees only the "colossal funnel" (133). When Hermina announces their engagement, Mr. Thwing shrinks into "a kind of relaxed impotence," then lapses into "an acute discomfort, which presently he traced: his encirclement by cups." Hermina's just having served coffee doesn't entirely explain the cups: "Mr. Thwing, unable somehow to drag his eyes off the large, absorptive, mammalian inescapability who was the wife of the man who was always saying he was just telling Em" does (136). Mr. Thwing, shriveled by impending marriage and cowed by support garments, excuses himself, goes to the kitchen, where Hermina is pouring cream into a pitcher, and suddenly asks for the key to her apartment (136–37). A discussion of Odin's apparatus arouses Mr. Thwing's attention: "'Say,' said Mr. Thwing, suddenly sliding up." But the machine is not available to be played with: "'Shucks. We could have some fun,' Mr. Thwing said" (139). Bored speechless by the end of the party, Mr. Thwing subsides in a revery, until "Hermina poked him covertly. . . . He straightened" (140). Teased out of context, these jolts sound like sniggering, but when Mr. Thwing delivers lines like "I'll be over shortly" (162) and "You are letting yourself *down*" (171), one's interest is scarcely prurient. De Vries has cultivated a mannerism, like Arcimboldo combining divers objects into paranoiac-critical portraits, that realizes Whitman's wish to make words "do the male and female act."[65]

*   *   *

So it is that I find it impossible to consider a painting other than as a window about which my first concern is knowing what *it looks out upon.*—André Breton[66]

This discussion of *Bugler* has emphasized the prospect that opens from within its frame. What of the painter, the framing devices he used, and the work's reception?

De Vries at thirty was full of contradictions. He praised surrealism in his criticism; he burlesqued it in fiction. He was an elite editor, a popular writer, and a deliveryman. His Wildean wit and whimsicality were counterposed by his Calvinist upbringing and education. If the contradictions of that extraordinary personality were resolved in a work of art, according to Herbert Read's principle, the result of its "entering into dialectical activity" could be "an act of renewal. . . . The renascence of wonder—. . . . I should not be afraid to adopt such a grandiloquent phrase to describe the general aim of Surrealism."[67] The rebirth of wonder is certainly what De Vries was after in his first novel.

In his practice of "good surrealism," De Vries makes fun of automatic writing while emulating Dylan Thomas's "images fused at astonishing high speed." Breton himself had reacted against automatism, claiming in "What Is Surrealism?" that surrealism had moved in 1925 from its "purely *intuitive* epoch" to its "*reasoning* epoch."[68] Surrealist publications promoting the collage as exemplified by Ernst's "collage novel" *La femme 100 têtes* suggested a form.[69] Having dealt with Ford and other surrealists, and no doubt having had the demystifying realization that surrealists were after all "a group of literary men under conditions of intense competition,"[70] De Vries cut up a surrealist or two and pasted them into the satirical picture. Calvinism, it turned out, had stiff competition from surrealism in providing a prospect from which to survey ordinary life—as Breton had said, "Living and ceasing to live are imaginary solutions. Existence is elsewhere"[71]—but one could get "elsewhere" and look back to see that surrealists, like divines, must eat, and that brute reality compels foolish compromises. In travestying Mr. Thwing's eagerness to find a message in every clue the world offers him, De Vries may be parodying both the paranoiac-critical method and Calvinist vigilance for signs of election.

Nothing could be more surrealist than attacking not only "bourgeois imbecility," but "everything," with "ferocious humor."[72] As Tristan Tzara, quoted by Edmund Wilson in *Axel's Castle*, declared, "We had already said that the true Dadaists were against Dada."[73]

Breton, who included De Vries's favorite Thomas De Quincey in his *Anthologie de l'humour noir*,[74] defined "objective humour" as

> a synthesis in the Hegelian sense of the imitation of nature in its acciden-
> tal forms on the one hand and of humour on the other. Humour, as a
> paradoxical triumph of the pleasure principle over real conditions at a
> moment when they may be considered to be particularly unfavourable,
> is naturally called upon as a defence during the period heavily loaded
> with menaces in which we live. With Swift and Lewis Carroll, the English
> reader is more fitted than anyone to appreciate the resources of that
> humour which in France is illustrated by the name of Alfred Jarry and
> which hovers over the origins of Surrealism under the influence of Jacques
> Vaché and Marcel Duchamp.[75]

The description fits the "triumph" of De Vries's wordplay, the adventures of Mr. Thwing, and De Vries's appreciation of surrealism as a
response to an age of menace. The dark side of objective humor is
present in James Thurber's definition of humor as well: as he told
Max Eastman, "neatly reworking Wordsworth, 'I think humor is the
best that lies closest to the familiar, to that part of the familiar which
is humiliating, distressing, even tragic. Humor is a kind of emotional
chaos told about calmly and quietly in retrospect.'"[76] These two ideas
of humor are not so far apart as might at first appear. A convenient
text for showing what they have in common, and linking both to
De Vries, is Cleanth Brooks's *Modern Poetry and the Tradition* (1938).
Chapter 2, "Wit and High Seriousness," claims that wit's most important function is "the ironical function," the most interesting wit
metaphysical wit; makes reference to "the conflict of opposites which
is the very life of metaphysical poetry"; and invokes the Eliotic notion that "the poet, the imaginative man, has his particular value in
his superior power to reconcile the irrelevant or apparently warring
elements of experience." The dialectics of nature/mind, pleasure/
pain, tragic/comic, and chaos/calm sketched in the Breton and Thurber quotations, presided over by irony and filtered through De Vries's
ambivalence toward modernism, energize De Vries's novel. Brooks's
conclusion, that "one is even tempted to indulge in the following
paradox: namely, that wit, far from being a playful aspect of the
mind, is the most serious aspect," would be assented to by Breton,
Thurber, and De Vries—except for its characterization as a paradox.[77]

   De Vries had the not inconsiderable problem of exercising his wits
to come up with a book that was both readable and writable. In
framing the work, he gerrymandered freely. As Constance Rourke
had noted of canonical American literature, "the touch of revolution
in popular comedy was there, . . . in the preoccupation with strange

or rebellious types who left tradition behind, belonging to all these writers. . . . A homogeneous world of the imagination had been created in which popular fancies and those of genius were loosely knit together." Solving the problems facing the creative writer in the wake of post-Eliotic self-consciousness and disillusionment would require an "understanding of the many sequences of the American tradition on the popular side as well as on purely literary levels."[78] As if rising to this challenge, De Vries strewed his novel with allusions to genius, put rebelliousness at its center, and populated it with popular-culture figures. The 1930s were "The Who-Done-Its' Big Decade" in Chicago literature;[79] De Vries alluded to Charlie Chan and Nick and Nora Charles. W. C. Fields was in vogue; De Vries had Mr. Thwing foul up at a pool table (42) and made things fall out of his pockets (29, 43).

Including painfully familiar, humble realities—"several irritating matters . . . a door lock, a stuck window, a rent arrears, a blown-out fuse" (63),—would allow the mundane to serve an ironical function: the juxtaposition of real and surreal. William Carlos Williams applauded in his preface to Ford's *Garden of Disorder* the "fantastic drive out of, while in the very process of entering the banal: using the banal to escape the banal."[80] De Vries could perform a Houdini's trick by using more baneful banalities and effecting more antic escapes than Ford, in a bid to be more surrealist than the surrealist. Breton had scorned the novel in his first manifesto, but in the second predicted "this other novel, in which the verisimilitude of the scenery will for the first time fail to hide from us the strange symbolical life which even the most definite and most common objects lead in dreams."[81] De Vries's would be commonplaces with a vengeance, ironic both inside and outside the frame as, according to the *London Bulletin*, Magritte's images were in painting:

> Magritte is not a painter in the sense understood by the aesthetes, but a man who uses painting to perfect astonishing experiences in which all forms of our existence find themselves taking part. . . . Magritte appeals to our everyday life, to the limits of our consciousness, and not to the theoretical abstractions which we may have constructed. . . . His images lie right in the middle of reality.[82]

Hence we see glimpses of Mr. Thwing's petty irritations, hear the "drizzle" of cocktail party conversation.

De Vries "framed" the surreal in *Bugler*, subjected it to the same parodic distortion to which the surrealists subjected everyday reality. Surrealism had a lengthy genealogy from which to call up rich, eccentric relations. Even the humble setting, the rooming house, was a parody of Breton's Gothic castle:

> Yes, there must be observatories of the inner sky. . . . This we may describe from the surrealist point of view as the *castle problem*. Human psychism in its most universal aspect has found in the Gothic castle and its accessories a point of fixation so precise that it becomes essential to discover what would be the equivalent for our own period. (Everything leads us to believe that there is no question of it being a factory.)[83]

De Vries used the factory in "Songs for Eight O'Clock," in which a laborer daydreams of a suburban Valhalla. In *Bugler*, the rooming house is for common readers a mock Castle of Otranto, for surrealist readers Peacock's Nightmare Abbey revisited.

Herbert Read had asserted in *Surrealism* that: "In dialectical terms we claim that there is a continual state of opposition and interaction between the world of objective fact—the sensational and social world of active and economic existence—and the world of subjective fantasy. This opposition creates a state of disquietude, a lack of spiritual equilibrium, which it is the business of the artist to resolve."[84] Of course, many surrealists "resolved" disquietude by flaunting it. De Vries mixed unreal with all-too-real, and turned his work inside out.

The novel's strongest self-reflexive tactic is to treat surrealism with surrealistic irreverence, exaggeration, and disjunction: putting Mr. Thwing to work at automatic writing is "surrealism squared." This tactic defamiliarizes both everyday life and the surreal. On the level of the plot, everything runs downhill: Mr. Thwing ends up in a grossly unsuitable marriage, sucked into the official art world and the middle class. If doctrinaire surrealists were destined to plant their flag at some new vantage point, they would need more sinew than Brezon provided. On the level of the ithyphallic action, however, things proceed upward. As if competing with Tristram Shandy, Mr. Thwing stirs from slumber on page 1, has many risings and fallings, and is just "on the verge" on the last page.

De Vries's first book is an epitome of what Victor Shklovsky called the laying bare of technique.[85] The text continually calls attention to itself, and there are several passages in which self-reflexivity becomes the explicit subject. One Jamesian example is a moment when Mr. Thwing "stared at the pattern in the rug, as though he could lose himself in its intricacy—or as though he were already lost in it and was, perhaps, trying to work his way out" (257). When Mr. Thwing shouts to Brabant, "We're all just barely hanging together. Do you hear! Just barely! I for one am just barely in one piece," Brabant replies, "Pull yourself together," and Mr. Thwing responds, "Pull *your*self together" (112). The exchange is worthy of Beckett's tramps. On one of his steamy visits to Lola, Mr. Thwing thinks of "the handful of male sand being sucked up by the sea, . . . the teeming and tidal female . . . he maybe glimpsed why he was always writing about the ocean . . . and for a moment he had a hallucination that he was wax dripping" (209). Later, when Brezon explicates Mr. Thwing's poems, he calls attention to "the nightmares of the dissolving candles and the loss in the obliterating sea" (237). Brezon continues, "In dreams the room, the house is always a symbol of the female" (237). The "always" may contain a note of derision for *The Interpretation of Dreams*, but Brezon is right about rooms and houses in *this* novel, with its gags about Hermina's room and her key. Mr. Thwing comes out and bluntly asks Brezon:

> "Do you think," Mr. Thwing tried again, "that we are right in the interpretation we are always giving our symbolisms? I mean—are they always as—" But he didn't want to risk mispronouncing the word, so he went on, "Well, the emphasis of your article, for instance." He leaned back with his hands clasped around his drawn-up knee and lounged in the cab. "I sometimes wonder if we might not overdo it. After all, the unconscious . . ."
> "The unconscious what?"
> "The unconscious *is* the unconscious," Mr. Thwing said, and slid up.
> "I do not think there is much mistake about the dominant impulse of the unconscious," Mr. Brezon said simply, and turned to the window again. (232–33)

This passage concentrates the very symbolic action Mr. Thwing fears may be overdone. The word repressed by Mr. Thwing's uncertainty the reader recalls: *phallic*, the symbolic principle of this fantasia, which takes the license to play freely with its readers and itself. As Rimbaud may be said to have tried out the century in advance, De Vries tried out postmodernism in advance.

* * *

One thing almost all surrealists have in common is an instinct for dramatic titles.—*Time*[86]

A book that tries to "to trace back to their sources the proverbs, maxims, and familiar phrases in ordinary English and American use" credits De Vries with inventing the phrase "But Who Wakes the Bugler?"[87] One of the few scholars who have written on De Vries's first novel says that "The book's title is taken from Irving Berlin's

'Oh, How I Hate to Get Up in the Morning,' suggesting at once the theme of escapism that De Vries is intent on and the popular sources of his subject matter,"[88] but this is a mistake. Berlin's lyric is "And then I'll get that other pup, / The guy who wakes the bugler up, / And spend the rest of my life in bed!"[89] There isn't any doubt who wakes the bugler—if there were it would be impossible to "get" him.

The reviewer was right who said *But Who Wakes the Bugler?* is "an interesting title which has no visible connection with the story."[90] There is no bugler, nor even a bugle. The display ad copy for the novel seems an unfair tease:

> Peter De Vries hates to write, but likes to read what he has written. He has written the story of Mr. Thwing, who uses a lie detector when he talks to himself, writes poetry when he is asleep, checks when he is awake, and love letters when he is tight.
> But who does wake the bugler?[91]

"What bugler?" a customer might demand of the publisher. One commentator tries theology: "Presumably the title of De Vries's first published novel . . . raises the basic cosmological question of the Prime Mover."[92] The question does arise, in the bird and egg images and other circular motifs, but only to show the vanity of the inquiry. (As Duchamp puts it somewhere, "If no answer, perhaps no question?")

It is not an idle amusement to attempt to explain the title. Is it a presentiment of *Godot*, the world waiting indefinitely for a wake-up call? Perhaps we are to think of the importance of the Red King's slumber in *Through the Looking-Glass*.[93] In the bellicose world of 1940, the title may ask how our ludicrous human nature can be conditioned to militarism (De Vries wrote in his poem "Conscript" of a draftee "Ravished with bugles . . . and drunk with valedictory"[94]), or, since the dramatis personae seem incapable of being roused to any martial cause, who wakes (i.e., lays out for burial) the bugler (who has died of atrophy and despair). Perhaps the question is rhetorical: for Mr. Thwing, no one wakes no bugler, and he will always only be on the verge.

De Vries's title properly belongs to the class of dadaist and surrealist titles that are deliberately enigmatic. It even enters a dialogue with those titles: *Why Not Sneeze?* asks one of Marcel Duchamp's most famous objects.[95] *Bugle* is slang for *nose*, so Duchamp's ridiculous question is answered with an equally ridiculous question, reminiscent of Sterne's ribald chapter on nosology in *Tristram Shandy*. The simplest, shortest, and most dadaist answer to the title's question, however, is the one with the most obvious relevance to Mr. Thwing: the bugler is awakened by Chanticleer, the cock.

*   *   *

Surrealist Fun
                    —Banner headline on a contemporary
        review of *But Who Wakes the Bugler?*

The contemporary reception of *Bugler* was favorable. Although De Vries's novel was not taken up by the surrealists—unsurprising, since the two editors most active in surrealism, Laughlin and Ford, had reason not to feel buoyant about it—at least De Vries was not attacked from that quarter.[96] Most reviewers simply called the novel entertainingly zany.

The one slur was a notice in *The New Republic:* "A tale of what you might call quimsey, with a poached-egg hero, a determined blonde and a boarding-house full of no doubt ludicrous types. There is a Mr. Thwing and a Mr. Thwackhurst and are you holding your sides yet?"[97] De Vries's whimsy didn't thrill everyone, but even those it did were hard pressed to name what De Vries was up to. *The New Yorker* referred to "A mad tale. . . . Wrap a wet towel around your head before you tackle it, and don't expect it to make sense."[98] Lisle Bell, in a funny, perceptive review, called "this madcap novel" an "omelette."[99] Beatrice Sherman, calling the book "first-class fun," confirms a blurb that "the book 'walks a tantalizing hairline between sanity and madness.' He might have added that it often wabbles over [*sic*] on the far side of the line, to the reader's greater delight." She describes the novel's characteristic maneuver—"This Thwing-De Vries style of combining: say prayer patter or the poetic or fantastical with very common sense is titillating and vastly amusing"—and notes that "its highly enjoyable humor is sometimes straightforward, but more often on the vague and subtle side, more lunatic than laughable," like Evelyn Waugh's.[100]

Ruth Hard Bonner began her review: "This hair-brained [*sic*] novel combines a Thurber-ish plot, and Thurber people with overtones of James Joyce and Lewis Carroll." She mentions the surrealism plot and remarks: "The publishers imply on the blurb of 'But Who Wakes the Bugler' [*sic*] that there may be hidden meanings in all this. We prefer to think that perhaps they are being taken in, just as Mr. Thwing took in Mr. Brezon of New Age. Mr. Thwing is sufficiently delectable and human and mad as he is, without undressing him in search of an allegory."[101] Dressed up or dressed down, Mr. Thwing is, according to Bonner, "welcomed to the bosom of" *New Age* magazine. The headline writer's screamer, "Surrealist Fun," may be the review's most convincing phrase. Sterling North's brief, complimentary notice in the *Chicago Daily News* bears a heading even more surrealist: "Typewriter Bites Local Fantasist." North links De Vries with Thurber and declares that "Mr. Thwing is worthy to go down in folklore with H*Y*M*A*N K*A*P*L*A*N, Paul Bunyan and Mike Fink."[102]

Among the connections that none of these reviewers made were those between Joyce and Thurber (implicit in "The Comic Prufrock") and between Thurber, Carroll, and surrealism. De Vries's daring trapeze act appears to the reviewers as undifferentiated "madcap humor." Even Jack Conroy, reviewing De Vries's second novel, in praising the "superlative" satire of *Bugler* does not specify whom he thinks is being satirized.[103]

The reviewer who comes closest, in spite of himself, is Fred Schwed, Jr.: "It may well be that this book will become known in the history of humor as the first wild bleat of a young voice which was soon to blossom into authoritative hysterics."[104] In the second manifesto of surrealism, Breton wrote "Praise be to hysteria."[105] He had a more pervasive project in mind than Schwed or Peter De Vries, but the reviewers' unanimity on the "madness" of De Vries's work is suggestive. Schwed agrees "here is our chance for a genuine Evelyn Waugh" but then shifts to the oneiric: "Mr. De Vries' extraordinary comic gift is based on the artful use of the nightmare as an instrument of fun." He is not able to connect to surrealism, though, and misses the parody in Mr. Thwing's poetry: "Mr. De Vries is interested in modern poetry, and I wish he could bring himself to blue pencil his precious poetry right out of his sterling humor." Although Schwed is plainly not interested in modern poetry, he recognizes the compatibility of chaos and contemporary art: the novel "is a remarkable document, damned by an unfettered fancy and sired by a half pint of gin on an empty stomach. The numerous sketches by Charles Addams are only a little saner than the text, which must be rated as an artistic achievement of no small magnitude."[106] Schwed anticipates what De Vries himself says in *Poetry* about "the drunken illuminations of surrealism, with its air of delirium and fragmentation."[107]

De Vries's college classmate John Timmerman, writing in *The Calvin Forum*, catalogs the madness—"the weirdest congeries of freaks that ever haunted a landlord"; "Mr. Thwing's boarding-house is a series of problems in abnormal psychology, a little wing of bedlam"— but tries to figure it out: "I believe it is difficult for any of our group to read even a novel without consciously or unconsciously looking for some deep philosophy or moral implication—even our stories must illustrate some thesis, must point some moral: we must feel 'The gods are just and of our pleasant vices / Make instruments to plague us.'" Timmerman plunks halfheartedly for the satiric reading:

> So I tried to ferret out some deep import in Thwing and company; but there is none or I can't see it. The book may be witty satire on all those who, like Mr. George H. Brezon, see something intelligible and significant in the recent cult of unintelligibility in poetry, music, and painting. It may be sharp ridicule of the inane gyrations in verse of Gertrude Stein and E. E. Cummings (at least Mr. Thwing punctuates). It may simply be a roaringly funny fantasy. Incidentally again, Mr. George H. Brezon's interpretation of Thwing's batch of words which look like verse at three feet is an extremely clever performance and shows the critic's pre-possession to find what he wants to find whether it's there or not.

It is. Timmerman's lively appraisal is wrong on several counts. De Vries liked the "gyrations" of E. E. Cummings and attacked the "cult of unintelligibility" canard in defending Dylan Thomas. And ragging "the critic" is an error. De Vries criticism has been skewed by the earnest hunt for a moral, not by a surplus of ingenuity. Timmerman expects from De Vries a "broader canvas and a wider range of life than the abnormal twilights of Thwing and company." Timmerman's is an intelligent voice issuing from within the fold De Vries had left before uttering this "first wild bleat." We hear in it a prejudice in favor of conservative, anagogic interpretations and against avant-garde, humanist readings and bewilderment about De Vries's multiple perspectives. Nothing could illustrate De Vries's shift from his origins more poignantly than Timmerman's incomprehension, his testimony to "funny fantasy" rather than "surrealist fun."[108]

* * *

All the Surrealist performances are so many finger exercises.—Herbert J. Muller[109]

In 1962, Peter De Vries told John K. Hutchens of the *New York Herald Tribune* that "those first three [novels] were only finger exercises, and I must have been conscious of it, as I concentrated on short stories to sharpen up."[110] Twenty years later, he spoke with a mixture of jocularity and gratification:

> With . . . self-deprecatory humor, De Vries talks about three of his early books that he no longer wishes to acknowledge. "For a while I tried to buy up extant copies and burn them, but now it costs too much." He

shows us a listing in a rare books catalogue for "But Who Wakes the Bugler?" The fledgling work is priced at a fancy sum, far greater than his current books command. It's the kind of irony De Vries appreciates.[111]

A further irony appears in Roy Newquist's *Counterpoint*. In their 1964 interview, De Vries takes pride in having "finished a novel" in a harried period; Newquist is specific—"That would be *But Who Wakes the Bugler?*"—and De Vries declines the opportunity to deprecate.[112] But De Vries's dispraise of his first novels in 1962 led students of his work to ignore or scant them ever since.[113] The omission of *Bugler* from discussion has adversely affected interpretation of all of De Vries's works. It was De Vries himself who damned the early books as finger exercises and applying the same standard at large would cost us not only "To a Young Ass" and *Franklin Evans* but also "English Bards and Scotch Reviewers" and everything in Chaucer except "Amen."

Meanwhile, outside the field of De Vries scholarship, Israel Shenker sketched the background to his 1969 interview of De Vries by calling *Bugler* a "classic," and a 1979 annotated bibliography of Illinois fiction applauds in *Bugler* "the zaniest group of crackpots ever to occupy the pages of a novel."[114] At least some later readers of *Bugler* who hadn't been told the author was just tuning up thought they were hearing an inspired performance.

The trio of scholarly commentaries on *Bugler*—those in Joseph Michael De Roller's "Lower-Case Absurd," T. Jeff Evans's "The Apprentice Fiction of Peter De Vries," and J. H. Bowden's *Peter De Vries*—suffer the consequences of ignoring De Vries's career at *Poetry* and his early published poems, stories, and essays. De Roller says the "pleasure" of *Bugler* lies in its "glimpse into an unrestrained imagination at play" and that it "prefigures De Vries's later work in its display of wild imagination, its sense of only slightly subdued hysteria," but trying to fit the novel into Northrop Frye's system compels him to call the book "flawed."[115] Evans's insistence that De Vries is a Comic writer intent on "return[ing] the [defiant] individual to society through reconciliation" and that any deviation from the pattern is a "falling off"[116] forces him to describe Mr. Thwing as "essentially conventional."[117] J. H. Bowden also depicts *Bugler* as conservative, yet sees "juxtaposition of . . . widely differing outlooks . . . makes the drama happen" and claims that reading De Vries creates "a heightened sense of unreality or art or insanity, which in De Vries's work may amount to saying the same thing three times, anyway."[118]

* * *

[Nathanael West's] was a brief expatriation, but it confirmed his avant-garde disposition and his interest in surrealism—though a part of his talent undoubtedly owes much to his friendship with the American humorist S. J. Perelman.—Malcolm Bradbury[119]

The reviewers of *Bugler* were on the right track toward "surrealist fun" but were not up to its challenges. Later commentators removed the book from its milieu. Literary scholars are beginning to reawaken to surrealism. Malcolm Bradbury entitles a chapter in his *Modern American Novel* "Realism and Surrealism: The 1930s." He discusses Djuna Barnes, Nathanael West, and Henry Miller as writers for whom "the quest for rational and orderly myth was illusory, and what was needed was not epical realism but grotesque surrealism." Bradbury applies the word *surrealism* broadly but never casually. In his treatment of *The Great Gatsby*, for instance, he asserts, "Fitzgerald's aim is surreal, the making bright of certain evanescent things so that they have the quality of a dream; but at the novel's end that dream is withdrawn, and another surreality, the nightmare of an unmitigated mass of material objects, takes its place."[120] The concerns of De Vries's work are similar to those of Bradbury's "surrealists."

Nathanael West's *Dream Life of Balso Snell* (1931) is, according to Bradbury, "a surreal comedy about an American poet innocent who wanders into the womb-like world of the Trojan horse through the posterior opening, and finds it 'inhabited solely by writers in search of an audience.'" There are resemblances, beyond poets lost in interiors, between De Vries's and West's first books:

This opens the (rear) door to pastiche and parody of many literary styles, a generalized mockery of art that dislodges past forms and even recent modernism, including the work of Joyce. It is a creative writer's notebook, a striking act of apprenticeship. West was always to be an idiosyncratic writer, with some obvious limitations: his desire to mock, undercut, make art into a kind of comic strip with puppet-like agents, often looks like bad writing, and at times, as in parts of *Balso Snell*, it is. Yet exactly those qualities, which displace prior artistic conventions and ideas of art's humanism, were to prove his real resource.[121]

There are too many parallels to enumerate. West had Perelman's friendship, De Vries, Thurber's; West visited Paris, Paris visited De Vries in the Chicago office of *Poetry*. But while West's first book is rough, De Vries's is smooth. West flaunted his insolence, but De Vries's flouting of convention was so polished that it slipped off the bourgeois verge. Whereas Balso Snell is raw, George Thwing is cooked, and to some tastes more palatable.

* * *

[Bachelard's theory of the literary imagination is similar to Breton's surrealism in that] what is essential is . . . the liberation from all previously fixed categories. Open rationalism, open realism, the open imagination.—Mary Ann Caws[122]

This discussion of Peter De Vries's first novel, which has gone on now at delirious length, suggests that all of De Vries's books should be read with reference to surrealism. Not to do so is to miss much of their humor and substance. Arguing this case may "prosecute" De Vries for a "crime" he never confessed in any interview. Yet he spoke up, in wartime, for a movement soon to have "the distinction of being denounced in Congress as an un-American activity."[123] De Vries must have known when he wrote for *Poetry* and *College English* that he ran a risk by befriending surrealism, yet he asserted the rights of the imagination.

Franklin Rosemont, for some years the chief American exponent of Bretonian surrealism, has observed that

The nation's history reveals a large number of "implicit surrealists," Americans whose lives and work appear in their own true light only in the light of surrealism. Many previously have been held to be "minor" or "tangential"—classifications suggestive of their remoteness from the bourgeois "mainstream." . . . The future surely holds in store many more discoveries of this sort, and the American surrealists have set themselves the task of searching for such material and recording it in their journal. Not all such "anticipations" are to be sought in the effects of obscure characters lurking in forgotten byways; untold wonders are waiting to be discovered even at the very heart of the "obvious."[124]

It is time that a major American writer close to the bourgeois mainstream and to surrealism be read in the light of surrealism. This is not to say De Vries will emerge as a surrealist or a surrealist in spite of himself. If Mary Ann Caws is correct in characterizing surrealism as "an act of faith in the superior reality of certain forms of mental association and of the dream,"[125] De Vries must be counted a skeptic. But as Roderick Jellema noted, "What Hawthorne said of Melville can surely be said of Peter De Vries: 'He can neither believe, nor be comfortable in his unbelief; and he is too honest and courageous not to try to do one or the other.' The friction generated by this tension produced the heat of Melville's creativity. It seems to do the same for De Vries."[126] Melville was, however, not only struggling with Calvinism: he is considered on good account to be a precursor of surrealism. The contenders for Melville's and De Vries's faith are multiple: such writers contend not with, in Jellema's phrase, one "absurd predicament,"[127] but with kingdoms of absurdities. And they know the curse of zeal. By 1950 "surrealism was achieving a form of consecration which was not to be entirely advantageous, since it tended to assume the character of an interment."[128]

De Vries's protean self and art have received many and various influences, lying between the extremes of Calvinism, in Kenneth Burke's terminology a "philosophy of binding," and surrealism, a "philosophy of loosing."[129] Not the least of these influences are the surrealism of the surrealists and the surrealism of everyday life.[130]

5

Surrealizations: The Unofficial Career
of Peter De Vries

Even in the [early] sketches . . . we see the wild free association, anarchic wordplay, maniacal non sequiturs, preposterous names, and surrealist juxtapositions of the accomplished pyrotechnician to come.—Peter De Vries on S. J. Perelman[1]

He strides in the mantle of S. J. Perelman, and it fits.—Malcolm Cowley on Peter De Vries[2]

DESPITE Malcolm Cowley and a few others, reviewers and critics depict Peter De Vries as a domesticated wit. But his works never have been conservative. De Vries's Thurberesque and Perelmanesque extravagances are the essential dynamics of his art, and he is more than a "laureate of suburbia."

"If I spent my time portraying life as it actually is, I think I would go insane with boredom inside of two weeks," said De Vries in 1956. "It is the question of reality passed through a filter."[3] His repugnance for literary realism recalls André Breton's. De Vries has often expressed views that tally with those of the surrealists. On Freud, for example, he said in 1966, "I think you have to judge Freud in the light of the validity of his discoveries—the importance of the unconscious and of sex in our lives. Both of these are corroborated by human experience. The collateral absurdities of psychoanalysis result from its determination to interpret absolutely everything in the light of them."[4] De Vries echoes the surrealists' assessment, which credited Freud with opening a new territory but excoriated psychoanalysts for walling it up as a private demesne.[5] In a *New Yorker* story, De Vries mocks analysts as preachers of a "Gospel of Responsibility"; the typical De Vries hero is a paragon of beguiling irresponsibility.[6]

Well-versed in Freud, De Vries makes frequent references to the unconscious: "I don't think I pursue any conscious 'purpose' or 'motivation' so much as an unconscious instinct of, and for, the absurd. I simply follow a comic scent where it leads."[7] De Vries likens himself to a beagle meandering on the trail, but he is not very far from recapitulating Breton's account of his and Soupault's dogged pursuit, often culminating in "a strong comical effect," of surrealist images. "Poetically speaking," Breton observed, "what strikes you about them above all is their *extreme degree of immediate absurdity.*"[8] De Vries has expressed a different opinion about what makes for successful writing: "It is control. The bane of comedy is facetiousness."[9] Yet the dominant theme in his remarks on writing is that there must be alternation between conscious and unconscious or "subconscious" forces: "It's when we're relaxed that the subconscious gets in its famous licks. . . . I write slowly fast. Bang away at white heat to get something down, and get it right later."[10] In "Exploring Inner Space," De Vries is careful to define "inner space" as "private consciousness and even unconsciousness." Taking Virginia Woolf as an exemplary writer in whom "a kind of psychic fission . . . releases the energy of the association," he describes writing as discovery: "I had sat down to write [a story] without the faintest idea that was what it was about. I had surmised it to be about something else altogether. Thus it was the practice of my craft that, ultimately, enabled me to understand the reality the craft was intended to illuminate."[11] This description of the writing process as expression and experiment is a Romantic and Transcendentalist view consistent with the practice of the surrealists, as is the reference to "my craft." De Vries has said "I've always liked virtuosity in a writer," and he has found it in avowed surrealists like Charles Henri Ford.[12]

Although De Vries's prose is universally acknowledged as meticulous, he has claimed, "The strongest single influence on my work is unmistakable—Debussy. Same emphasis on texture rather than structure; accumulated nuance rather than organized continuity; the chord as an experience in its own right apart from melody. That clear it up for you, sweetheart?"[13] The same tone carries into his interview with Roy Newquist:

> N. Recently . . . I came across a review of *Reuben, Reuben* that elaborated on the fact that you "lacked cohesiveness." Can you comment on that?
> *De Vries:* That is because of my influences.
> N. You mean literary? You've been compared to Thurber, Benchley, Lardner, Lewis, Marquand—
> *De Vries:* No. I don't derive from any of them. I would say my main influences spring from two sources: Debussy and Sibelius. From one the emphasis on the individual nuance rather than the melodic whole, the chord being its own justification quite apart from any duty to a supporting

continuity. From Sibelius, *carte blanche* to be as free-form as I please. Anyone wishing to call that "lack of cohesiveness" is welcome.[14]

De Vries constantly alludes to all the named writers and is putting Newquist on. Nonetheless, emphasizing nuance and openness *is* common to De Vries and the composers. As to emphatic chords, *Madder Music*'s hero rigs a piano to explode when "the famous 'mystic chord' of Scriabin's" is struck (143–45).

In *Peckham's Marbles*, the spectacularly unsuccessful novelist Earl Peckham is asked by a newspaper reporter named Looply, "Who would you say your major influences are?" "Debussy and Ravel," replies Peckham, in a spasm of satirical impulse. "The other's expression indicated that he realized his leg was being pulled" (99). But Peckham suddenly realizes, after he has made the statement, that there is some truth in it. De Vries's interviews and novels mirror each other in an Aladdin's castle of reflections. The subject is often antinomy: "There are two sides to any question, and one simultaneously takes them both," mused De Vries to Ben Yagoda on a drive around Westport.[15] Twenty years earlier, Tom Waltz espoused the same Montaignian idea in *Let Me Count the Ways* (123). Like a good surrealist, De Vries delights in subverting the rational critical faculties, and his characters often champion works of imagination and contradiction against the assaults of interrogation and analysis.[16] Yet De Vries is himself an able critic. In the following effort to describe what is distinctive in De Vries's novels, I have taken his cue to follow "chords" rather than "the melodic whole" and to soft-pedal the Scriabin.

One of the primary themes of surrealism is that of the poet as seer. De Vries claimed in his essay on James Thurber: "The truly original poet is often prescient. . . . Poetry is sometimes an antenna by which the race detects actualities at which it has not quite arrived."[17] He gave laconic voice to the same theme when he was asked in 1964, "How would you like yourself to be evaluated" in 2064? "My needs are modest," De Vries replied. "A good artist predicts as well as reflects, and all I ask is that they say, 'We know now what they couldn't see then. He was six months ahead of his time.'"[18] Only ten years later, Richard Boston could observe that De Vries's 1950s novels "were not only right up-to-date but seemed actually to anticipate events. *The Mackerel Plaza*, for example, effectively parodied the beliefs and disbeliefs of Dr. John Robinson's *Honest to God* some years before that book was actually published. . . . *The Tents of Wickedness* . . . anticipated Women's Lib by nearly a decade."[19] De Vries's reflections on the relations between taste cultures in America, most especially in *I Hear America Swinging,* raucously prefigure sober socio-logical treatises,[20] and from his first novel he pioneered catch-22 logic and the self-reflexive techniques of postmodernism.

De Vries must also be credited with scores of predictions and satires-before-the-fact that proved as true as if his ideas had been lifted by admen, inventors, and editors. In *Into Your Tent I'll Creep,* Al Banghart vows to write a rock-and-roll song about a *Playboy* center-fold (142) about fifteen years before the veritable "Angel in the Cen-terfold." Al pretends to be an immigrant to sell his wares with the spiel, "I lawv zis cawntree" (147), a line a real immigrant used on TV viewers in commercials of the late 1980s. In *The Cat's Pajamas,* Hank Tattersall sells canned fresh air door-to-door (158) as an exercise in absurdity several years before enterprising canners employed the same scheme for profit. The college English instructor Tom Waltz in *Let Me Count the Ways,* by winning popular essay contests with mawk-ish effusions, prefigured the career of Erich Segal. In *Forever Pant-ing,* De Vries predicted gratuitous sex in TV advertising with Dolly Smackenfelt's "Swamp Tease" enticements (88–89, 182). Inventing for *I Hear America Swinging* an avant-garde magazine named *Gargoyle* (110), De Vries wrote just about six months ahead of the founding of *Gargoyle.*[21] Paul Theroux was moved in a review of *Madder Music* to "wonder whether since Peter De Vries began writing novels the American people have become more and more De Vriesesque," De Vries's "violent farces" and "vocabulary of desire" sardonically limn-ing the dark side of the American psyche.[22] De Vries proved a receptive "antenna" for trends ridiculous enough, George Henri Brezon might say, that Americans would enact them.

Besides designing a wardrobe of motley coats for the rest of us to grow into, De Vries fashioned a comic persona for himself. He consistently declared that his goal was "to amuse the reader as much as he could":[23]

I don't think about what I am or what I'm trying to do, except to amuse an intelligent reader with what I hope is some truth we both know about life.

I'd rather offer the reader an honest surfboard ride than pack him into a diving bell and then lower him into what turns out to be three feet of water. . . . My aim generally is refreshment, and anybody looking for nourishment is on his own, and perfectly welcome.

How funny you are is all that counts.

I guess you'd have to call me that [i.e., a "confessed humorist"]. What I aim for is to amuse. . . . I can't remember not wanting, as a child, to amuse people.[24]

De Vries could be impatient with attempts to categorize the type of amusement he provided: "Call it satire, humor, or comedy—I don't care." He could also put on a mild, avuncular manner: "I don't think I have enough lemon in me to be a satirist." He once rejected the label "Black Humor" as "another bumper sticker"; his humor is "blue." Nevertheless, he regarded the poet Gowan McGland of *Reuben, Reuben* one of his best characters partly because McGland's "attitude is one of sardonic amusement with the world, however tragic it is," an attitude close to De Vries's own: "The ocean of human folly is bottomless."[25]

De Vries did not want to fasten readers into a diving bell, but he peered into depths: "The oblivious person, the fool, the man who slips on the banana peel is not funny in himself. There must be someone of wider consciousness watching the oblivious one. . . . There can be layers and layers of this deepening perception, like the cow on the evaporated milk can."[26] The juxtaposition of perspectives becomes dizzying in De Vries's work. "We human beings are all absurd variations of one another in any case, and this is what comedy of all kinds puts down on paper."[27] "What I want to show is something perfectly plain: that we're all absurd variations of one another."[28] More than this, "'My protagonists are all more or less versions of myself,' [De Vries] admits. 'I've cut myself up into segments. So many pieces I don't know how I get around any more,'"[29] not excepting a female protagonist: "I share enough traits with Daisy [of *Sauce for the Goose*] to call the characterization autobiographical."[30] De Vries's avowal of his mixed cast of sharps and gulls as versions of himself and his exploitation of mischief for amusement refute the contention that De Vries is a Calvinist in spite of himself. There are no elect, although everyone would like to feel elected—there are only absurd variations. Wearing the mask of Comus, De Vries goes Lautréamont one better, showing that art *is* "made by all."

All art is not equal, and De Vries included among his favorite authors Anthony Powell ("comedy-without-facetiousness"), Elizabeth Bowen ("style, sensibility, a wild, lyrical wit"), Kingsley Amis, Fitzgerald, and Faulkner.[31] "I cut my eyeteeth on Thurber, Ring Lardner, and Mark Twain. They have to be counted among my favorites," De Vries said, not leaving out his early "overdosing" on De Quincey: "I like Faulkner's use of rhetoric, even when it spills over into self-parody, as it often does. Not even the dithyrambic jags in *The Wild Palms* are too much for me, who as a high-school adolescent would overdose on De Quincey. Certainly an odd first enthusiasm for a humorist. Odd."[32] Not so odd: De Quincey's extravagance, the "wild" side, the "dithyrambic jag," is present in all De Vries's favorites, not excluding the suave, "cool" Anthony Powell.[33]

De Vries maintained a dynamic comic credo:

> Nobody has been funnier than Faulkner, nor has anyone a better grasp of the human predicament than Mark Twain. And didn't Yeats say Hamlet and Lear are gay? Frost said of this basic principle of playfulness (in discussing Edwin Arlington Robinson, of all people), "If it is with outer seriousness, it must be with inner humor. If it is with outer humor, it must be with inner seriousness. Neither one alone without the other under it will do." Any comic worth his salt knows this instinctively, even without being able to put it in Charlie Chaplin's words: "If what you're doing is funny, don't be funny doing it." Any attempt to isolate the "serious" from whatever you want to call its opposite is like trying to put asunder what God hath joined together. The reverse is equally foredoomed.[34]

In this view, the comic principle (and for that matter, the tragic) is juxtaposition. De Vries was generous to *The New Yorker* as his tutor in managing his comic means:

> It was a school I went to. . . . To the extent that what I do has any merit whatsoever, it was purified of its defects by the standards I had to meet in writing for *The New Yorker.* . . . I learned that the bane of real humor is facetiousness. It's the Charlie Chaplin principle—if what you're doing is funny, don't horse around while you're doing it or you'll deprive it of its humor. Specifically, what I had to learn was to cut the comedy.[35]

Although De Vries no doubt learned much from writing for *The New Yorker,* James Thurber found him already "The perfect *New Yorker* writer" in 1944. De Vries cannot have been insensible of his precocity (precociousness appears as a theme in several of his novels), nor of his own and Charlie Chaplin's facetiousness. The Sydney Smith epigraph to *The Tents of Wickedness* even promises facetiousness: "You must not think me necessarily foolish because I am facetious, nor will I consider you necessarily wise because you are grave." In lavishing credit on *The New Yorker* De Vries voiced homage to Thurber and gratitude for support. He may have been adding a hint of Eustace Tilly to his public persona as Eastern wit. De Vries's identification with *The New Yorker* may register in some readers' minds as a rejection of surrealism, but there is no basis for such a view. As Walter Blair and Hamlin Hill point out, in discussing Thomas Pynchon's *V.,* "Such surreal fantasy—especially when the protagonist attempts unsuccessfully to confront and conquer it—hearkens back to the Walter Mittys, the Balso Snells, and the Benchley persona of the genteel, high-culture humorists of the *New Yorker* mode of comedy."[36] In any case, the gloss of De Vries's *New Yorker* polish cannot obscure a rough and shaggy wildness in his works, which contain gags, frolics, irreverences, and indecencies that could never have been admitted into the pages of the Ross or Shawn *New Yorker.*

De Vries's ambivalence toward sophistication, frequently exploited in his novels, is succinctly expressed in a statement he wrote for an exhibition of his manuscripts:

> A distasteful distaste for the milieu into which I was born, and in which I was repressively reared, bred the natural desire to flee it for a more congenial line of country, one regarded by the authors of my being as Sin itself. It had been expected of me that I would say with the psalmist, "I would rather be a doorkeeper in the house of my God than dwell in the tents of wickedness." Having successfully opted for the latter scene, there was nothing for me to do but satirize it, and thus in some shaky accommodation propitiate the household gods being simultaneously flouted. The critic was right who said I was against both morality and immorality.[37]

So much for not having "enough lemon in me to be a satirist." No victim of a foolish consistency, De Vries satirizes moralists, immoralists, and amoralists; creatures of the town, the city, and the country; highbrows, lowbrows, and middlebrows. The sense of wonder reigns in his books, spinning out "unerring puns, malapropisms, hyperbole, metaphors, parodies, slapstick, mimicry, and one-liners. What should be judged is not the book," suggests one reviewer, "but the voice emanating from it. It is a manic voice, capable of countless timbres, inflections, and speeds."[38]

De Vries's voice is devoted largely to play and pleasure. "I'm past admiring [in literature] anything I don't enjoy," De Vries told Newquist in 1964; "divorce of appreciation from enjoyment . . . is the curse of academic literary analysis." He said to Douglas Davis, "I recently read a couple of serious-type articles about what I am actually up to, and I can only conclude that my stuff is really over my head" and to an audience at Calvin College,

> There are actually teachers who assign my books, and graduate students who write learned theses on them and get doctoral and master's degrees—all of which goes to prove what I've been saying in these books all along, that everything is going to hell in a handbasket. One such thesis, which I read recently . . . said that I was moving toward a neo-Manichean dualism. Of course, I was the last to know.[39]

De Vries worked not toward, but through, the solemnities of systems and isms. Invoking them, he flashed his credentials as one who had looked into the void and seen the difficulties of living with or without dogma, so as to gain authority for his assertion, against the odds, of the prerogative of laughter.

De Vries's laughter is not that of social correction but of astonishment. It does not subtract from human possibilities but augments them. It does not seek to limit diversity but celebrates it. The surrealist farce exists not to ridicule or co-opt the avant-garde, but to become it, to join in its antiauthoritarianism. Melvin Maddocks said of De Vries in 1981 that "no other ism has yet been able to tempt him from the chastity of his sole conviction: skepticism."[40] While this skepticism applies to surrealism, from the first De Vries's work has shared with André Breton's an impulse toward "complete insubordination."[41]

The extreme form of insubordination is madness. Without ever romanticizing insanity, De Vries included episodes of madness in every one of his books. It might be said that lunacy is the leitmotif of his work. Suffering up to and beyond the breaking point is the central human experience confronted, with heroic laughter, in De Vries. As Edouard Roditi observed in the October 1943 *Poetry,* "art and psychopathology . . ., without being the same, follow the same or similar patterns."[42] Dudley Fitts, discussing hallucination in Rimbaud in the April 1944 *Poetry,* remarks, "It is like symbolic substitution in certain kinds of mental disease; it is one of the technics of surrealism."[43] The investigation begun by André Breton in World War I field hospitals continues in De Vries's novels.

Dick, the narrator of *The Tunnel of Love,* suffers from psychosomatic laryngitis (3). Andrew Mackerel and Joe Sandwich get dizzy from Ménière's syndrome, the disease from which Jonathan Swift suffered (*Mackerel Plaza,* 114; *The Vale of Laughter,* 85–86, 93, 97, 200–203), and both spend time in the sanitarium. Jim Tickler's father is a somnambulist whose "nocturnal tangents" are "surrealist charades" (*The Glory of the Hummingbird,* 11). Alma Marvell drives her psychiatrist crazy (*Through the Fields of Clover,* 268–74), and Emma Wallop bewilders her marriage counselor (*Mrs. Wallop,* 241–43). Chick Swallow's amateur psychology drives his pal Nickie crazy (e.g., *Comfort Me With Apples,* 229–35; *The Tents of Wickedness,* 142–46). Chick's attempted suicide ends in a fever dream described in parodies of Kafka and Joyce (*The Tents of Wickedness,* 242–58); Eddie Teeters's similar bout with "the poetry of delirium" (*The Prick of Noon,* 139–47) has been termed "a sustained surreal tour de force."[44] Joe Sandwich and Hank Tattersall share the Daliesque worldview that there is "interconnection between things . . . thought dissimilar or even opposite, like tragedy and comedy . . . desperation being the common denominator" (*The Vale of Laughter,* 212; *The Cat's Pajamas & Witch's Milk,* 62). *Reuben, Reuben*'s Gowan McGland suffers from a variety of psychosomatic ills and depression. McGland's would-be chronicler, Alvin Mopworth, is paradoxically *expelled* from a mental institution for acting maniacal (431).

Patients driving their doctors around the bend and doctors prodding their patients out of the asylum for acting sick are not merely jokes but part of De Vries's problematizing of madness. Andrew Mackerel's imaginative extravagances—"I was in the country of those dark specialists in rumination who had left their phosphorescent print on a corner of nineteenth-century French literature" (*The Mackerel Plaza,* 191)—that is, his fear that he is a victim of "malignant satyriasis" (203) and his penchant for double entendres land him in an asylum. He is ejected by a doctor with catch-22 flair: "Committed! You must be crazy. . . . No, I'm sorry Mackerel . . . I have no choice but to release you" (219). Mackerel, while a strange fish, is no stranger than his supposedly normal antagonists, the fundamentalist Turnbull and the Babbitts of Avalon, Connecticut (60–62, 152, 167). Tillie Selzer rebukes Hank Tattersall for his fashionable despair (*The Cat's Pajamas & Witch's Milk,* 171–79) but ends up in an asylum herself after getting into a fight with a fellow organizer of the Mental Health Ball (288). Bob Swirling is cured of his delusion that he is Groucho Marx by a conspiracy of friends, but for good reasons he finds life among the sane so irksome that he emerges "a patently happy man" in the new role of W. C. Fields, a trickster hero again (*Madder Music,* 219–20). De Vries's perennial concern with madness and sanity, illusion and reality, far from having evolved out of a naive distinction between romantic illusion and commonsense reality, took its departure from an acute appreciation of the problematic nature of such a distinction. In *The Handsome Heart,* Brian Carston's insanity proves more sane that his sane brother Charles's greed and lust (176–79; 203–7). In *Angels Can't Do Better,* Peter Topp acknowledges that "consciousness is a weird compost of fact and hallucination" (88). Anyone tempted to suppose that De Vries's novels are apolitical might reflect that basic political questions—Who gets to define reality? Whose version of reality is privileged?—are fundamental to them.

De Vries is famous for inventive imagery, and his images often drive two realities together, like Lautréamont's famous chance encounter of an umbrella and a sewing machine on a dissection table: "He could scarcely see the sidewalk with its humanity like a twitching moss." "*A halibut's head looks like a human head,* and that's why nobody is allowed to take them ashore with the heads on" (*The Handsome Heart*, 106; 14 [cf. 8, 211]). Similar Magritte-like images appear in *Angels Can't Do Better:* Peter dreams that "when I answer the door there is a naked man there with a derby on and a cigar in his mouth and he says, 'Can you repair fish?'" (96). A repeated image of a swirling flock of starlings (1–3, 7–8, 14, 56–58, 96–97, 129, 137, 171–73) recalls Lautréamont's well-known image from Book Five of *Les Chants de Maldoror,* which James Laughlin had just published in English translation the year before De Vries's novel.[45] These images from De Vries's early novels are representative of his defamiliarizing juxtapositions.

The sensory perceptions in De Vries's works are often phantasmagoric, and literary associations add to the vertigo. De Vries is celebrated for his allusiveness, and he often juxtaposes frames of reference and cultural levels. In *The Handsome Heart,* the name of Gutzon Borglum (sculptor of Mt. Rushmore) appears (20) amid references to Mozart, Beethoven, Toscanini, Houseman, and Thomas Wolfe, and allusions to Shakespeare, Whitman, and Twain. *The Tents of Wickedness* is a tour-de-force told in the parodied voices of Faulkner, Fitzgerald, Greene, Hemingway, Joyce, Kafka, Marquand, and Proust in what amounts to a surrealistic overstanding of the originals: De Vries stands somewhere between Pierre Menard rewriting *Don Quixote* and Marcel Duchamp drawing the moustache on *La Gioconda.* *The Cat's Pajamas'* Hank Tattersall lives in a maelstrom of kitsch and high culture. In *Slouching Towards Kalamazoo,* Anthony Thrasher, of Ulalume, North Dakota, falls behind in his eighth grade work because he spends his time reading Nietzsche and Kierkegaard and is "moving toward a Manichean dualism" in his thinking (102). The grace notes are often "readymades"—"Gascoyne" in *The Cat's Pajamas* a likely reference to David Gascoyne, "Ulalume" a possible surrealist connection,[46] "Manichean dualism" an appropriation of a critic's fancy. And De Vries's works teem with allusions to writers popular with the surrealists, such as Swift, Huysmans, Baudelaire, and Lewis Carroll.

De Vries's plots are farces with a difference, like a Marx brothers version of *Nadja,* or *Main Street* altered by Magritte. The endings are tricky, tending to open up the antinomies that have been held precariously in balance during the action. A prime example is *Madder Music,* whose plot consists of the twists Robert Swirling takes through a "pathological amnesiac condition," or fugue state (3). The language matches: the narrator calls Swirling's dialogue "surrealist patter" (13), and Swirling's style seeps into the narrator's voice.

De Vries does not attempt to map illusory psychological depths, preferring to follow the trail of the absurd. For the reader, this trail meanders from "absurdity Gulch" (*The Handsome Heart*, 93) through "the first [TV] commercial of the Absurd" (*The Cat's Pajamas & Witch's Milk*, 39) and beyond. Because the domain of the absurd is everywhere, De Vries's basic move is to surmount logic, to point to gaps and built-in contradictions. In *Madder Music* as elsewhere, the upholders of reason and convention, and the conventions themselves, fall prey to the failures of logic: dull Dr. Josko cannot cure Swirling, and the plot, unable to contain Swirling, sets him free as W. C. Fields.

* * *

The omelet with *bones* in it that Mackerel eats with Molly Calico belongs to a world in which surrealism has been made available on a franchise basis.—Frederic Raphael[47]

The surrealist farce does not spare bohemia: De Vries takes lusty swipes at "plaid music" (*The Cat's Pajamas & Witch's Milk*, 25) and *Vogue*- and *Cosmo*-approved *objets trouvés* that become the rage in Grand Rapids (*Sauce for the Goose*, 11), and George Henri Brezon is only the first of a legion of the avant-garde De Vries marches into the vale of laughter. In *The Vale of Laughter*, in fact, Joe Sandwich is characterized by his foil, Wally Hines, as "the original Dadaist. Joe remained the object of my interest, the focus of my horrified curiosity. He belonged to that class of miscreants who fascinate while they appall" (275–76). The trouble with Wally is that he is so much less interesting than Joe, and commentators are generally agreed that Joe the trickster is the more sympathetic character. Peter Topp, who runs a surrealistically silly campaign for alderman in *Angels Can't Do Better;* Andy Mackerel, the avant-garde clergyman; Hank Tattersall, the *homme revolté;* Emma Wallop, the avant-garde film producer; Gowan McGland, the avant-garde poet—and many others—all belong to the class "miscreants who fascinate while they appall." Their problem is not that they have departed from social norms, but that, retaining ordinary vanity, self-deception, and fatalism, they did not go far enough. Their conservative antagonists in Avalon, Decency, Woodsmoke, Slow Rapids, and Ulalume appall but do not fascinate.

In *The Tents of Wickedness*, Chick Swallow opines that "The task of rearing a child must have taught [Sweetie] a lot. Taught her that the conformity we often glibly equate with mediocrity isn't something free spirits 'transcend' as much as something they're not quite up to. That concentration calls for broader shoulders—and, for all I know, more imagination—than revolt" (267). Many critics have swallowed this straight as an apology for conventionality. To do so they must ignore Chick's inveterate hypocrisy: as Jack Kent Boyd points out, Chick isn't "up to" either convention or revolt; both Chick and his foil, Beth Appleyard, are "weak advocates for their respective causes" of bourgeois respectability and bohemian freedom.[48] Like the personages in scripture, De Vries's characters can be quoted on both sides of the important issues. "We are all surrealists at bottom," muses the antihero of *Peckham's Marbles* (125). As a sampling of six novels will show, what is important in De Vries is not so much such pronouncements as the dialectical play of their oppositions in surrealist farce. Hank Tattersall, echoing Joe Sandwich, says "Mirth and grief have a common manifestation, the convulsion" (*The Cat's Pajamas*, 62). Both echo Breton's "Beauty will be convulsive or it will not be."[49]

* * *

The Blood of the Lamb is probably De Vries's best known and most discussed novel. It begins as a bildungsroman that contains some of the funniest scenes in De Vries but culminates in the grinding ordeal of a widower who must watch as his only child, Carol, is consumed by a cruel illness. A volatile compound of wit and hilarity, ferocity and grief, it is often seen as ushering in a "darkening strain" in De Vries's work.

Although "darker strains" invaded the earliest of De Vries's works, there does lurk in this book a deeper rage and a more harrowing sorrow than in its predecessors. There are enough autobiographical elements in the protagonist, Don Wanderhope, to have elicited a good deal of biographical criticism, which tends to focus, for good reason, on De Vries's religious upbringing. Yet the sense of disquiet universally recognized by the novel's readers has not been adequately explained. Why is this novel so deeply unsettling to so many readers? What distinguishes it from other meditations on emergencies of life and death? How can we account for its being so chameleonlike that the same crucial scenes were excerpted in both an avant-garde anthology of black humor and a *Reader's Digest* condensed book?[50]

"This, it seems then, is my Book of the Dead," Don Wanderhope says near the end of his narrative; "all I know I have learned from them" (243). Wanderhope is dragged down by the weight not only of his many losses—his brother; his parents; his lover, Rena; his wife, Greta, a suicide; his spritelike daughter—but also by the burdens they bequeathed to him. ("The old have nothing to tell us," Don tells us, in one Thoreauvian aside, made immediately into a joke: "it is more commonly we who are shouting at them, in any case"

[120].) He is cursed by the wounds of his losses—"Time heals nothing" (246)—and his efforts to bear the immovable objects and ideas of the past. Yet he is blessed by the special understanding he has gained from his transactions in and with the past, moments of knowledge incommunicable at the time but now recorded as the esoterica of "my Book of the Dead." *The Blood of the Lamb* is a hermetic text, an arcanum of private experience, told by way of secrecy, concealment, mystery, and paradox.

Don's brother, Louie, dies reassuring his devout mother that he is secure in his faith, while sharing with Don by a surreptitious sign the secret of his resolute unbelief (30). Don's "insane" liaison with the dying Rena Baker in the tuberculosis sanitarium where both are patients is clandestine (105–10). Greta's parents deceive Don into marrying their daughter, a secret she guiltily discloses to him (131–34). Carol's fatal diagnosis, leukemia, is concealed from her, but Don thinks her friend "Omar knew" (202), and Carol's secret is that she did know, as Don learns (240–42). Don observes that "we live this life by a kind of conspiracy of grace," which maintains the pretense of a meaning to human existence in denial of persuasive evidence to the contrary (214–15). The special case of this is "the sacred hoax . . . that Everything Was Fine" that obtains on the children's ward (179). Don must disguise his revulsion at the spectacles of suffering and stupidity he witnesses on the ward (206–26). And he is always confronting the inscrutability shared by surrounding nature and religious icons. But as Don's bitterness increases, his narrative counts the ways in which his private knowledge inevitably grows through exposure to extremities of experience best described as surreal. Thus, his narrative runs the gamut from pathos to irony, from the banal notion of "shared moments" to the refinements of "objective chance." It is in effect his *summa*, a palimpsest in which his various levels of development are simultaneously present. Some readers respond more strongly to the pathos, others to the irony, but all sense a disturbance in their usual categories.

A famous scene near the beginning of the novel is that in which Don and his father, owing to a mishap at the city dump, find themselves buried in rubbish, like Ham and Clov in Beckett's *Endgame*, "save for the principals' being engulfed in a valley of abomination rather than individual containers of it" (50–51). As father, son, and machine (their garbage truck) roll down the embankment of the wasteland, Mr. Wanderhope singing the doxology (52), they strike a "comic emblem" that makes a "good example of the way De Vries blends slapstick and surrealism to create a scene of comic absurdity."[51] De Roller and other critics see in this emblem a version of the existentialist absurd, making reference to Beckett and Camus, but junk was an icon of modernism for Eliot and Fitzgerald and a protopostmodern "collage of detritus" for surrealists:

> What is the relationship of surrealism to the postmodern condition?
> If the early surrealists—Magritte, Roux, Ernst, Dali, Duchamp, and Miro—can be so popular today with their visions of the pineal eye, floating body parts, and disembodied power, it is because their artistic imaginations are brilliant anticipations of the postmodern destiny as detritus and aleatory sacrifice. . . .
> Albert Skeer's review *Minotaure*, which appeared from 1933 to 1939, was not only an extraordinary demonstration of the surrealist imagination, but, in its privileging of the mythic figure of the minotaur as the principal theme of its covers (by Derain, Bores, Duchamp, Ernst, Miro, Dali, Matisse, Magritte, Masson, and Rivera), it successfully painted the collage of detritus that defines the disappearing postmodern subject. The covers of *Minotaure* are a brilliant cryptology of the key social codes governing the contemporary condition.[52]

De Vries's emblem is as replete a collage of cultural signs as that described in this discussion of "Panic Surrealism." The chief difference is that De Vries's emphasis is given to the human rather than the "contemporary" condition. While Carol, the sacrificial lamb singled out by chance, will be a victim not only of her disease but of an impersonal, insensitive brand of modern technological medicine, "the art of prolonging sickness" (206), ultimately the narrator sees Carol's fate and his own as "brief links . . . in the *eternal* pity" (246, emphasis added). The absurd and the surreal are perennial. As the militant atheist Stein declares, in a line echoed in later De Vries works, "What baffles me is the comfort people find in the idea that somebody dealt this *mess*" (207–8, emphasis added).

Don Wanderhope, whose name mixes that of Byron's hero with *wanhoop*, the Dutch word for "despair,"[53] is a wanderer between the realms of belief and unbelief, the leap of faith and the rack of reason. As a child in a community and family obsessed with religion, he had trembled to hear his father's and brother's expressions of doubt. In youth, he sought to climb the "ladder of sensibility" (59) and thought of himself as "a sort of reverse Pilgrim trying to make some progress *away* from the City of God" (66). In this pilgrimage he makes considerable progress. One of his early declarations of freedom takes the form of "Chicago Bohemianism," a phase in which he associates with "intellectuals who had become Marxist-oriented" (121–23). While his reminiscences about the *New Masses* and such figures as Maxwell Bodenheim are laconic (Bodenheim is, for example, the only workers' champion who had ever actually worked), he recounts the episode as an integral part of his story. Don's marriage to Greta, which had been contrived by her parents, quickly deteriorates. Greta converts to "Bible-banging evangelism" (139), but after they move to New York, where Carol is born, and then to Westchester, Greta turns to drink, adultery, and finally self-destruction (143–53). Wanderhope's illusions and disillusions along his path are resolved in a skeptical stoicism he distills in a brief "manifesto" at the request of his college newspaper:

> I believe that man must learn to live without those consolations called religious, which his own intelligence must by now have told him belong to the childhood of the race. Philosophy can really give us nothing permanent to believe either; it is too rich in answers, each canceling out the rest. The quest for Meaning is foredoomed. Human life "means" nothing. But that is not to say that it is not worth living. What does a Debussy *Arabesque* "mean," or a rainbow or a rose? A man delights in all of these, knowing himself to be no more—a wisp of music and a haze of dreams dissolving against the sun. Man has only his own two feet to stand on, his own human trinity to see him through: Reason, Courage, and Grace. And the first plus the second equals the third. (166–67)

Armed with this humanist, rationalist credo, he must face the ordeal of Carol's illness.

The final five chapters of Don Wanderhope's story are a phantasmal account of Carol's acute leukemia conveyed in a glossolalia of medical jargon mixed with common language dense with allusion. The ward is a "slice of hell" (215), a "hell of prolonged farewell," attended by "ministering vampires from Laboratory" (206). "How slapstick can tragedy get?" wonders Don at the spectacle of *"leukemic children in funny hats"* at a birthday party (226). "Twice," Don avers, "I had the uneasy experience of witnessing a crackup" among the parents, one of them set "in perhaps the most amazing midnight I had ever lived through, yet one possessing, in the dreamy dislocations of which it formed a part, a weird, bland naturalness like that of a Chirico landscape, full of shadows infinitely longer than the objects casting them" (220–21). When he accuses Stein of sadism, Don describes the torment he himself writhes in: "One doubts that you don't enjoy thinking or saying what you do, at least a little, Stein. The side of man that loves to hate, to rub in the horrible, even revel in it. Psychiatrists have even got a name for it, I think. Algolagnia, or something like that" (213–14). The "or something like that" is disingenuous; Don knows as much about Freud as about Calvin (he links the two names on 113) and in any case would know about algolagnia from extrapsychiatric sources. For, though all the commentary on *The Blood of the Lamb* emphasizes Wanderhope's biblical allusions and religious conflicts, Don alludes just as often to an antipathetic literature and frame of reference; while the Christian apologists invariably focus on the spiritual conflicts awakened by Carol's suffering, Wanderhope confronts the physical agony.

Carol is dreaming as she dies. "All her dreams are pleasant," her nurse murmurs in the tone of sentimental reassurance. But as Carol fades, Don Wanderhope is "thinking of an old line of poetry. 'Death loves a shining mark.' Now the flower-stem veins were broken, the flower-stalk of the spine destroyed. But through the troll I saw the fairy still" (234). The "old line of poetry" is Edward Young's *Night-Thoughts*, book 5, line 1011. In his anguish Don recollects a poem "greatly admired by Sade, Robespierre, Blake, Novalis, Wordsworth, Lautréamont, et al." and which Breton said is "surrealist from cover to cover."[54] The allusion contributes to the scene's pathos and over-rules it: the passage speaks in what Breton calls *"the surrealist voice . . . that continues to preach on the eve of death and above the storms."*[55]

Wanderhope's elegy for his dead, which had earlier passed through a Whitmanesque phase—"here is a branch of early lilac" (201); "a brown thrush began his evening note" (204)—finds its cynosure and speaks of it in the antithetical voices of sentiment and surrealism. At the crisis in a central De Vries work, Wanderhope's inner voice is surrealist. But suddenly, in a final moment alone with Carol, Don surreptitiously prays over her: "The Lord bless thee and keep thee" (234).

The most famous and audacious scene in the book follows Carol's death. Wanderhope gets drunk in a bar. Remembering the birthday cake he had meant to bring to Carol but left on a pew in St. Catherine's church, he enters the church, retrieves the cake, goes outside, and flings it at the face of Jesus on the crucifix hanging above the church door:

> It was miracle enough that the pastry should reach its target at all, at that height from the sidewalk. The more so that it should land squarely, just beneath the crown of thorns. Then through scalded eyes I seemed to see the hands free themselves of the nails and move slowly toward the soiled face. Very slowly, very deliberately, with infinite patience, the icing was wiped from the eyes and flung away. I could see it fall in clumps to the porch steps. Then the cheeks were wiped down with the same sense of grave and gentle ritual, with all the kind sobriety of one whose voice could be heard saying, "Suffer the little children to come unto me . . . for of such is the kingdom of heaven." (237)

Much has been written about this scene. Most of the commentary focuses on the "come unto me" rather than the acidulous linking of "kind sobriety" and "suffer," even though the book emphasizes torment, not salvation. Indeed, there is a discussion earlier in *The Blood of the Lamb* "on the sacred subject of the thrown pie" of silent film comedy, in which Omar asserts that the whole routine is a "ritual" (191–92); Carol repeats that opinion to her father later, when both are watching TV in the hospital (224–25), and the description of Jesus conforms to the early, "ritualized," description. What critics have not noticed is that the ritual Omar chooses for his analogy is not a clean affair like the burning of incense or a choric procession, but a blood sport: "You see it isn't a fight in the sense of something in which you defend yourself, but basically like your bullfight in Spain, where it isn't a sport either as we here think of it with our S.P.C.A. attitude—it's a *ceremony*" (192). Omar is a tiresomely precocious boy whose idea of offering consolation to Don after Carol's death is to present him with a copy of *Zen: The Answer?* (245). But the novel's sanguine imagery—blood, stigmata, bloodstreams, a blood bank, vampires, brick-red necks—suggests that in spite of his fatuousness Omar has chosen an apt example: "your bullfight in Spain" conjures up not only Hemingway but Picasso, the minotaur, and *Minotaure*, mutual teasing and bloodying, and the certainty of there being no intervention by a society for the prevention of cruelty.

Neglected also by critics is the aftermath of Don's gesture:

> Then the scene dissolved itself in a mist in which my legs could no longer support their weight, and I sank down to the steps. I sat on the worn stones, to rest a moment before going on. Thus Wanderhope was found at that place which for the diabolists of his literary youth, and for those with more modest spiritual histories too, was said to be the only alternative to the muzzle of a pistol: the foot of the Cross. (238)

"The diabolists of his literary youth" may include De Quincey: opium-smoking is mentioned (224–25). Whoever the diabolists are, they are precursors of surrealism, patrons of the surrealist tenor of the cake-throwing episode. For the participation of Jesus in a pastry-throwing contest is a surrealist juxtaposition. Although the Reverend Andrew Mackerel argues that Jesus was a master of repartée (*Mackerel Plaza*, 135) and at least one book has been written on *The Humor of Christ*, as Richard Boston says, "most references to laughter in the Bible are disparaging."[56] Boston raises the question: Did Jesus laugh?

> . . . Chesterton is agreeing that Jesus did not laugh. Like most people other than Sir Thomas Browne he instinctively finds the idea of Jesus

and laughter mutually exclusive. It is because they *are* incompatible that the French painter Clovis Trouille is able to use them for surrealist ends in his painting "Le Grand Poème d'Amiens." Juxtaposition of opposites is a standard surrealist trick—the flat-iron with tin-tacks soldered to its surface; the fur-lined tea-cup and saucer; the confusion of indoors and outdoors, as with the room that contains a large tree and water lapping across the floor, or the street scene with a double-bed in the middle of the road. Trouille's painting shows the interior of Amiens Cathedral, with Jesus standing in one of the aisles. He is wearing a loincloth and a crown of thorns, clearly having just descended from the cross. And he is clutching at his sides and roaring with laughter. One either finds the picture funny or shocking. Either reaction is a recognition of what we instinctively know—that Jesus does not laugh. . . . A biblical laugh is usually one of . . . contempt or indignation, rather than mirth or jocosity.[57]

De Vries's Jesus does not laugh. It is essential to the silent film "ritual" that the target of the hurled pie not laugh; it is for the audience to laugh. De Vries's scene, following on the crowning disaster of the novel, smashes together two antithetical terms, Jesus, the laughter-excluding term, and pie-throwing, the term dictating that the audience laugh. While readers feel scandalized, Don Wanderhope realizes his situation is both in and aloof from his world. No less for him than for the André Breton of the first manifesto, "It is living and ceasing to live that are imaginary solutions. Existence is elsewhere."

Wanderhope becomes a Christian. When we next see him, it is autumn, several months after Carol's death, and he carries a crucifix in his pocket (239). But the final pie has not yet been thrown. The following spring, Don finds a tape recording left for him by Carol, in which she gently tells him she knew she was dying and that he had helped her more than he knew with his credo of Reason, Courage, and Grace, which she had discovered and read (241). She proceeds to read his own words back to him: "I believe that man must learn to live without those consolations called religious." This disembodied, surreal, visitation naturally overthrows Don's faith and reason at once. Reason is mocked, for it is unreasonable that Carol should have chanced on the magazine and been deprived of the very consolation that her father would be driven by her death to seek; and now he himself is deprived of religious consolation by the reflection that Carol was compelled by his statement to face death stoically and had had the courage to do so. Bereft now of family and all faiths, Wanderhope concludes his narrative in a paroxysm of contempt for the world (242–43) succeeded by a praise of compassion: "How long, how long is the mourner's bench upon which we sit, arms linked in undeluded friendship, all of us, brief links, ourselves, in the eternal pity" (246). It is a double ending: funerary sculpture with frosting dripping down it. The novel has shown that "undeluded friendship" is likely to be another illusion and dramatized the contradiction between "eternal pity" and the eternal withholding of pity from the characters. Just a page earlier, the narrator gives us a flintier sentence: "A wood thrush sang in the *merciless* summer boughs" (emphasis added).

Such antinomies as faith and reason, mercilessness and pity, cannot be resolved in the current state of affairs with its unrelenting humiliations, but surrealist techniques help to pose the important questions and riddle received opinions. At the extremes of experience, surrealist techniques are recording devices for surrational occurrences. Surrealism is, in such instances, realism. The surreal, if grasped, is shocking; interpretations of *The Blood of the Lamb* have insulated it. The novel's most scandalous elements, such as the brutal implications of the bullfight, the "diabolists," and the absurd dramatic reversal with the tape recording, have been studiously ignored.

* * *

De Vries's 1965 novel, *Let Me Count the Ways*, shows the number of ways De Vries can exhibit his involvement with surrealism without anyone taking much notice.[58] Tom Waltz, the central character, avers, "I am prey to fantasies" (117), and his narration is an exercise in defamiliarization:

> Yesterday I saw a man in the street trying to put out an umbrella that had caught fire. That part was all right. Nothing unusual about that. But for a moment I thought that these details were being photographically registered on some kind of aspic embedded in two sockets in my head and transformed into comprehension by a scoop of albumin directly behind them, and that was scary. I had had to wait till the sensation passed. (127)

Tom's father, Stan, reveres Ingersoll, Paine, and Darrow (11); Tom's mother Elsie attends the Gospel Mission (5). "O.K. we'll compromise. We'll bring him up an agnostic" (10), proposes Stan. Tom becomes a walking thesis-antithesis who thinks to himself, "At last I was beginning to understand how Hegel felt at the end of his life. 'Only one man understood me,' he said, 'and he didn't understand me'" (270). In a book based in part on the humor of Tom's involuntarily echoing his father's behavior, Stan gets the last word, another paradox: "The universe is like a safe to which there is a combination.

But the combination is locked up in the safe" (307). Both father's and son's accounts of themselves are surreal.

Stan is a quixotic furniture mover, self-taught ignoramus, and fetishist. At one point, he takes an interest in an abstract painter named Ona Mervin, who fatuously poses the moving crew as they trundle her old piano to the dump: "There she got some interesting shots of three mystic figures carrying a piano across a bloated landscape in the fading light of day. The long shadows we cast gave it a haunting surrealist quality she called out as she darted around clicking the shutter" (44). Lautréamont's Mervyn is a caricature bourgeois "son of fair-haired England,"[59] and Ona is a caricature bourgeois artist in the tradition of *The Great Gatsby*'s Mr. McKee.[60] Stan is capable of entering (and, by way of comment on the state of literacy, winning) a poetry contest with Elizabeth Barrett Browning's most famous sonnet (110–12). Embarrassment at the discovery of his theft provokes in Stan a psychosomatic "hangover" of twelve years' duration. He baptizes himself in the kitchen sink (58). He is arrested as a peeping Tom for hiding in the backyard and peeping at his own wife (97). The son of this remarkable father teaches English at a college named Polycarp. He disgraces the English Department by winning a sentimental essay contest (185), thereby hastening the death of his mentor, Norm Littlefield (194, 208), but owing to a lack of talent on the faculty Tom is made acting head of the department (211). When he bumblingly leads Littlefield's funeral cortege on a high-speed chase through town, causing Polycarp's president to have a heart attack, Tom is appointed acting college president (222). Tom doesn't allow his high estate to prevent him from calling on the school guidance counselor, Miss Holroyd, to discuss his "two childhoods." Bored, he decides to subvert her questions:

> Q: Do you shed tears when you listen to music, or read a book or watch a movie?
> A: Hair.
> Q: How would you describe your relations with the opposite sex?
> A: 1066. (231)

This preposterous interview (228–32) conforms to the doctrine set forth in Breton's first manifesto:

> Language has been given to man so that he may make Surrealist use of it. . . . The forms of Surrealist language adapt themselves best to dialogue . . .

Q. "How old are you?" A. "You." . . .
Q. "What is your name?" A. "Forty-five houses." . . .

The words, the images are only so many springboards for the mind of the listener.[61]

Tom cannot even wear a cast on his leg conventionally; his cast is infected with ants, a Daliesque file of which he observes "coursing upward in a thin line from the floor to my bed" (164). When, to save his broken marriage, he visits Lourdes to seek a cure for his neurosis, Tom is cured and converted after being stricken by a "miraculous" illness. His affliction is actually brought on by his having replaced a loose tooth filling with airplane glue, a determination his wife, summoned from America, makes swiftly, thus out-diagnosing the physician, priest, and even veterinarian previously consulted (296–304). *Let Me Count the Ways* gives a ragging to both the establishment and such congenitally irresponsible persons as Tom, and it counts on the reader to take as a springboard the words of a proletarian narrator who relates, "There we were, McGurk, Art Salerno and me, exemplars of some voluntarily assumed despair or whatever, phantoms in a surrealist landscape" (Stan, 46) and a professor-narrator who backs up the assertion "life is in the end a soap opera" with examples from Shakespeare, El Greco, Beethoven, and Joyce (Tom, 260).

* * *

Among the least responsible De Vries antiheroes is Stew Smackenfelt ("*Smaak* means taste, *veld* field" [78]), who "had the hots for my mother-in-law. I wanted to go to bed with her" (101). Stew's mother-in-law, Ginger, is actually Dolly Smackenfelt's aunt and adoptive parent, but the theme of De Vries's 1973 novel *Forever Panting* nonetheless is "incest" (6). Stew and Dolly are divorced and Stew marries Ginger, but he finds that he cannot "deny the unmistakable: he had the hots for his step-daughter," his former wife, Dolly (177); and Stew and Dolly are eventually reunited (271–74). With this slender, scandalous plot, De Vries continues the assault on totem and taboo he had begun in *Mrs. Wallop*. He does so histrionically; Stew is an actor who embodies Sartre's assertion—which De Vries had used as an epigraph in *The Tents of Wickedness*—"We can be nothing without playing at being" (1).

So playful is Stew that "I even have a name for my own id. . . . I call him Blodgett" (3). Blodgett is freely exercised in the novel. The protagonist is not only interested in "Freudianity" (e.g., 3, 267), but his "sanity hung by a single thread: the belief that he was Edwin

Booth" (24); he has the delusion that he is Sir Walter Raleigh (221); and his idea of relieving stress is to polish "a 'suite' of impressions . . . in which he recited 'Ulalume' as each of several stars would do it" (25). There is Thurberesque fun with Freudian jargon (e.g., "pseudo-masochist" [51]), and the narration is crammed with allusions, many to surrealism. The second paragraph of chapter 2 is a microcosm of this rococo style:

> Naturally his being Edwin Booth gave him access to many another identity as well. . . . In the croaking contralto in which he had done Lady Teazle in college years, he would sometimes order groceries over the telephone; as Huncamunca, pleas for fuel oil in the bitter weather. He did a peevishly cerebral, existentially offhand Hamlet very much of our time indeed, articulating the soliloquies with an urbanely implied *Weltschmerz* as he plowed the remote corners of the house in the laudanum hours. If the classical and the naturalistic represent the two basic schools of acting—chewing the scenery as against throwing your lines away—Smackenfelt could—now get this—Stewart Smackenfelt could *throw* chewing the scenery *away*. Wallace Stevens' self-disclaiming rhetoric was another example, Dali's mock floridity still another, of this devilishly suave, insanely difficult art. In real life, being married, he was of course the Socrates each man plays to the Xantippe of his choice, for it is a fact universally acknowledged that a husband is the most ridiculous thing on earth, except for a bachelor. (24–25)

The School for Scandal, Tom Thumb, Hamlet, Stevens, and Dali weave together with 1960s Shakespeare productions, Coleridge's habits, Jane Austen's first lines, and perhaps even Duchamp's *The Bride Stripped Bare by Her Bachelors, Even*. De Vries includes flamboyant self-congratulation at having achieved the "devilishly suave, insanely difficult art" of "throwing away" histrionics: insouciant melodrama, soap opera crossed with *Godot*.

There are references to de Chirico (14), Chagall (41), and Picasso (134), and an elaborate satire on the dilettante surrealism of Zap Spontini, whose mural is mistaken for the work of vandals (254–66) and who ends up trashing his own painting. Casual reference is made to "a touch of surrealism in everyday life" (35) and "surrealist juxtapositions" (137). In one surreal sequence, Stew mistakes a soap capsule for a tranquilizer and hiccups bubbles through an opening-night gala (239–43). References to Dali (25, 110), and De Vries's later use of the phrase "Dali fantasy" (*Madder Music*, 97; *Sauce for the Goose*, 142), highlight Dolly Smackenfelt's name:

> Drowsy fantasies of Dolly, inordinately erotic, shaded swiftly into slumber in which, at some point, he dreamed of her (or some woman) as

turning naked on a spit in a rotisserie window in which Spontini, cast as a hatted chef, basted her with melted butter, drawn from a pan by means of a bulbed siphon, as she had revolved till golden brown, for the delectation of a sidewalk audience. (235)

The pun on Dolly is a Daliesque double image. Another example of De Vries's semiprivate joking is his use of the name Blodgett for Smackenfelt's id. J. J. Lamberts, in a publication of the Christian Reformed Church Board of Publications, notes, "Now if Western Michigan readers seem to detect any symbolism in the choice of this particular name, they are welcome to do so."[62] John Wood Blodgett (1860–1951) was one of the first citizens of Grand Rapids from 1890 to 1951, where he "was considered 'the biggest financial figure'" and was known, like Smackenfelt, for his generosity. A part of the symbolism Lamberts does not emphasize, in his Pauline reading of De Vries, is the business in which Blodgett made his fortune and was so prominent an expert as to have served as president of its National Manufacturers Association and advisor to Herbert Hoover in 1930, when De Vries was at college in Grand Rapids: lumber.[63] Not only is Stew well endowed, but when he picks up a large sliver in his haunch doing floor exercises, "Blodgett" goring his host adds to the traditional wound-in-the-thigh motif (135–39).

With a nod to Henri Bergson, Stew calls exercise "an unnatural act. The body loathes artificially imposed regimentation" (103). Consistent with his aversion to mechanical exercise is his revulsion from the "computerized hell," the "Kafkaesque nightmare" of the corporate world, which he briefly joins and quickly begins to subvert, getting himself dismissed when he tries to fire the "Boss" (170–74). On the other hand, Stew gets into brawls with the spontaneous Spontini. Smackenfelt is ultimately more conundrum than character, a patchwork of imitations and roles who remarks, "I sometimes wonder whether I'm right for the part" (274). That metafictional twist throws identity-crisis, scene-chewing fiction of the 1960s and 1970s away. It is nothing less than a comic rendition of Rimbaud's "Je est un autre," or Roland Barthes's "The linguistic *I* can and must be defined in a strictly a-psychological way . . . the *I* of discourse can no longer be a place where a previously stored-up person is innocently restored."[64] The title *Forever Panting* not only emphasizes the satyr-play element of the scene on Keats's Grecian urn but also recognizes the mutability of seemingly static figures, the shiftiness of supposed innocence.

* * *

In *I Hear America Swinging,* a "quack manqué" marriage counselor abets and complicates the sexual revolution in Middle City, Iowa, where his reward for incompetency is a booming practice. Bill Bumpers's clientele is composed of rustics eager to queue up for misinformation dispensed by a cross between a Thurber psychologist and a Mencken chiropractor.

Bumpers is a contemptible and amusing hedonist. His name suggests he should be large, like a bumper crop, but he is small (129); he should be a shock absorber, but he is the importer of "a kind of shock treatment" to his advisees (e.g., 188) and has "mentally . . . what garage mechanics call in the case of automobiles a fast idle" (122); and he should be a brimming cup—and indeed he *is* full of himself, and often of liquor. Bumpers's doctoral dissertation in sociology on "Causes of Divorce in Southeastern Rural Iowa" is ridiculed by his thesis committee at Demeter University, so he turns it in as an "anti-thesis . . . the first thesis of the Absurd" and has it accepted by the English Department as an antinovel, *The Apple of Discord* (3–15). Thus armed with a Ph.D., he sets up as "Dr. Bumpers," marriage counselor, in Middle City (17). He presently falls victim to the same phenomenon he had described to his committee as "the unexpected that lies in ambush for all intellectual endeavor" (7). He recommends to one client that she have her husband read the Bible; the man decides on the authority of Judges that he wants to take a concubine (50–51), and Bumpers finds himself counseling a ménage à trois. Bill suggests to a hired man that he go into art criticism as a "primitive critic" to exercise his creativity and soon finds himself contending with the "psychic strain" of the man's growing celebrity as the "Grandma Moses of exegesis" (67–75). Bumpers gives a pop psychology book to another client only to have the man's sexual paranoia reverse into satyriasis (175–78). The cures Dr. Bumpers achieves are deliriums. As the primitive critic, deriding a surrealist imitator at a local art gallery, "saw fit to lead the entire troupe in a circle of the showroom singing at the tops of their voices 'Hello Dali, well hello, Dali, it's nice to have you back again,'" Bumpers thinks messianically, "My work here was finished" (203).

The book is filled with surrealist references and allusions, such as Huysmans and Barbey D'Aurevilly (110–11), *Animal Crackers* (87), and "a sometime sanatarium [*sic*] inmate who thinks he is all four Marx Brothers" (189). Cousin Clem, the art critic, becomes a fountain of surreal knowledge: "One show he presently covered exhibited the recent pieces of a surrealist celebrated for his 'eerie nuances,' as the catalogue copy put it. 'Them nuances look like the same old ances we been getting from Dali and Tanguy,' Clem drawled, pitching an apple core into a sandpot as he moseyed on out the door" (69–70). Soon Clem has grown even more sophisticated: he opines, "Them visual verities and that there implicit trust in the hegemony of the random carry suspicious echoes of Max Ernst's early experiments with *frottage*" (91) and makes offhand reference to "the urinal motif, say" (92). His job as a "primitive" now in jeopardy owing to his widening knowledge, Clem starts avoiding another rube "whose conversation . . . ran to reminiscences of artists he had met or befriended in his time, men like Arp and Miro and Giacometti" (94). But Clem cannot resist showing off in describing a new show described in its catalog as "the most iconoclastic anti-art we have seen since the Dadaists. . . . Events such as this should bring that much closer to realization the hope expressed by Marcel Duchamp in a letter to Alfred Steiglitz, that people would come to despise painting" (96). Clem's exegesis is so powerful that his editor tells him, "It's brilliant of course. Superb. You're fired" (96). There is plenty of mockery to go around: spoofing of dada, satire on derivative artists-on-the-make and their credulous audience, and laughter at the trend-conscious editor. The greatest scorn, though, is heaped on the latecoming men of mode. The epitome of this type is Bill's old friend and "bad influence," Artie Pringle, who, harkening back to an earlier fashion, attends seances at one Madame Baklava's: "Last week we tried for hours to communicate with Max Ernst—for my money the best of the whole surrealist lot. But it was a clinker. Nothing. Zero." Bumpers explains: "Max Ernst is still alive" (109).

The latter-day avant-garde receives many jibes in *I Hear America Swinging*, but the novel swings freely left and right. Artie's diction in describing Ernst—"for my money"—is typical of the characters' meretriciousness. Half the women of the countryside have set up in businesses that trade in the greediest way upon their wholesome image. In bonnets and granny glasses, each "did her thing with home-style foodstuffs, cut-throating, price-gouging" (35), and generally being capitalists, from Ma Sigafoos with her Bloody Mary Mix (28) to Ma Tinklehoff and her tartare sauce (34) to Ma Godolphin, a "Ma" monopolist and "tycoon" (35, 155). Philosophy becomes the babel of "Crackerbarrel Philosophers" (78–82). The sharpest jabs are aimed at exploitation, commodification, the confederacy of dunces that avant- and arrière-gardes may join together, and hypocrisy. Just after fantasizing a Caribbean idyll with a new flame, Bumpers imagines he can finance his romance "by the skill with which I could persuade the numberless couples seeking my counsel to relinquish the romantic dreams of their youth" (122–23). He is a marriage counselor who joins in an orgy (113–21).

This fabulist novel is based on an Iowa so enamored of sophistication that its farmers think "Alfalfa's terribly *démodé*" (57); its marketers trade at a feed and grain store named Oat Cuisine (200); and its jaded gossips remark, "There goes that there *ménage à trois*" (61). De Vries began superimposing culture on culture in stories written during the period in which he was praising surrealism.[65] The gaiety of the conceit and the outrageous fun that ensues place De Vries much closer to the avant-garde artists lampooned in *I Hear America Swinging* than to the academics, psychiatrists, and businesspersons lambasted in it. Bumpers is right in pointing out that all intellectual endeavor is susceptible to ambush, and this scandal drives De Vries's works as it does the works of the surrealists.

Perhaps the most surprising aspect of *I Hear America Swinging* is a matter no one has seen fit to write about: the novel's revelry in ordure, or, to use a phrase once applied to Jonathan Swift, its "excremental vision." As *But Who Wakes the Bugler?* out-Dalied Dali in phallic symbolism, *I Hear American Swinging* vies with Dali in scatology. The basis of the joke—and it *is* a joke, not a trope in a moral tirade—is that American mores have become those of the barnyard. Much of the action, which includes three, four, and more persons in the same bed, occurs at a farm the owners—the Browns—call Pretty Pass. At one point they drink to the "new sexual freedom" with the toast "Mud" (58). Hattie Brown's mother criticizes her son-in-law with "he prunes himself on being sophisticated" (52). Clem, who is described by Mrs. Brown as "anal retentive" (to which her husband replies, "Well the horse isn't," in complaint that Clem refuses to clean the barn), also "prunes" himself on his celebrity (75). One of Clem's coinages in art-crit jargon is "defecated inheritances" (96). Bumpers and a hired man get into an altercation about cleaning a henhouse (150–51). The design of Middle City's new Civic Center calls for "ceiling murals and friezes everywhere, even the walls of the washrooms. Parallels with the Roman Empire and all that. Emphasis on bathrooms" (159). Bumpers uses the following unfortunate phrases: "Someone who can get to the persecution streak of yours, give you some insight into it, as we [professionals] say, with the aim of purging your life of it" (169); "People were beginning to *look* like Oliver Hardy, as they kept repeating it was another fine mess I had gotten them into. But at least Sigmund Freud might be credited with some smattering of comprehension about it" (178); "Ma [Godolphin] grew a little more relaxed, and seemed receptive to my assurances that everything would come out all right in the end" (179). A Freudian would have no trouble finding many more such images and expressions. The nadir of this "merde-ism" is reached with the preternaturally silly climax to Bill Bumpers's and Ma Godolphin's affair of "ever more riotous debaucheries" (182): "I stood aghast at her now unmistakable plan. She wanted to be ravished in the mud wallow. . . . Her breathing quickened, and her voice was hoarse as she said: 'Defile me'" (183). This roll in the "quagmire," "muck," "bog," "slew," and "*boue*," described at length, has a happy ending: the husband, discovering the pair of bemired lovers, is elated to see his wife is having an affair and exclaims, "I wasn't imagining things! I'm not crazy, I'm not paranoid, thank God, thank God, I'm not paranoid!" (187). To round out the motif, Bumpers accepts Artie's invitation to attend a black mass:

> I was late for the service, slipping as unobtrusively as possible into the last pew when the mass was well in progress. Pew being the last three rows of chairs lined up at the end of Mrs. Renaldi's very long living room. . . . Two choirboys lighted scarlet candles while another presided over an incense pot in which smoldered leaves of henbane and nightshade mingled with acrid resins and asphalt, odors dear to our master, Satan. Anti-fragrances they might have been called. (191–92)

As part of the excrementory motif, *Bumpers* assumes a new meaning: bum-purse, the receptacle emptying into the narrative. Artie had lectured Bumpers on *The Exorcist*, "The flick is a breakthrough in that it postulates revulsion as a legitimate objective of art. What Andy Warhol did for boredom this does for disgust" (108). While Artie's artsy analysis is pretentious tripe, *I Hear America Swinging* in fact studies the revolting. De Vries, like the "original Dadaist" Joe Sandwich, often "*pretends to do what he's doing*" (*The Vale of Laughter*, 314).

Swift's "excremental vision" was an expression of contempt for the world sustained by transcendent belief. De Vries alludes to Swift by way of the name Godolphin, "an esteemed name. Not without its aristocracy, if memory serves," Bill says (64). De Vries certainly remembers that the Earl of Godolphin was one of the Whigs against whom Swift turned in turning Tory. But De Vries's tale does not encourage or suggest belief in a transcendent reality other than that created by the audacity and imagination of the *I* in *I Hear America Swinging*. As for the corrupting influence of art, Bumpers does not sow more discord than he digs up. He does not deserve the credit he takes for the delirium of Middle City, for decadence (including decadent surrealism) and depravity were in full swing when he arrived. De Vries's surrealist farce poses imagination against imitation.

Of course, the protagonist, a marriage counselor in spite of himself, is a bad priest of the imagination. Like the fenders on a car, Bill Bumpers's end is in his beginning: his "nostalgic farewell," at the end of what he calls "The Palindrome of Billy Bumpers," recalls his "First Love," of which he "can most luminously remember the crystal purity" (204–7). But "the end of innocence" soon arrived, as Bill read his sweetheart Baudelaire. As he muses, with his new bride asleep beside him, he thinks that perhaps, on the return to Iowa from their honeymoon, he might look up his childhood sweetheart (210–11). His incorrigibility makes for a mock-rueful ending, the twin allures of innocence and experience prominently on display. In a novel that so vividly argues that culture is a veneer and counterculture a sham, it is sadly appropriate that the narrator close by describing a situation that is in effect acultural: he watches shadows on the ceiling, like a man chained in Plato's cave, then, bothered by "the sinuous play" of the shadows and disturbed by his thoughts, and apparently oblivious of the wife to whom he is already unfaithful in his mind's eye, he gets up and pulls down the shade, sealing himself into solipsism.

* * *

In *Consenting Adults, or The Duchess Will Be Furious*, we meet a hero with grander illusions. "This was all predicted by Pascal. Pascal said that the loss of God would lead to two things. Megalomania or erotomania, or both," the hero is told (195). Ted Peachum, who has felt the emptiness of the universe as a "cold wind from Aldebaran [sending] a shiver through my blood" (26), has yielded to both: a messiah complex and a libido so excited that he gets involved in a ménage à trois and an affair with triplets at the same time. A nihilist with a messiah complex is not merely a brain-teasing incongruity. Together with Ted's Jarry-like impudence—he thinks of his triplet consorts as "the luscious trinity" (200)—the conceit makes this one of De Vries's most entertaining surrealist farces.

Self-described as "hallucinative" (7), Ted Peachum narrates a story full of personas *manqué:* a "barber *manqué*" (5), "exterminator *manqué*" (18), "haberdasher *manqué*" (57), "bricklayer *manqué*" (71), "novelist *manqué*" (79), "one-legged railroad-crossing tender *manqué*" (117), and some "actresses *manquées*" (202). This motif is social satire manqué, for the pun on *monkey* edges into Marcel Duchamp territory. Ted is an irritable and pugnacious narrator who launches into frequent "outbursts" accusing readers of fetishism, prejudice, ignorance, and bad faith. While drily calling our attention to his own virtues, such as a "gift for metaphor," he condemns his reader as a "secretary-treasurer," a complacent bureaucrat.

One reason for Ted's belligerence is defensiveness. "For as long as

I can remember, my father hibernated," Ted begins (3). It is from the ignominy of seeing his father featured as a curiosity in *Life* that he must raise himself (10–11). Like his namesake in *The Beggar's Opera*, Peachum is moved to "peach on" us, his fellow hypocrites. De Vries's Peachum is also a receiver of stolen goods: his words are rife with plagiarism. But he is ultimately not a malicious, but an absurd, man.

The "Duchess" of the title refers to the duchess in *Alice in Wonderland* (5, 29, 80, 91), who is realized here as a Mrs. d'Amboise, a chiropractor's wife and sculptor of Pocock, Illinois, for whom Ted Peachum poses (12). Mrs. d'Amboise intends to marry her daughter, Columbine, to Ted when they are ready; at the book's start, Ted is just sixteen and Columbine ten (17). Ted, who comes to feel that "the d'Amboises had made a kinko out of me" (141) by encouraging his interest in a ten-year-old, alludes to *Alice* even when he doesn't appear to mean to do so (e.g., "jabberwocky," 27) and is teased that Lewis Carroll "liked little girls. You could write another *Alice in Wonderland*" (151). Reference is also made to *Lolita* (73), and Ted is fearful of becoming a Humbert Humbert (92), certainly a hazard for him. Thus there is both scandal and sacrilege in Ted's frequently invoked notion that he is followed by a clique of "disciples" (e.g., 69). In one representative sequence, Peachum, a mover, carries a plank across town, like Christ his cross, while addressing his "disciples" and banging passersby as in a "silent-film farce" (116). There is also a character called The Prophet who is given to pithy exhortations such as "'So get your ass in gear,' saith the Lord" (47). The profanation continues with Mrs. d'Amboise's insistence that Columbine "was violated by Santa Claus" in a department store (her son corrects her: "No, she was *molested* by Santa Claus," 129) and Ted's confession that he has fallen in love with triplets ("three nymphs out of Mallarmé") on Christmas day. He describes the Peppermint sisters, his new inamoratas, as "the hottest little pieces in Christendom" (202–5).

Peachum's behavior is deplorable and his speech outrageous, but the tone of these passages is not that of savage indignation but raucous merriment. Like the surrealists, De Vries seems instinctively to rake up scandal, to embarrass received opinions by striking juxtapositions. Here, his collage containing elements of the Bible, *Alice in Wonderland*, and *Lolita* imitates the state of a cut-up culture. There are set-pieces on the embarrassment of philosophy. Peachum's megalomania extends to encompass not only "the Galilean" (211) but the peripatetic philosophers as well: he gives a lecture on General Semantics while treading down the street not under the philosopher's archetypal chair but a huge overstuffed armchair, and he concludes with a Camuian defense of the relativistic philosophy of Peter De Vries's old acquaintance of *Poetry* days, S. I. Hayakawa (97–102). Ted's philosophy of American culture is succinct: "If we can think of this great country of ours as polarized between two sets of James brothers . . . Frank and Jesse at one end and Henry and William at the other, why, we begin to get some sense of the enormous spectrum in between" (210; cf. 73, 133). A moral might be drawn from the conjoined absurdities that make up Ted Peachum, but to pin him down would miss the point. Like Dali's symbolic figures, De Vries's characters are springboards, not dead weight.

Peachum's erotomania not only engages him in explicitly described and ridiculous flings ("think of Rube Goldberg constructions *vivants*," 199) but impels him to attempt to violate a police officer in her prowl car (113). Far from holding this infraction against him, Officer Arpeggio assists Peachum in retrieving his hibernating father's comic book collection and reassures Ted that his fetishes are explicable and he is not crazy (148–58). But of course, he is—with what Dali called "the best kind of crazy."[66] Peachum intones that "there is something to be said for insanity, always granting that being a secretary-treasurer is the norm" (215). He has been crazy enough to marry Columbine (he is now twenty-seven; she, twenty-one), partly out of sympathy for her in the anorexia nervosa into which she has sunk. The marriage gives every promise of felicity, and Peachum's farewell to the reader is buoyant and unmarked by the certainty of future infidelity with which many De Vries narrators sign off. Accommodating to the prevailing tastes, he acts in a soap opera and she is a fashion model, but Peachum retains his surrealist imagination.

Consenting Adults is suffused with surrealism. Ted ogles a woman in a supermarket through "boxes of breakfast cereal arranged in a construction with holes in it, like a Henry Moore sculpture" (57). A German acquaintance has "a fondness for George Grosz" (66; "fondness" and Grosz is a surreal disjunction). The narrator lets a dangling verb phrase stand, for the sake of "the surrealist effect I want to convey" (87). As Peachum talks to his duchess, a "girl ran by rolling a hoop with a stick, something I had never seen outside a de Chirico painting" (96; a disciple named Haverstick becomes Ted's "Judas" by marrying the nightstick-carrying Officer Arpeggio [158]). Ted claims he is "not a little marked by the ennui Magritte claimed to have been the motive power behind his paintings" (159). This mood is soon dispelled when Ted runs into "a stocky man in late middle age, well dressed in a dark pinstripe suit and Homburg"—a figure out of Magritte—who turns out to be a producer, Frank Candlestickmaker, who hires Peachum as an actor (160–61). A "Chagall with its villagers afloat in midair" hangs over the bed of Ted's ménage (180, 214). The last chapter begins with a surrealistic bus ride from New York to Chicago on which Peachum creates havoc by his recitation of arcane facts on subjects like the painter Albert Ryder, Auden, Rimbaud, and the various James brothers (208–13). Noticing "a man . . . paging through an art magazine, at the moment open to a reproduction of a painting showing a fried egg floating through a revolving door," Peachum recites, "Surrealism . . . may be the last of the mayonnaise of Romanticism oozing from the disintegrating club sandwich of the Western psyche" (211). Turning his attention to a woman who happens to be reading a copy of *Exile's Return*, in which Malcolm Cowley relates his adventures among the surrealists,[67] Peachum offers "Malcolm Cowley is the Pope for those of us who are catholic in our tastes" (211). Asked to desist by an "oaf," Ted is himself a buffoon, whose free associations are as intriguing and as rich as the surrealism he calls "mayonnaise." And Ted's hibernating father, friend Ambrose with his homeopathic cure for existential anxiety, wife who vibrates like a tuning fork and has Daliesque doorbell breasts, and Ted's own phantasmagoric perceptions, antics, and priapic tall tales, are themselves surreal.

In the end, Ted Peachum seems to have but one regret:

> Still, I often wish I'd made the race. That was the road not taken. Whenever I have premonitions of impending tepidity, fears that I will wind up a secretary-treasurer in a situation fraught with safety, I wonder if staying in politics mightn't have kept me more adventurous, more risk-willing. A race for senator in the cards, perhaps, who knew? A run for the governorship on the Surrealist ticket? (218–19)

It is hard not to read this as a mock-testament of Peter De Vries, who once entertained political ambitions. Peachum, so glib in describing others as *manqués*, appears in any case to be a surrealist governor of Illinois manqué. But De Vries, like the Romantic poets he often alludes to, in turning from politics to art relinquished nothing of his desire to reform the art of thinking.[68] There was no possibility of a reformer being elected in Chicago in the 1930s and little chance of an American *Mad Love* to be published or widely read. De Vries's response to these realities has been a succession of rebellions, the surrealistic realizations of his works.

Consenting Adults ends with a message to loyal readers:

You the unknown reader I salute in farewell. You are silly like me . . .,
praying for the wisdom to survive your follies. . . . *Mon semblable, mon
frère.* . . . [Peachum imagines his own death in the remote future.]
I must die with a paradox on my lips or it will kill me.
"Yes?"
"A self-disparaging egomaniac."
"Ah."
I nod. "Yes. I guess that about wraps it up," I whisper. And so. . . .
. . . . . . *Abstract me, silent ships.* (219–21)

In the story "The Art of Self-Dramatization," De Vries identifies
"Abstract me, silent ships!" as a line

from Baudelaire (in the excellent George Dillon translation)[69] that has
stood me in such good stead in so many crises in my personal relations,
especially with women. The bit of pantomime that regularly accompanies
its utterance [an arm laid across the eyes] is by now a perfectly timed
and polished bit of fakery in which I only *seem* to be blotting from view
a world no sensitive man can endure. In reality, it is a shield from under
which to observe the reactions of the person I am trying to impress.
(*Without a Stitch in Time,* 236)

While Peachum continues to try to impress us, De Vries impresses
on his faithful readers the extent of Peachum's fakery—and accuses
and convicts himself of self-dramatization. But in having Peachum
revert to *Flowers of Evil,* De Vries is a trickster's trickster. "Abstract
me, silent ships" flings a Baudelairian challenge to the reader: De
Vries, who causes a fire to start in a smoke-alarm system (89–90), is
just as averse as Ted Peachum to "a situation fraught with safety."

* * *

Peckham's Marbles sets De Vries's favorite allusions, dunces, and
themes spinning. Earl Peckham is a splendidly failed novelist who
yearns for fame and fortune but clings to the theme of despair and
his elitist style (180). He is the sort of artist Mencken described as
offering "some commodity that only a few rare and dubious Americans want, and then weep[ing] and beat[ing] his breast because he
is not patronized."[70] In action set in Westchester, Connecticut, site
of the Dappled Shade asylum, and New York City, with forays to
Cedar Rapids, Omaha, and Denver, Peckham engages in an affair
with a successful writer of trashy romances named Poppy McCloud.
Because she has always craved the critical respect Peckham earns,
he becomes her writing coach. To the horror of Poppy's publisher,
she soon raises "the specter that haunts all publishers—a volume of
poetry" (171). As her fiction improves enough to be published in *The*

New Yorker, Poppy's book sales plummet; when Peckham publishes *his* next volume, *The Ghastly Dinner Party,* reviewers say that he is writing under Poppy's influence (198). Nobody wins at these games, and Peckham settles down playing Groucho to the dowager he marries for money, Nelly DelBelly (232, 243–53). In De Vries's last novel, as in his first, a phallic antihero (here "Peck-'em") joins with a Junoesque wife in a charade of marriage.

De Vries alludes prominently to Dylan Thomas (83, 129); S. J. Perelman (57, 59); Fitzgerald, Twain, and Eliot (174); Kafka (175); W. C. Fields (85); Max Beerbohm (99); and even, again, *Moby-Dick* (176). Running jokes on Peckham's "Svengali eyes" and dreams of Manderlay underscore Peckham's adolescent yearnings (though he is forty-two [84]). References to Tennessee Williams emphasize the tawdriness and cynicism of Peckham and his friends; Big Daddy's preserve even sends a representative to *Peckham's Marbles,* Father Tooker, an unctuous and mercenary Episcopal priest (56–59, 224–29). His ideal parishioner is Mrs. DelBelly, a high-toned and not so old Christian woman who objects to Peckham's putting up a working-class Catholic-Italian couple for country club membership with "Christians, are you mad? What's that got to do with it?" "Everything," replies Peckham: "Our Lord enjoins us to charity, love for all our fellow creatures. Doesn't he?" "But he didn't belong to a country club" (243). Peckham, an "atheist leaning toward agnosticism" (111), is perfectly insincere in his speech for Christian charity; he is being blackmailed by Mrs. Spinelli, who saw Peckham make advances to his wife's niece (236). Hypocrisy is De Vries's main target, but plain ignorance will do: an editor rejects Peckham's parody of "To His Coy Mistress" with the note, "A parody of Andrew Marvell will be well over the heads of most magazine readers anywhere, wouldn't you say. How many would have ever heard of Andrew Marvell, let alone know that he is one of our most important American poets" (161).

Among the favorite themes treated in *Peckham's Marbles* is the perverse desire for style at the expense of substance. When Peckham insists on a "bloodbath" of black comedy, rather than a "sitcom" reconciliation with Poppy, he destroys their relationship (191–94). By goading Poppy into insulting him, Peckham believes he can "pick up all the marbles." His mistake is Tom Sawyer's, that of doing things "by the book." Nelly is right to say that he "ought to have his marbles examined" (74), and Earl eventually notices some "marbles missing" (218). Earl's refuge is the theory of humor. The atheist Peckham and hypocrite Tooker discuss whether God has a sense of humor, and

Peckham espouses Aristotle's theory: "we laugh at that which if there were more of it, would cause us pain" (59).

Certainly *Peckham's Marbles* makes readers laugh at what otherwise would be painful. Its mocking applies to itself: "And, of course, tomorrow is another day," the narrator pronounces in family-epic style, winding up for the big finish (250). Peckham's life is "best described by the word he most hated in the English language—*bittersweet*" (253). But the ending is not pure fleering. Peckham "is like all of us, organically programmed to be both predator and prey, an arrangement we are powerless not to visit on our fellows" (253). The scandal of the notion of a deity that created beasts and then created other beasts to feed on them recurs often in De Vries. The narrator here, who sounds like the narrator of *But Who Wakes the Bugler?* in his knowledge of the intimacy of the avant-garde with the ordinary, savors scandal.

When Peckham first sizes up Nelly DelBelly, "Discreet inquiries revealed they were of divergent faiths. She was an Episcopalian, Peckham a Dadaist. But who could say that in this era of ecumenism the two denominations might not soon one day merge?" (13). Indeed, when we first see Peckham and his Nelly married, they are in Father Tooker's church on Epiphany Sunday: "as a Latter Day Dadaist," Peckham thinks, "what difference did it make where you were?" (233). The merger of ersatz Latter Day Dada with Episcopalianism is a phenomenon not far different from the "Christorama" in *Mrs. Wallop* (155, 257) or the Christian Atheism of *Slouching Towards Kalamazoo:* binary opposites tend to merge, as De Vries has often written. Comedy and tragedy, mirth and grief, love and loathing, reverence and profanity, are often indistinguishable. These perceptions are not new, but they receive special emphasis in *Peckham's Marbles:*

> [Peckham's] improvisations had become increasingly more labyrinthine, not uniformly enthralling to his hearers except for intellectual soulmates capable of appreciating contents idiotic by design and thus intended in a surrealist-dadaist vein to travesty folk pith, especially of the imported kind. Television was forging a nation of clods turning, when they read at all, to increasingly imbecile bestseller lists. (89)

Like Peckham, De Vries has worked a surrealist-dadaist vein. It is hazardous to ascribe any character's views to De Vries, yet when Peckham surmises that "we are all surrealists at bottom" (125), there seems no reason to argue. If *we* refers to De Vries's characters, Peckham is certainly right. De Vries has played Prospero to hundreds of Calibans and Ariels.

As in *Consenting Adults* a dangling modifier created a surrealist image, in *Peckham's Marbles* the language unhinges:

"Why are you always having brief whispered discussions behind closed doors which are broken off when I open them?" The syntax provided Peckham a surrealist image of portals unhinged as [Nelly] regally bore down on them, but little relief from the crisis apparently enveloping them anew. (244)

The surreal is latent everywhere, but the power of the surrealist image is squandered under current conditions. Peckham, like his ancestor Mr. Thwing, is powerless to rescue himself from an effete existence. The narrator leaves us in the tone of Fitzgerald: "For we are all swimmers ephemerally buoyed by what will engulf us at the last; still dreaming of islands though the mainland has been lost; swept remorselessly out to sea while we spread our arms to the beautiful shore" (253). Anyone who wishes may blame Peckham's failure, his drifting, on his dadaism. To do so is to read De Vries as "art." But De Vries plainly practices antiart. His surrealist farce twists the tails of all parties campaigning for literary election. The problem with Earl Peckham is not that he compromised his bourgeois standards but that he compromised his dadaism into Latter Day Dadaism and never gave a thought to running on the surrealist ticket.

6

In "The Extravagant Vein
in American Humor"

Harlow Twitchell has announced his candidacy for President on the
Surrealist ticket. "My campaign will be different," he declared. . . .
"Instead of going around the country eating barbecued ribs and
wearing ten-gallon hats, I shall eat ten-gallon hats and wear barbecued ribs." —*Madder Music*, 94

THE phrase "running on the Surrealist ticket," which appears in
Madder Music and *Consenting Adults*, is a surrealist juxtaposition. The
"Surrealist ticket," like Marcel Duchamp's homemade stock certifi-
cates, counterposes an antiaesthetic against a totemic form, conjuring
up the candidates and ballots of an electoral *corps exquise*. Surrealism
cannot take credit for all comic incongruities. Juxtaposition is necessary but not sufficient to identify a body of work as surrealist.[1] The
"Surrealist ticket" belongs to the broader class of comic incongruities
and could surely be discussed as such—but how?

> Anyone who enters a university library looking for simple answers to
> basic questions about comedy and laughter finds a labyrinth of contradic-
> tory explanations and a morass of terminology from which there is no
> escape. Like the reader of *Tom Jones* or *The Ordeal of Richard Feverel*, he
> wanders through an almost perfect symmetry of binary oppositions, of
> mirrored and inverted arguments, and of flawed and unreliable guides.
> Virtually everything that could be said about the subject has been said—
> every position, its counterposition, and their synthesis.[2]

Among the paradigms of comic theory, the one most revealing about
De Vries is the one closest to surrealism. In *The Act of Creation*, Arthur
Koestler argues that "all patterns of creative activity are tri-valent:
they can enter the service of humour, discovery, or art."[3] The basic
pattern of creativity Koestler describes is that of "the clash of . . .

166

two mutually incompatible codes, or associative contexts. . . . *[T]he perceiving of a situation or idea . . . in two self-consistent but habitually incompatible frames of reference,*" a mode of perception Koestler calls "bisociation." Koestler believes that "the capacity to regress, more or less at will, to the games of the underground [i.e., the unconscious], without losing contact with the surface, seems to be the essence of the poetic, and of any other form of creativity."[4] For Koestler *all* comedy—all acts of creation—spring from juxtaposition achieved by descent into the unconscious. In *Mathematics and Humor,* John Allen Paulos assents to Koestler's "incongruity theory," embellishing it with his own "catastrophic theory model of jokes and humor" and "metalevels" and "meta-meta-levels" in the equations of humor.[5] Perhaps the tersest statement of the case is Kenneth Burke's phrase "perspective by incongruity," the "crucial strategy" in comedy, which Burke applies in his criticism and explicates in his subjects.[6] The perspective of "bisociation," "catastrophe," and "incongruity" is compatible with Freud's analysis of wit and humor. Joke-work—condensation, multiple use of the same material, double meaning, displacement, unification, representation by the opposite, and so on—is bisociative.[7] So is humor, which Freud sees as the simultaneous perception of the child and the adult, the ego and the superego, in the self.[8]

"Running on the Surrealist ticket," then, works for Peter De Vries on several levels. In *Angels Can't Do Better,* he makes Peter Topp a caricature of a Surrealist candidate. The thirty-four-year-old author looks back at the twenty-four-year-old reformer and comforts them both with humor for the disappointment of political hopes. In *Madder Music,* the "Surrealist ticket" is a gag for the stand-up comic Pomfret to extemporize; in doing so, he makes what Freud calls a joke by analogy, a species of "indirect representation," relying on a "strange juxtaposition or the attribution of an absurd epithet."[9] That is wit without humor. When Ted Peachum in *Consenting Adults* repines that he never ran on the Surrealist ticket, both wit and humor are at work. On the joke level, Peachum simply reiterates Pomfret's analogy, but on the humor level Peachum is reassuring himself that he has been wise to pursue the course he has chosen; a Surrealist will not defeat a Democrat or a Republican. And on the meta-level, "Surrealist ticket" objectifies and blackens the humor by evoking the gulf between inspiration and politics.

A representative De Vries juxtaposition—even one in which the word *surrealism* appears—can be examined profitably without recourse to surrealism. The radical doubleness of his works—often termed "tragicomedy," "seriocomedy," or "tragifarce"—is harder to deal with, however. It is important to involve surrealism in discussions of De Vries to avoid a critical impasse, to do justice to De Vries's complexity, and to recognize surrealism as having helped to form a major American humorist. It is also important—perhaps, that is to say, amusing—to add De Vries's evidence to Koestler's and the surrealists', to show that surrealist perception is contiguous, to their mutual hazard and potential gain, with mundane perception. "Criticism on Surrealism seems to me to be in its early stages," the French critic Jacqueline Chénieux Gendron recently wrote, and De Vries's works have implications for that criticism.[10]

In *Forever Panting*, Stew Smackenfelt wrestles with Zap Spontini in a "dogfight" (263–64). Many of De Vries's other characters have taken on surrealism as a sparring partner. Occasionally surrealism is the punching bag, but more often it rebuts the attack and shows up its opponent. De Vries's calling of the action has sharpened round by round, in all the surrealist categories H. R. Hays laid out in *Poetry* in 1939: association, amazement, "nightmare" cinematic effects, relaxed playfulness, blending of juxtaposed images, and incongruity of style.[11] The effect is surrealistic, as if we saw the Wallace Beery of *The Champ* climb into the ring and go toe-to-toe with Arthur Cravan.

Queensbury rules do not apply; Oscar Wilde frequently visits De Vries's pages. But didn't the surrealists despise aesthetes? Isn't Wilde's presence a blow against seeing De Vries in surrealist terms? This objection falls to Edouard Roditi's "Oscar Wilde's Poetry as Art History," which De Vries published in *Poetry* in March 1946. With reference to Rimbaud, Huysmans, Whitman, Baudelaire, Mallarmé, Eliot, and even the "mad King Ludwig," Roditi relates Wilde to the avant-garde.[12] But surely De Vries's connection with Eliot, "who is quoted or alluded to in every novel,"[13] should ultimately repel any effort to associate De Vries with surrealism? Wasn't Eliot a classicist?[14] In actuality, De Vries's affinity for Eliot strengthens his connection to surrealism. As William Skaff has shown, "Eliot's mind encompasses just about every important avant-garde intellectual movement of his time." Skaff argues that "Eliot's criterion for art resembles that of those other explorers of the unconscious, the Surrealists. . . . Eliot's poetic is not specifically Surrealist, but it is *generically* surrealist, beyond the point of merely sharing certain resemblances."[15] De Vries's references point to the early Eliot, rather than to the author of *Christianity and Culture*.[16] And "Eliot of the baleful influence" (Kenneth Koch's epithet) shared with De Vries a great admiration for the archsurrealist of the cinema, Groucho Marx. Eliot's, like De Vries's, allusions often intersect "the orbits in which Surrealist taste travels."[17]

It is peculiar that De Vries's references to surrealism have gone unremarked and his resorts to surrealist techniques unexplored. This lack of interest needs explanation. After all, a high proportion of De Vries readers are probably *New Yorker* readers, and the *New Yorker* tradition has not lacked surrealist elements. As Jesse Bier points out in *The Rise and Fall of American Humor*, "the conjunctions of realism and surrealism" in American humor between the world wars, some of the best of which ran in *The New Yorker*, "are not to be dismissed as curiosities." The tradition was carried on by S. J. Perelman after World War II in work Bier relates to "the comic fantasies of Groucho Marx, whom Perelman knows, and to the grimmer surrealism of his brother-in-law, Nathanael West."[18] Blair and Hill, in the section of *American Humor* devoted to *The New Yorker*, point out that "the most obvious element that Lardner passed along to the writers for *The New Yorker* was his reliance on and popularization of abnormal states of behavior."[19] A formidable trio—Benchley (*"Sheer madness is, of course, the highest possible brow in humor"*), Perelman (he "exploited the antics of a persona gone mad in a world that also had gone mad"), and Thurber ("I would be the last person to say that madness is not a solution")—engaged in "surreal fantasy" that prefigures Heller, Barth, Vonnegut, Pynchon, and Hawkes.[20] But surrealism is seldom more than mentioned in discussions of those writers, either.

We are led to the conclusion J. H. Matthews reached regarding painters with surrealist connections:

> Critics incline to share a tendency to minimize their favorite painters' debt to surrealism. . . . We have the distinct impression that art critics who speak with respect of Max Ernst, André Masson, and Joan Miro, for instance, aim to detach these artists from the surrealist movement, as though affirmation of artistic merit as well as of respectability must presuppose severance of all ties with the surrealists . . . as if [surrealism] were a stigma to be erased by convenient forgetfulness.[21]

Matthews reports that "quite a few surrealists have not stopped short of pronouncing evidence of this kind proof of a 'conspiracy of silence' . . . surrounding surrealism and isolating it." If Matthews is right that most critics lack the methodology to discuss surrealism, then Koestler, Burke, and Matthews himself can help. To the degree that the problem is "the willingness—not to say the eagerness—of former surrealists to forget their origins,"[22] artists can break the silence. De Vries's works have hardly been silent about surrealism, and he has declared in a letter to me, "I'm frequently aware of surrealist elements and strokes in my work, but your treatise clearly makes a case for its embodiment in that school."[23] Ignoring his surrealist elements has hurt interpretation and, worse, diminished enjoyment of his work. Surrealism delights in disorder. It is not a happiness pill or form of escapism; many of its works are grim. But surrealism confronts the scandals of existence to overcome them. It takes up the absurd as a cudgel against the Absurd, the banal as a shield against Banality, Black Humor as a way of curing black humors. Peter De Vries has joined the fray with the same arms and in the same spirit.

Surrealism was a healthy influence on De Vries. It is beginning to receive its due, one hopes without being consecrated or exploited into uselessness, in cultural studies and in the press. André Breton's opinions are even appearing in reference books.[24] Freud, who had a disagreeable interview with Breton in 1921 and exchanged pointed letters with him in late 1932, was unimpressed with the magus of surrealism.[25] But in 1938 Stefan Zweig brought Salvador Dali to meet Freud, and "the famous painter made a sketch of him on the spot, maintaining that surrealistically Freud's cranium was reminiscent of a snail!" The next day, Freud wrote Zweig

> I really owe you thanks for bringing yesterday's visitor. For until now I have been inclined to regard the surrealists, who apparently have adopted me as their patron saint, as complete fools (let us say 95%, as with alcohol). That young Spaniard, with his candid fanatical eyes and his undeniable technical mastery, has changed my estimate. It would indeed be very interesting to investigate analytically how he came to create that picture.[26]

If even Freud's mind could be changed by élan and "technical mastery," many might be swayed by the writer who announced to Harold Ross, "I can imitate a wounded gorilla," and whose technical mastery, already evident in 1940, has governed twenty-six books.

The recuperation of surrealism's influence, and the reading of surrealism in De Vries's works, must contend with three obstructions to clarity. The first is the fuzziness that sets in when the world comes to resemble surrealist parodies of it:

> One of the constituents of Post-Modern culture is the license to talk about anything in the context of anything else, for where international banking has become more surrealist than Surrealist art, older categories of relevance cease to apply.[27]

Jessie Bier once remarked, "It would not be possible for Chaplin or Groucho Marx or W. C. Fields to match the extravagance of the President of Guinea";[28] and what can a surrealist do with a vice president who says "What a waste it is to lose one's mind—or not to have a mind. How true that is"?[29] Yet, as H. R. Hays predicted in 1939, no writer who had "submitted to [surrealism's] influence" would "be dismayed as the world becomes increasingly surrealist."[30] What is dismaying is the removal of surrealistic works from their historical context and the denial of their surrealism.

The second obstruction to clarity is confusion between surrealism and the contents of the cloud of dust it raised. In 1945, Breton deplored "everything that, with the aid of fashion and confusion, tends today to simulate Surrealism by confining itself to counterfeiting its procedures from the outside."[31] In other words, "imitators beware." De Vries is a surrealist "outsider" but no imitator. He protects the genuine from the counterfeit by mocking via his "bohemian bourgeoisie" the imitations Charles Newman described in *The Post-Modern Aura:*

> [T]he modernism which began as the destruction of the Bourgeois worldview becomes the Bourgeois idiom *par excellence,* a kind of mass produced and ready made surrealism—familiar images in unfamiliar contexts—images which are not juxtaposed as much as they are simply disconnected from their source: the Avant-Garde as a spectator sport, the Picasso in the corporate courtyard, Modernism as the new Bourgeois Realism.[32]

"Ready-made surrealism" is a tawdry parody of surrealist art but has been taken for and even enshrined as the real thing. De Vries saw what was happening at least as early as 1940, when he wrote about it in *But Who Wakes the Bugler?,* and since then two generations of commentators have enjoyed the opportunity to harangue or congratulate each other about the co-optation of the vanguard. But De Vries's chidings of surrealists' shortcomings and punishing satires on imitators must not be mistaken for assaults on the original spirit of surrealism.[33]

The third obstruction to clarity is the most problematic: the persistent difficulty of defining *surrealist.* J. H. Matthews regrets that casual application has reduced the term "to the point at which it loses any meaning and becomes . . . synonymous with 'strange,' 'weird,' or even 'fanciful.'"[34] That is the way *surrealist* has usually been applied to De Vries. Even Matthews admits, "The surrealist content of a given work, pictorial or written, is best discovered by the viewer or reader of that work, and, for identification, will require on his part a certain predisposition that the creative artist is under no obligation to share."[35] Requiring a "predisposition" to recognize *surrealist* content would seem to make definition hopeless, unless we reflect on the success of a predisposition to perceive exaltations of martial butchery as *classic.*

Scholars of surrealism continue to confront the problem of definition. In *Surrealism and the Novel*, Matthews, seeking to go beyond Breton's antirealism, notes

> Nostalgia for an unattainable ideal pervades [Alain] Jouffroy's novel [*Une rêve plus long que la nuit*], as it does *The Confessions of an English Opium Eater*. Jouffroy shares with Nerval and De Quincey an anguished sense of estrangement which comes from the need to reconcile dreamed desire and lived experience.

The frame of reference Matthews describes is congruent with that in De Vries's novels. Matthews says that Jouffroy's novel "militates against the argument that surrealism and realism must be forever incompatible," and there is warrant for extending credit to De Vries for effecting a similar "tribute to the spirit of surrealism." Finally Matthews decides that "it is futile to search for a fully representative surrealist novel. It is no easier to define what a characteristic surrealist novel ought to be."[36] But the family resemblance his study describes is coherent, and it extends at least to *But Who Wakes the Bugler?*, *The Handsome Heart*, *Madder Music*, and *Consenting Adults*.

In *The Imagery of Surrealism*, Matthews says we will "know whether a work merits classification as surrealist" by

> the profound community of aim shared by all: "to reach the land of desire that everything, in our time, conspires to conceal." . . . [W]e can see that, as *La Clé des champs* emphasizes, a surrealist work qualifies, really, by the "spirit in which it has been conceived."[37]

The surreal work is true, not to a medium, form, or theme, but to the artist's "inner model":

> [S]o many "literary analyses" obstinately [seek] to reduce the "obscurities" of a poem when what matters above all is that, on the affective plane, *contact* be established spontaneously and that the *current* flow, arousing the person receiving it to the point of creating no obstacles for him in those very obscurities.[38]

De Vries has lodged many briefs against interpretation and prefers electrical to hermeneutical linkages: "All connections are fused" (*Comfort Me With Apples*, 4).

Mary Ann Caws discussing in *André Breton* the "elements which are easily discerned in surrealist works" names "mysticism, alchemy, antibourgeois revolution, black humor, eroticism, and reliance on the play of contraries." To these she adds the influences of Freud, Hegel,

Rimbaud, Marx, and Lautréamont and enumerates the antinomies surrealist works seek to overcome while preserving the tensions they create: waking/sleeping, reality/dream, reason/madness, objective/ subjective, perception/representation, past/future, collective sense/ love, life/death. All these criteria describe De Vries's theater of operations as well as Breton's. One of the key points Caws makes is that despite his reputation as the pope of surrealism, Breton was ready to move on if surrealism were eclipsed—was in favor of provocation because he saw the hazard for surrealism of exhaustion of its initial impulse and absorption, parasitism, and systematizing. Thus, for Caws as for Matthews, "The criterion on Surrealist art is not, as is often thought, any particular technique, but rather the spirit in which it was conceived." That spirit of nonacceptance of the commonplace implies a "moral intent to transcend 'ordinary human conditions,'" the theme of each De Vries novel. In fact, De Vries's books are truer to that spirit than works more conspicuously, but derivatively, surrealist. Caws asserts that "Surrealists must somehow manage to retain their "haughty feelings of discontinuity . . . their aloofness from the human situation and from the judgment of others . . ., and yet not lose contact with the non-Surrealist world."[39] De Vries, whose furniture movers give lectures on existentialism and whose college professors sell produce, is a wily manager of the transactions between the surrealist and nonsurrealist worlds: he is, as Matthews said the surrealist novelist should be, an "interrogator of enigmas" seeking to "glimpse the other side of the coin."[40]—or a "connecting thread" between the surreal and the nonsurreal. Bringing about "a kind of poetic explosion of meaning and form," the hallmark of the original surrealist poet,[41] is precisely the effect De Vries achieves. "The key to the mental prison can be found only by breaking with [the conventional] ridiculous means of knowing: it resides in the free and unlimited play of *analogies*," said Breton,[42] and this free play was De Vries's mode long before postmodernists claimed it. Breton asserted in 1945 that "only an absolute purity of means, at the service of unfailing freshness of impression and of a limitless gift for effusion can make possible a leap out of the rut of the known and, with an impeccable arrow of light, point in the present-day direction of liberty."[43] Effusion, even garrulousness, has seldom been wanting in American writers. As to freshness, De Vries never copied surrealist works, but, in creating surrealist farce, gave new twists to what Breton called the "amazingly prehensile tail" of Romanticism.[44]

Chénieux-Gendron wonders if "in the last analysis, perhaps Surrealism is only a role."[45] If so, De Vries's literary gestures sometimes enact that role. It is not a supporting role, but perhaps "the catalyst of a liberated world." Chénieux-Gendron's Foucauldian perspective stresses the surrealist transgression of the social "prohibition of desire; the division between reason and madness; and the will to truth"[46]—these all are transgressions committed in De Vries's works. More than do American writers on surrealism, Chénieux-Gendron emphasizes "the life of the [surrealist] group" as one of the "crucial points of any definition of surrealism."[47] As the works of De Vries show, going back to the surrealist *naif* Mr. Thwing, an American surrealist is in danger of being thrown "back forever upon himself alone" and confined "entirely within the solitude of his own heart."[48]

Charles Newman quotes Constance Rourke—"Though extravagance has been a major element in all American comedy, though extravagance may have its incomparable uses with flights and inclusions denied the more equable view, the extravagant vein in American humor has reached no ultimate expression"—to dramatize his own claim that "It is clear that with the Post-Modern, the 'extravagant vein' *has* certainly reached a kind of 'ultimate expression.' While increasingly puerile in many forms, such humor nevertheless represents an astonishing aesthetic response to modern life."[49] Neither puerile, nor making ultimate claims for itself, nor attracting attention commensurate with its genius, De Vries's astonishing work has been expressing the extravagant vein since 1940.

In 1939 Kenneth Burke wrote, "In so far as art contains a Surrealist ingredient (and all art contains some of this ingredient), psychoanalytic co-ordinates are required to explain the logic of its structure."[50] The measure of truth in Burke's statement is diluted by the factor that as soon as artists know the "psychoanalytic co-ordinates," the "logic" of their work is complicated by their conscious manipulation of them.[51] Their ambiguities and ironies grow "unstable," and they often become shakier still when Freudian critics explain them. Nevertheless, Freudian literary analysis can be helpful with some aspects of De Vries's extravagance. De Vries, knowledgeable in Freud, insists he is a "humorist" rather than a satirist (or, in Freudian terms, a tendentious wit). Freud says about humor that

It refuses to be hurt by the arrows of reality or to be compelled to suffer. It insists that it is impervious to wounds dealt by the outside world, in fact, that these are merely occasions for affording it pleasure. This last trait is a fundamental characteristic of humour. . . . Humour is not resigned; it is rebellious. It signifies the triumph not only of the ego, but also of the pleasure principle, which is strong enough to assert itself here in the face of the adverse real circumstances.[52]

This accords with De Vries's "rebellious" practice in causing Don Wanderhope to fling pastry at a crucifix while remembering the words "suffer the little children." Freud makes observations even more suggestive when applied to De Vries:

> If we turn to consider the situation in which one person adopts a humorous attitude towards others, one view which I have already tentatively suggested in my book on wit will seem very evident. It is this: that the one is adopting towards the other the attitude of an adult towards a child, recognizing and smiling at the triviality of the interests and sufferings which seem to the child so big. Thus the humorist acquires his superiority by assuming the role of the grown-up, identifying himself to some extent with the father, while he reduces the other people to the position of children. This supposition is probably true to fact, but it does not take us very far. We ask ourselves what makes the humorist arrogate to himself this role?
>
> Here we must recall the other, perhaps the original and more important, situation in humour, in which a man adopts a humorous attitude towards himself in order to ward off possible suffering. Is there any sense in saying that someone is treating himself like a child and is at the same time playing the part of the superior adult in relation to this child?
>
> This idea does not seem very plausible, but I think if we consider what we have learnt from pathological observations of the structure of our ego, we shall find a strong confirmation of it.[53]

De Vries's characters share the trait of trying on various roles rather than committing to any one. They never grow up. "I'm my own best butt," De Vries says, aligning on Freud's "co-ordinates" as both father and child. The son of a troubled father, De Vries fills his books with hibernating, permanently hung over, somnambulating fathers and irresponsible, rationalizing, escapist sons who take on troublesome wards, whose doppelgangers write them letters, and who converse with their ids. Of course, we have "enthroned the disreputable character as one of the royal figures of American humor"[54]—the formal cause of De Vries's reliance on the type—but his male characters appear to be overdetermined by his early life experiences. According to Freud, the meaning of humor is "Look here! This is all that this seemingly dangerous world amounts to. Child's play—the very thing to jest about," and the superego of the humorist thus "is in fact repudiating reality and serving an illusion."[55] *The Handsome Heart*'s Dr. Grimberg sounds as if he had taken a lesson from Freud's observations on humor. Certainly his therapy—taking Brian back within the walls of the hospital—makes the man the child of the father, expressing by the opposite De Vries's probable sense of his own family experience: the child was father of the man. Both are redeemed by De Vries's sense of humor, a faculty Freud says has in it "something fine and elevating."[56]

So keen, then, were De Vries's conflicting feelings of hostility toward and affection for his father that he sought and found extravagant and redemptive means to express them. To say so is to pay homage to De Vries's triumph, but it does not advance the understanding of his work. To cope with the literary fathers, De Vries cultivated his great ability for parody, refining the skill for which he is perhaps best known. Jesse Bier quotes from De Vries's famous Faulkner parody "Requiem for a Noun" as an example of "marvelously expressive and refined" literary parody.[57] But De Vries takes parody much further than author-by-author take-offs, into the realm of what Linda Hutcheon calls an "integrated structural modeling process of revising, replaying, inverting, and 'trans-contextualizing' previous works of art" characteristic of twentieth-century parody.[58] Hutcheon has developed her theory of parody with extensive references to modernist and postmodernist works, including surrealist works, and her formulations can be applied with great explanatory power to De Vries's work and its reception.

Hutcheon says that parody "can, indeed, function as a conservative force in both retaining and mocking other aesthetic forms; but it is also capable of transformative power in creating new syntheses, as the Russian formalists argued."[59] This is an apt statement of De Vries's case and shows why the same De Vries excerpt could appear in both a *Reader's Digest* condensed book and a volume compiled as a deliberate assault on bourgeois taste: different readers responded to the different forks of the parody. As Hutcheon puts it, "parody, while often subversive, can also be conservative; in fact, parody is by nature, paradoxically, an authorized transgression."[60] "Authorized transgression" describes De Vries's need to reckon with his ambivalence toward his father, overcome religious scruples about writing, and develop a form that would enable him to contend with his literary mentors. For, as Hutcheon points out, "The parodied text today is often not at all under attack."[61] When De Vries has Tom Waltz extemporize "Shakespearian claptrap" in *Let Me Count the Ways*, he praises Shakespeare while the English professor buries him; for parody, as Hutcheon says, has "the potential power both to bury the dead, so to speak, and also to give it new life."[62] The family trees can grow apace:

> On the level of structure, for example, Brecht's *Threepenny Opera* is a parodic reworking and updating of *The Beggar's Opera* (itself a parody of Handel). But would Gay's work necessarily be known to the German

audience that Brecht wanted to reach with his political message? Would they, in other words, see it as a doubled operatic parody (as well as a bourgeois satire), even if Brecht . . . and his modern critics did?[63]

Similarly convoluted rhetorical questions arise about De Vries, who names the protagonist of *Consenting Adults* Ted Peachum.

In a favorable review of Hutcheon's book, Matei Calinescu uses Wayne Booth's terms to point out that "parody, in [Hutcheon's] sense, is an artist's criticism: a direct and immediate way of studying another artist's work, of both 'understanding' and ironically 'overstanding' it."[64] This observation helps place De Vries's work securely in the self-reflexive and intertextual realm, where it situated itself before that realm was "discovered" and claimed, like the Mississippi, by the French. Booth's terms also parallel Freud's analysis of the humorist as simultaneously adult and child, "overstander" and "understander," and, for that matter, Koestler's and Paulos's "meta-level" and "object level." In sum, what many critics have insisted on seeing as De Vries's divinely comic perspective can be described in the sufficiently powerful and dignified terms of a decorous humanism—or in purely technical aesthetic terms. On the other hand, anyone is free to demur at Booth's plea that we attempt to understand what we essay to overstand.[65] But anyone who has avoided thinking about the surrealist content and technique—the extravagant—in De Vries's books is certainly overstanding, without understanding, his work. As the beguiling works of De Vries come to be better understood, none of their tension as springboards should be lost. On the contrary, they should become springier. As Anthony Burgess said, "As somebody once said about something else, the whole of life is here."[66]

The encounter of De Vries texts and deconstruction, a long-overdue match, remains a lively possibility. If Calinescu is right in characterizing parody as a form of literary criticism, then De Vries himself practiced critical deconstruction for fifty years, and his work poses an interesting problem for a deconstructionist. The confrontation of their texts may unravel the bindings of their covers. De Vries found a way to "overthrow . . . the traditional sign system" without producing total "non-sense,"[67] as he bridged the gap between the surreal and the ordinary and thereby reproblematized the "revolution of the word." There is a growing literature on the pun, De Vries's most plentiful store of verbal ammunition. It is a large and largely unexplored topic in De Vries and warrants study. Walter Redfern's *Puns*, which quotes several of De Vries's, has prepared the way.[68] On a level having less bisociative energy, perhaps, is De Vries's enthusiasm for dropping adscititious words into his characters' mouths. The study of De Vries's jawbreakers is best begun via *The Oxter English Dictionary,* in which nineteen entries cite De Vries—based on only three of his novels.[69] The shimmery effects of De Vries's prose and its free play with meaning draw readers into a state of what has been called polysemania: "an abnormal awareness of possible ambiguity; an uncontrollable tendency to bring to mind the inappropriate or unintended sense of a word in any context."[70] John Ellison Kahn's article on this phenomenon in *Verbatim,* though it does not mention De Vries, wonderfully concentrates the mind on multiple meanings and is a good preparation, like sandpaper on the fingertips of a safecracker, for reading De Vries.

There is a direct linkage between De Vries's polyvalent language and the theme of social class relationships and taste cultures. De Vries often mixes dialects and takes bisociative leaps among categories, such as having characters call Baudelaire a brand of refrigerator (*Comfort Me With Apples,* 17), order lobster thermopane (*Reuben, Reuben,* 45), and observe "sexual morays" (*Let Me Count the Ways,* 14). These speakers all have got stuck somewhere on the "ladder of sensibility" up which Don Wanderhope (*The Blood of the Lamb,* 59) and many others are climbing, sometimes to the point of altitude sickness. It is a theme De Vries approached early (e.g., "Different Cultural Levels Eat Here"[71]) and that must have fascinated him ever since he attended the Dutch school, lived in the Chicago Irish neighborhood, and read the diabolists and the bohemians.

Bohemians and other artists and would-be artists receive, like everyone else, mixed reviews in De Vries's surreal criticism of life. De Vries's treatment of art and its status in society is noteworthy not only for its range of reference and its impolite commentary on the influence of money over artistic production but also for its sustained meditation on the diachronic dimension of artistic production and reception—a meditation through wit and humor in advance of the cultural studies movement. De Vries shows the dissemination, and debasement, of elite culture and avant-garde culture, as we have seen. But he is concerned also to show the peculiar shifts in perception and taste that occur over time, with comical results for the myth of artistic priority. A case in point is the composer in *Comfort Me With Apples* who "claimed to have first heard and been unable to stand Bartok, then liked him, and finally outgrown him, all in the course of a single composition" (80). Another, in the same novel, is Chick Swallow's assessment of his wife, Crystal: "Another gauge of her progress into a more companionable modernity lies in her use, now, of the word 'wonderful,' for something quaint appreciated on another level" (275; cf. 16, 278–80). In *Into Your Tent I'll Creep,* a campy, "wonderful" restaurant is the scene of "inverted snobbishness"; Al Banghart is reassured by his wife that he needn't feel ashamed of visiting with new, more genteel companions the place where he used to hang out: *"You went there on another level"* (138). In *The Prick of Noon,* Eddie Teeters's tacky attempts to imitate the middle class win him respect as a parodist of "bourgeois vulgarity," encouraging him to believe "I was at bottom a smart cookie capable of doing things on two levels" (168). The shiftiness of cultural levels, and their crossing each other like a pianist's hands crossing above the keyboard, play with the theme that our culture has entered a fugue state.

Religion and philosophy is a rubric under which a great deal of De Vries criticism has been written. De Vries's characters run the gamut from fundamentalist to nihilist, and readers have tended to identify with the characters and to emphasize the ideas closest to their own beliefs. De Vries's portraits of piety appear to sustain Freud's remark at the close of *Civilization and Its Discontents:* "One thing only do I know for certain and that is that man's judgments of value follow directly his wishes for happiness—that, accordingly, they are an attempt to support his illusions with arguments."[72] The pious in De Vries are rationalizers and illusion mongers no less than his scoffers and rebels. In 1978, De Vries said that his favorite of the lines he had written was "in *Let Me Count the Ways* where the husband [Stan Waltz, a quoter of Ingersoll] explains, *And then, as luck would have it, I belted her one."*[73] Getting oneself off the moral hook is a talent all of De Vries's characters share; in De Vries's books, a moral sense is as independent of belief in the supernatural as it is in the documents of official surrealism.

There is one eschatology De Vries studied closely: the final days of literacy. De Vries's valedictory to literacy is not the Beckettian "End Game Strategy" Newman discusses in *The Post-Modern Aura,* which cancels previous literature.[74] On the contrary, as Anthony Burgess pointed out in 1981, De Vries "is one of the few novelists we have left who are joyfully aware of the books others have written."[75] De Vries also was bemusedly aware that many Americans know about only one pair of James brothers, and their number appears to be growing. But the 1980s fad for "cultural literacy" probably fractured De Vries, who had been cataloging Dantesque levels of cultural ignorance since the 1930s. In a National Public Radio interview after Allan Bloom's *Closing of the American Mind* came out, Mortimer Adler sputtered indignantly that he had said "everything Bloom has to say in this silly book" in a *Harper's* article thirty years before. De Vries may have had similar sensations about Bloom's book and E. D.

Hirsch's *Cultural Literacy.*[76] De Vries's books assume a constant preva-
lence of dunces. The threat of an imminent dark age is a traditional
comic and satiric ploy, but De Vries noted trends as alertly as the
watchdogs. In 1929, just at the beginning of De Vries's career, I. A.
Richards's *Practical Criticism* revealed the abysmal performance even
of English public school students in construing classics of English
literature.[77] It is easy to follow through recent decades the literature
deploring the postliterate sump into which we are sinking. But
Mencken had already described *boobus Americanus,* and his Latin no-
menclature recalls jokes running from Juvenal to Pope to Byron. We
are always sinking. Nevertheless, the present moment does seem to
us more inimical to literature than previous eras, and De Vries sometimes adopts the bleaker view. In *The Portable Curmudgeon,* Jon Winokur includes him in an honor roll of "World Class Curmudgeons" and
quotes him to the effect that "my father hated radio and couldn't
wait for television to be invented so he could hate that too."[78] In
"Exploring Inner Space," De Vries laments that literacy "is going to
hell in a handbasket" and inveighs against "the boob-tube."[79] In
the novels, De Vries has things both ways: a reassuring presence of
painstakingly integrated allusions whose presence implies an ongoing
tradition and plenty of rueful jokes about encroaching postliteracy.
The effect can be funny and eerie, as when an editor in *Peckham's
Marbles* calls Andrew Marvell an American poet. What if the *Dunciad*
is coming true? "My secret ambition is to sell a million copies of
every book . . . and then also have a small, select cult of aficionados
who look down on my mass audience."[80] It is not inconsistent with
dada to confide such a "secret ambition" to *People* magazine, and it
is entirely consistent with surrealism to reveal the scandal of the
"absence" of literacy in its presence.

Humor and comic faith serve De Vries not only as aesthetic impulses but also as cognitive strategies and moral guides. Reading the
books of Peter De Vries is an exercise in the "'comic' theory of
education" that Kenneth Burke, in his "Definition of Man," says
would ask us to center our attention on the understanding of our
"natural temptations." Burke places a high value on comic education.[81] As Robert McMahon points out in "Kenneth Burke's Divine
Comedy," "for over four decades Kenneth Burke has been teaching
us that every literary form implies a philosophy and that every work
of philosophy has a meaningful literary form." In his treatment of
St. Augustine, Burke "comically criticizes the dogmatic willingness
to anathematize an opposition as heretical." As McMahon points out
in discussing Burke's 1961 *Rhetoric of Religion,*

Cold-war rhetoric simplified the world into two opposing ideologies. . . . Burke, in contrast, urges on us principles of comic criticism that envision the opposition in ourselves. . . . Burke refuses the comfortable simplifications of either-or for the ironic complexities of both-and. Such comic criticism of the Them in Us refigures Us as well as Them. Being comic, it proves undogmatic. It prefers complex, if discomfiting, self-other understandings to the oversimplifications of programmatic political action.[82]

In March 1964, when Burke's "Definition of Man" was on the stands in the winter 1963–64 *Hudson Review*, Peter De Vries said "The problem of the sexes is coexistence, and it is the same as for the two great political powers: Not to let rivalry become enmity."[83] His novels illustrate the philosophy of "both-and" in a style that combines the analytic potency of aggressive wit with the synthesizing strength of tolerant humor. It is not compatible with political dogma, as, finally, surrealism was not compatible with the Communist Party.

"The point is to live, Camus and Mayakovsky affirmed. And one way to live is through laughter," Richard Boston in his *Anatomy of Laughter* affirms. "Laughter defies the pain of human existence and relieves it. . . . A twentieth-century writer who has notably put forward the claims of laughter in fair weather and foul is Peter De Vries. . . . It is the bleakness that gives edge to his comedy, and that makes it courageous."[84] As William R. Higgins points out, "Like the humor of Aristophanes, Swift, and Twain before him, De Vries's comedy contains much horror and terror"; but De Vries does not capitulate to the nihilism of the modern black humorists.[85] In Paul Theroux's opinion, De Vries's Watergate-era novel *The Glory of the Hummingbird*, the work of "our most dedicated satirist," offers us, "when the derangement of melancholy seems almost overwhelming, the gift of laughter." De Vries confronts "the stupendous follies of our age" with courage: "Comedy, for the De Vries character, is a form of boldness; a sense of humor provides an opportunity for heroism; only the brave crack jokes. How welcome a rarity in a savage time, when book clubs are mugging their members with horror stories, for De Vries's annual novel to be a celebration of comedy as power."[86] And Melvin Maddocks notes that De Vries's "comedy redeems and justifies the business of living"; more than simply affirming, it "has a kind of headlong compulsiveness to it. . . . Farce snowballing with a kind of attendant horror—Kafka crossed with the Keystone Kops."[87] The "celebration of comedy as power" in De Vries's works is contingent on their "headlong compulsiveness" in bringing together opposites, from the elevated to the mundane, from the restrained to the unfettered.[88]

Being "the gagmeister of the American novel"[89] has cost De Vries. But critics do him little service to base a defense on a "seriousness underlying the comedy." The comedy *is* the "seriousness," and there is no reason to be grave about it. Paul Gray calls De Vries

> at once the liberal humanist, tolerantly condoning free expression and yearnings of the flesh: he is also the hooded inquisitor, meting out appropriate punishment whenever anyone tries to have a little fun. . . . Perhaps the only force that can embrace these opposites is the meliorism of humor.[90]

More precisely, De Vries employs the medium of farce to comprise the volatile opposites. In so doing, he has created a complex, comically educational version of farce's "irrational vision."[91] De Vries has managed this feat sometimes in tandem with, sometimes ironically opposed to, sometimes in virtual collaboration with, the surrealists.

Not only does De Vries belong in discussions of surrealism, but surrealism deserves prominence in discussions of our recent and our classic literature. De Vries, in reoxygenating the mythic figures in the extravagant vein of American humor, has brought the Mike Finks into the Age of Anxiety and the Sut Lovingoods into the Sexual Revolution. *I Hear America Swinging, Forever Panting, Consenting Adults,* and *The Prick of Noon* are priapic tall tales that feature the more knowing successors of Jedediah Homebread, Jerusalem Dutiful, Jack Downing, and Sam Patch. While De Vries's ad men, brokers, and thespians generally exemplify weakness, not, as do so many of their ancestors, villainy, they afford similar opportunities for reflection on the "kinds of turbulence" Burke says "threaten to undo us."[92] Huckleberry Finn's Pap does not appear in De Vries but has been portioned out among De Vries's Dukes and Dolphins and Huckleberrys. One of De Vries's many catch phrases refers to bestiality of the Sut Lovingood variety:

> Blodgett is the beast that sleeps in all of us (dozing lightly in some). (Stew in *Forever Panting,* 6)

> The beast that sleeps in all of us (dozing lightly in some) had certainly wanted out, back there in that awful house. Had very nearly gotten loose, too. There was no mistake about it: *at that moment his fingers had wanted to close round that soft white throat.* (Alvin Mopworth in *Reuben, Reuben,* 305)

> I suggested that all these abnormalities, from harmless peeping to rape and murder, were exaggerations of normal instincts. That we're all prowlers, thieves, rapists, and murderers at heart, or have a dash of it in us.

This is the beast sleeping in each of us, dozing lightly in some. (Stan Waltz in *Let Me Count the Ways*, 95)

When not wrestling with the beast, though perhaps while "slouching towards Kalamazoo," De Vries's characters grapple, often raucously, with quiet desperation. De Vries does not sanitize the unconscious or disguise our banality. Nor are his books, as surrealist works stand often accused, escapist. The laughter they provoke may be the last resort of effete cultivation or the first fruits of a comic education: that is up to us. De Vries offers testimony to the proposition that to be a surrealist in America is to be *on another level*—or on no "other" level at all?—an American.

Notes

Chapter 1. Introduction

1. Peter De Vries, "An Interview with Peter De Vries," interview by Douglas M. Davis, *College English* 28, no. 7 (April 1967): 524–28; Peter De Vries, "Peter De Vries," interview by Roy Newquist, in *Counterpoint* (Chicago: Rand McNally & Co., 1964), 145–54; Peter De Vries, "An Interview in New York with Peter De Vries," interview by Richard B. Sale, *Studies in the Novel* 1, no. 3 (Fall 1969): 364–69.

2. Kenneth Burke, *Language as Symbolic Action* (Berkeley and Los Angeles: University of California Press, 1966), 20.

3. *New York Times* headlines are a laboratory of the phenomenon: "Remembering War as a Surreal Muddle," banner headline on 24 April 1992, sec. B, p. 1; "CLEANUP BEGINS IN LOS ANGELES; TROOPS ENFORCE SURREAL CALM," banner headline on 3 May 1992, top of p. 1; "THE SURREAL HORROR OF THE RWANDA REFUGEES," headline on the front cover of the *New York Times Magazine,* 5 June 1994.

4. Peter De Vries, "'You Overhear Cliches, and Dislodge Them'": An Interview with Peter De Vries," interview by John K. Hutchens, *New York Herald Tribune Book Review,* 18 March 1962, 5.

5. Peter De Vries, *Madder Music,* 94; *Consenting Adults,* 218–19. All references to Peter De Vries's books are to the first editions; see Works Cited.

6. Wilbur Merril Frohock, *Strangers to This Ground* (Dallas: Southern Methodist University Press, 1961), 9–11, 171–72.

7. See, respectively, Nancy Down, "The Search for Authenticity in the Satiric Worlds of Nathanael West and Peter De Vries" (Ph.D. diss., Drew University, 1986), 215–16; T. Jeff Evans, "Peter De Vries in American Humor," *Whimsy VI,* Proceedings of the Sixth (1987) Conference on International Humor (Tempe: Arizona State University, 1988), 13–15.

8. See, e.g., Roderick Jellema, *Peter De Vries* (Grand Rapids, Mich.: William B. Eerdmans Publishing Co., 1966), 12–15.

9. See, e.g., J. H. Bowden, *Peter De Vries* (Boston: Twayne Publishers, 1983), 167.

10. See, e.g., Craig Challender, "Peter De Vries: The Case for Comic Seriousness," *Studies in American Humor* 1, no. 1 (April 1974): 40–51.

11. Although the following list of overt references is the result of a systematic survey, some mentions of surrealism or surrealists may have been overlooked. Approximate surrealists are not included nor are general allusions. Some interesting references to dada are included. *But Who Wakes the Bugler?* (1940), 61–62, 144–45, 220–49; *The Handsome Heart* (1943), no references; *Angels Can't Do Better* (1944), 165; *No But I Saw the Movie* (1952), 223–24; *The Tunnel of Love* (1954), 22, 87, 103; *Comfort Me With Apples* (1956), no references; *The Mackerel Plaza* (1958), 35; *The Tents of Wickedness* (1959), 198; *Through the Fields of Clover* (1961), 54, 168, 216; *The Blood of the Lamb* (1962), 220–21; *Reuben, Reuben* (1964), 145–46, 418; *Let Me Count the Ways*

(1965), 44–46, 230; *The Vale of Laughter* (1967), 275, 280, 307; *The Cat's Pajamas & Witch's Milk* (1968), 51, 111, 171; *Mrs. Wallop* (1970), 228, 254, 268; *Into Your Tent I'll Creep* (1971), 10, 162, 236; *Without a Stitch in Time* (1972), 4–5, 104–5; *Forever Panting* (1973), 14, 25, 35, 41, 110, 137, 261; *The Glory of the Hummingbird* (1974), 11, 38, 111, 133, 229; *I Hear America Swinging* (1976), 69–70, 91–92, 96, 109, 203; *Madder Music* (1977), 13, 15, 28, 94, 97, 180, 181; *Consenting Adults* (1980), 87, 96, 159, 180, 211, 214, 218–19; *Sauce for the Goose* (1981), 31, 118, 142, 169; *Slouching Towards Kalamazoo* (1983), 205; *The Prick of Noon* (1985), 68; *Peckham's Marbles* (1986), 13, 89, 125, 233, 244.

12. See Douglas M. Davis, ed., *The World of Black Humor* (New York: E. P. Dutton & Co., Inc., 1967), 152–73.

13. De Vries, interview by Hutchens, 5; *Who's Who in America*, 45th ed., 1988–89, vol. 1 (Wilmette, Ill.: Marquis Who's Who, 1988), s.v. "De Vries, Peter" omits mention of the first three novels.

14. Cornelius John Ter Maat, "Three Novelists and a Community: A Study of American Novelists with Dutch Calvinist Origins" (Ed.D. diss., University of Michigan, 1963); Arnold Roy Hoffman, "The Sense of Place: Peter De Vries, J. F. Powers, and Flannery O'Connor" (Ph.D. diss., Michigan State University, 1970); Jellema, *Peter De Vries;* Jack Kent Boyd, "The Novels of Peter De Vries: A Critical Introduction" (Ph.D. diss., University of Arkansas, 1971); Joseph M. De Roller, "The Lower-Case Absurd: A Study of the Novels of Peter De Vries" (Ph.D. diss., University of Rochester, 1976); Nancy Down, "The Search for Authenticity"; J. H. Bowden, *Peter De Vries.*

15. See *Poetry* 52–67 (April 1938–March 1946); De Vries continued as contributing editor through vol. 70 (September 1947).

16. Constance Rourke, *American Humor: A Study of the National Character* (New York: Harcourt, Brace and Co., 1931), 299; discussed by Charles Newman in *The Post-Modern Aura* (Evanston, Ill.: Northwestern University Press, 1985), 79.

17. Aldo Leopold, *A Sand County Almanac* (1949; reprint, New York: Ballantine, 1984), xvii.

18. André Breton, "Manifesto of Surrealism," in *Manifestoes of Surrealism*, trans. Richard Seaver and Helen R. Lane (Ann Arbor: University of Michigan Press, 1969), 14.

19. Henry David Thoreau, *The Writings of Henry David Thoreau*, vol. 5, *Excursions and Poems* (Boston: Houghton Mifflin and Co., 1906), 231.

20. Peter De Vries, "What's All That About Commuters?" *New York Herald Tribune Book Review*, 30 August 1959, 2.

21. Peter De Vries and Katinka Loeser, "Peter De Vries & Katinka Loeser," interview by Sybil Steinberg, *Publishers Weekly*, 16 October 1981, 8.

22. See T. A. Straayer, "Peter De Vries: A Bibliography of Secondary Sources, 1940–1981," *Bulletin of Bibliography* 39, no. 3 (September 1982): 146–69; see also Ben Yagoda, "Peter De Vries: Being Seriously Funny," *New York Times Magazine*, 12 June 1983, 42–56; George Will, "D is for Dodo," *Newsweek*, 9 February 1976, 84 (in which Will calls De Vries "my favorite novelist"); and Michiko Kakutani, reviews of *Slouching Towards Kalamazoo*, by Peter De Vries, *New York Times*, 22 July 1983, sec. C, p. 23, and of *Are You Listening Rabbi Löw*, by J. P. Donleavy, *New York Times*, 12 October 1988, sec. C, p. 21.

23. A[ndrew] H[ook] and E[ric] M[ottram], "Peter De Vries," in *The Penguin Companion to American Literature*, ed. Malcolm Bradbury, Eric Mottram, and Jean Franc (New York: McGraw-Hill, 1971).

24. William R. Higgins, "Peter De Vries," in *Dictionary of Literary Biography*, 2d

ser., vol. 6, *American Novelists Since World War II*, ed. James E. Kibler, Jr. (Detroit: Gale Research Co., 1980), 79.

25. Joe Queenan, "Then the Spoon Speaks Up," *New York Times Book Review*, 15 April 1990, 12; Frank Muir, ed., *The Oxford Book of Humorous Prose* (Oxford: Oxford University Press, 1990), 881.

26. Horton Davies, *The Mirror of the Ministry in Modern Novels* (New York: Oxford University Press, 1959), 171. Davis finds Elmer Gantry "unacceptable" treatment of the clergy (177) but finds satire of church liberals entirely satisfactory.

27. Jellema, *Peter De Vries*, 9, 11, 21–22. Like Davies, Jellema devalues Sinclair Lewis ("quite an insignificant observer, and a very limited artist," 9). The gratuitous dispraise is no favor to De Vries, in whose works appear many Lewis touches.

28. John H. Timmerman, "Tragicomedy and Saving Grace," *Christian Century*, 26 November 1975, 1079.

29. Ralph C. Wood, *The Comedy of Redemption: Christian Faith and Comic Vision in Four American Novelists* (Notre Dame, Ind.: University of Notre Dame Press, 1988), 230, 278. Similarly, James D. Bratt, in his *Dutch Calvinism in Modern America: A History of a Conservative Subculture* (Grand Rapids, Mich.: W. B. Eerdmans Publishing Co., 1984), sees De Vries "in the agnostic camp" (181) but "a secular Jeremiah, a renegade CRC [Christian Reformed Church] missionary to the smart set" (179).

30. Wood, *Comedy of Redemption*, 230. Wood notes (240) Tillie Seltzer's use of the word "surrealism" in her slam at Hank Tattersall's nihilism in *The Cat's Pajamas*, but he does not reconcile the accusation with De Vries's being "discerningly surreal."

31. J. H. Bowden, preface to *Peter De Vries* (n.p.); Bowden argues De Vries is antiromantic but aligns him with Steppenwolf (167).

32. Wood, *Comedy of Redemption*, 278, 270.

33. Peter De Vries, "Voice in Babel," *Poetry* 62 (July 1943): 214.

34. Anthony Burgess, review of *Sauce for the Goose*, by Peter De Vries, *New York*, 28 September 1981, 64. Burgess celebrates the "sheer artistry" of *The Blood of the Lamb*, "a joyful masterpiece made out of great personal pain," in *The Novel Now: A Guide to Contemporary Fiction* (New York: W. W. Norton & Company, Inc., 1967), 201.

35. Max Byrd, "Reconsideration," *New Republic*, 23 October 1976, 31.

36. Al Hine, "Serious Frivolity," *Saturday Review*, 15 May 1954, 14; Whitney Balliett, "The Egg in the Omelette," *New Yorker*, 12 May 1956, 157; Al Hine, "Exurbia Impaled," *Saturday Review*, 5 May 1956, 20; Wilbur Merril Frohock, *Strangers to This Ground*, 166–72. Frohock touches on surrealism in discussing "the Great Topos" of the displaced person but does not connect it with De Vries. He borrows "inner-directed" and "outer-directed" from David Riesman's *The Lonely Crowd*.

37. Abigail Ann Hamblen, "Peter De Vries: Calvinist Gone Underground," *Trace* 48 (1963): 20–24; Kingsley Amis, "What We Need Is Savage Laughter," in *Opinions and Perspectives from the New York Times Book Review*, ed. Francis Brown (Boston: Houghton Mifflin Co., 1964), 279; Melvin Maddocks, "Chase Scenes by Kafka," *Christian Science Monitor*, 22 July 1965, 11, quoted in *World Authors 1950–1970*, ed. John Wakeman (New York: The H. W. Wilson Co., 1975), s.v. "De Vries, Peter"; Don Coray, "Only When I Laugh," *The Reformed Journal* 15, no. 9 (November 1965): 24; Charles Child Walcutt, *Man's Changing Mask: Modes and Methods of Communication in Fiction* (Minneapolis: University of Minnesota Press, 1966), 248–49.

38. Joy Rome, "Peter De Vries: Compassionate Satirist," *Unisa English Studies* 9, no. 3 (September 1971): 23; Wesley Kort, *Shriven Selves* (Philadelphia: Fortress Press, 1972), 50–51, 148–49 (Kort never mentions surrealism); Penelope Gilliatt, "Art, the Always-with-Us," *New Yorker*, 16 January 1971, 97.

39. Paul Showers, review of *Without a Stitch in Time, New York Times Book Review,* 24 December 1972, 3, 17, excerpted in *Contemporary Literary Criticism,* vol. 2, ed. Carolyn Riley and Barbara Harte (Detroit: Gale Research Co., 1974), 114; Penelope Gilliatt, "The Unbudgeable Blodgett," *New Yorker,* 16 July 1973, 78; Alan Green, "The Giddy Heights of Humor," *World,* 17 July 1973, 39, excerpted in *Contemporary Literary Criticism,* vol. 3, ed. Carolyn Riley (Detroit: Gale Research Co., 1975), 126; William Walsh, "The Combination in the Safe," *Encounter* 40, no. 1 (January 1973): 75–80; for Spender, see "Selected Notices," *Horizon* 7, no. 40 (April 1943): 277–82, 287–89, cited by De Vries in "Voice in Babel." For the moral implications of surrealism, see André Breton, "Manifesto of Surrealism," esp. 44 n.; André Breton, *What Is Surrealism?* trans. David Gascoyne (1936; reprint, New York: Haskell House, 1974), esp. 49–50; David Gascoyne, *A Short Survey of Surrealism* (1935; reprint, San Francisco: City Lights Books, 1982), esp. 136; Herbert Read, introduction to *Surrealism,* ed. Herbert Read (London: Faber and Faber Limited, 1936), 34, 51–56, 86–87; and Paul Eluard, "Poetic Evidence," in *Surrealism,* ed. Read, 171–83.

40. Fred Rodewald, "The Comic *Eiron* in the Novels of Peter De Vries," *Quartet* 6, no. 41 (Winter 1973): 34–38; Craig Challender, "Peter De Vries: The Case for Comic Seriousness," *Studies in American Humor* 1, no. 1 (April 1974): 50; Calvin De Vries, "Peter De Vries: The Vale of Laughter," *Theology Today* 32 (April 1975): 18; Robert M. Strozier, review of *I Hear America Swinging, New York Times Book Review,* 9 May 1976, 5; Byrd, "Reconstruction," 30.

41. Stuart Sutherland, "The Comedy of the Commonplace," *Times Literary Supplement,* 30 January 1981, 107.

42. Rhoda Koenig, "A Satire on Feminism," *New Republic,* 14 October 1981, 38–39; Melvin Maddocks, "Galloping Lust, Crawling Remorse," *Time,* 21 September 1981, 81.

43. E.g., Burgess, review of *Sauce for the Goose,* 63–64; Whitney Balliett, "Convulsive Merriment," *New Yorker,* 19 October 1981, 200–204.

44. Respectively, David Macfarlane, "The Architect of Chuckles," *Maclean's,* 25 July 1983, 54; Harriett Gilbert, "A+," *New Statesman,* 19 August 1983, 26; Lucille Crane, review of *Slouching Towards Kalamazoo,* by Peter De Vries, in *Best Sellers* 43, no. 6 (September 1983): 201; and "Adult Fiction" notice in *Booklist* 79 (15 March 1983): 929.

45. Respectively, R. Z. Shepard, "Uncle Gatsby in Connecticut," *Time,* 22 April 1985, 69; review in *Library Journal,* 15 May 1985, 78; Whitney Balliett, "Climbers," *New Yorker,* 10 June 1985, 139; and Clancy Sigal, "Paronomasiamania," *New York Times Book Review,* 19 May 1985, 16.

46. "Bookends," *Time,* 13 October 1986, 102. I appreciate Renee Huntley's pointing this notice out to me.

47. See De Roller, "The Lower-Case Absurd," 60, 77–79; Down, "The Search for Authenticity," 212 (Down does not pursue the surrealistic leads); and Boyd, "The Novels of Peter De Vries," 148–49, 185, 292, 160, 291. De Vries says "I do not at all apologize for the change of tone, from comic to tragic, midway in 'The Blood of the Lamb'" (interview by Hutchens, 5). For Lacan, see Gascoyne, *A Short Survey of Surrealism,* 126. In his interesting discussion of "Four Renegade Novelists" in *Dutch Calvinism in Modern America,* James D. Bratt describes De Vries as "scarred by the catechisms of both Calvinism and Modernity" (182). Bratt also asserts that De Vries's work from *I Hear America Swinging* on "is becoming increasingly monochromatic and formulaic" (181). Ignoring or underestimating De Vries's surrealist heritage is done at the risk of misapprehending and undervaluing his work.

Chapter 2. The Literary Life of Peter De Vries

1. Clarence A. Andrews, *Chicago in Story* (Iowa City: Midwest Heritage Publishing Company, 1982), 124, 145, 368 n.

2. J. H. Bowden, *Peter De Vries* (Boston: Twayne Publishers, 1983), 4; cf. Ben Yagoda, "Peter De Vries: Being Seriously Funny," *New York Times Magazine,* 12 June 1983, 42–56.

3. Peter De Vries, letter to author, 11 November 1988. (The name De Vries means "The Frisian, i.e., one who came from the province of Friesland," and is associated with the meanings "curled hair" and "free"; Elsdon C. Smith, *New Dictionary of American Family Names* [New York: Harper and Row, 1956].)

4. J. H. Bowden, *Peter De Vries,* 2. Cf. Yagoda, "Peter De Vries"; "Adrift in a Laundromat," *Time,* 20 July 1959, 100; and Allen B. Borden, "Peter De Vries," *Wilson Library Bulletin* 33, no. 7 (March 1959): 460.

5. Borden, "Peter De Vries," 460.

6. Rochelle Girson, "The Author," *Saturday Review,* 24 March 1962, 20.

7. Peter De Vries, "Peter De Vries," interview by Roy Newquist, in *Counterpoint* (Chicago: Rand McNally & Co., 1964), 146–47; see also *World Authors 1950–1970,* ed. John Wakeman (New York: The H. W. Wilson Company, 1975), s.v. "De Vries, Peter."

8. Cornelius John Ter Maat, "Three Novelists and a Community: A Study of American Novelists with Dutch Calvinist Origins" (Ed.D. diss., University of Michigan, 1963), 10–16; cf. Arnold Roy Hoffman, "The Sense of Place: Peter De Vries, J. F. Powers, and Flannery O'Connor" (Ph.D. diss., Michigan State University, 1970), 25; see also James D. Bratt, *Dutch Calvinism in Modern America: A History of a Conservative Subculture* (Grand Rapids, Mich.: W. B. Eerdmans Publishing Co., 1984).

9. See the "Chronology" (n.p.) in J. H. Bowden, *Peter De Vries;* De Vries, interview by Newquist; and J. J. Lamberts, "I Love You Just the Same," *The Banner,* 4 October 1974, 14–15.

10. De Vries, interview by Newquist, 147.

11. Peter De Vries, introduction to *Lions, Harts, Leaping Does and Other Stories,* by J. F. Powers (New York: Time Inc., 1963), xv–xvi. The De Vrieses' address was 7759 Halsted Street (Peter De Vries, letter to author, 11 November 1988).

12. De Vries, introduction to *Lions,* xvi.

13. I am grateful to Sister Dolores Koza, S.S.J., of St. Leo's parish, for sharing this information in our telephone conversation of 17 October 1988 and for sending me the pamphlet "St. Leo the Great Parish" commemorating the centennial, in 1985, of the parish.

14. Girson, "The Author," 20.

15. Ter Maat, "Three Novelists," 19.

16. De Vries, introduction to *Lions,* xvi–xvii.

17. Yagoda, "Peter De Vries," 44.

18. Peter De Vries, "'You Hear Cliches, and Dislodge Them': An Interview with Peter De Vries," interview by John K. Hutchens, *New York Herald Tribune Book Review,* 18 March 1962, 5.

19. Borden, "Peter De Vries," 460.

20. *World Authors,* 387–88.

21. J. H. Bowden, *Peter De Vries,* 4. Variations on the nickname were "'Dewp' and 'Daddy Dew Point,' both apparently related to a chemistry experiment for finding dew point, one he had trouble with. The nickname also refers to his being

a good basketball player" (Jan De Vries, letter to author, 4 December 1994). Presumably *Dew Point* is a pun for "Two-Point," a complimentary epithet for a player who scores lots of baskets.

22. "St. Leo," 7–8.

23. Borden, "Peter De Vries," 460; J. H. Bowden, *Peter De Vries*, 2.

24. J. H. Bowden, *Peter De Vries*, 2–3, 23.

25. "The Literary Club," *Violet and Maize* 7 (June 1927): 67. I am grateful to Jan De Vries for this source, a magazine published by Chicago Christian High School to celebrate the school's clubs and activities.

26. "Talk with the Author," *Newsweek*, 20 July 1959, 99.

27. De Vries, interview by Hutchens, 5.

28. Thomas De Quincey, *The Confessions of an English Opium-Eater* (London: J. M. Dent, 1907), 194.

29. David Perkins, ed., *English Romantic Writers* (New York: Harcourt, Brace, and World, Inc., 1967), 722.

30. Peter De Vries, letter to author, 1 December 1988.

31. Andrews, *Chicago in Story*, 145–53.

32. De Quincey, *Confessions*, 157.

33. "Adrift in a Laundromat," 100.

34. Borden, "Peter De Vries," 460.

35. Roderick Jellema, *Peter De Vries: A Critical Essay* (Grand Rapids, Mich.: William B. Eerdmans Publishing Co., 1966), 40.

36. John J. Timmerman, "As I Knew Them," *Dialogue*, April 1975, 20–22; Lamberts, "I Love You," 14–15.

37. Timmerman, "As I Knew Them," 20; The Calvin College and Seminary *Yearbook 1930–31* (Grand Rapids, Mich.), which names Peter C. De Vries as a senior (62), notes that chapel was compulsory: "All students are required to attend the devotional exercises held in the auditorium each school day at 9:40 a.m." (26).

38. Peter De Vries, letter to author, 15 March 1989.

39. Jellema, *Peter De Vries*, 14.

40. J. H. Bowden, *Peter De Vries*, 4; Borden, "Peter De Vries," 460.

41. Timmerman, "As I Knew Them," 21; J. H. Bowden, *Peter De Vries*, 4.

42. Borden, "Peter De Vries," 460.

43. Timmerman, "As I Knew Them," 21.

44. Jellema, *Peter De Vries*, 14.

45. Timmerman, "As I Knew Them," 21.

46. J. H. Bowden, *Peter De Vries*, 4–5.

47. Lamberts, "I Love You," 14.

48. J. H. Bowden, *Peter De Vries*, 4–5. According to the Calvin *Yearbook 1930–31*, Stob was a year behind De Vries (62, 64).

49. Timmerman, "As I Knew Them," 20–22.

50. J. H. Bowden, *Peter De Vries*, 5.

51. Ibid.

52. Frederick Manfred, "An Interview With Frederick Manfred Conducted by Leslie T. Whipp, May 7, 1987" (East Lansing, Mich.: The Midwestern Press, The Society for the Study of Midwestern Literature, Michigan State University, 1992), 51–52.

53. Timmerman, "As I Knew Them," 21.

54. Manfred, interview by Whipp, 52. The chronology indicates that De Vries visited Calvin three years after he graduated. Manfred recounted this anecdote in a question-and-answer period following his reading in the National Public Radio broad-

cast series *Live from Prairie Lights* at the Prairie Lights Bookstore in Iowa City, Iowa, on 25 September 1992.

55. Frederick Manfred, letter to Peter De Vries, summer 1940, in *The Selected Letters of Frederick Manfred 1932–1954*, ed. Arthur R. Huseboe and Nancy Owen Nelson (Lincoln: University of Nebraska Press, 1988), 109.

56. Jack Kent Boyd, "The Novels of Peter De Vries: A Critical Introduction" (Ph.D. diss., University of Arkansas, 1971), 4; see also *Contemporary Authors*, vol. 17–20, 1st revision, ed. Clare D. Kinsman (Detroit: Gale Research Co., 1976), s.v. "De Vries, Peter."

57. Andrews, *Chicago in Story*, 146.

58. De Vries, interview by Newquist, 147.

59. Boyd, "Novels of Peter De Vries," 4.

60. De Vries, interview by Hutchens, 5.

61. De Vries, interview by Newquist, 146.

62. Peter De Vries, "Talk with Peter De Vries," interview by Lewis Nichols, *New York Times Book Review*, 29 April 1956, 28.

63. J. H. Bowden, *Peter De Vries*, 5.

64. *World Authors*, 387; De Vries, interview by Newquist, 147–48; De Vries, interview by Hutchens, 4–5.

65. Boyd, "The Novels of Peter De Vries," 5; J. H. Bowden, *Peter De Vries*, 6.

66. De Vries, interview by Nichols, 28.

67. Arthur Evans, "479,825 for Kelly; A Record," *Chicago Daily Tribune*, 27 February 1935, 1. On 2 April 1935, Kelly won the general election by "the greatest margin in Chicago's history" and carried all fifty wards; see Roger Biles, *Big City Boss in Depression and War: Mayor Edward J. Kelly of Chicago* (DeKalb: Northern Illinois University Press, 1984), 39.

68. "Fusion in Chicago Will Run Douglas," *New York Times*, 16 February 1935, 7.

69. Evans, "479,825 for Kelly," 1.

70. Ibid.

71. See *World Authors*, 387–88; M. H. Abrams, *Natural Supernaturalism: Tradition and Revolution in Romantic Literature* (New York: W. W. Norton, 1971).

72. J. H. Bowden, *Peter De Vries*, 86.

73. Edward Morris, "Delightful, Delicious, Delectable, De Vries," *Writer's Digest*, January 1978, 8.

74. Edwin T. Bowden, *Peter De Vries: A Bibliography 1934–1977*, Tower Bibliographical Series, no. 14 (Austin: Humanities Research Center, The University of Texas at Austin, 1978), 57.

75. Peter De Vries, "Art's a Funny Thing," *Esquire* 5 (February 1936): 59, 124, 127. See Celia Hilliard, "Sophistication Sells: *Esquire*'s Chicago Success Story," *Chicago*, May 1980, 134–40, and Andrews, *Chicago in Story*, 261–62. That De Vries actually visited Gingrich is established by Peter De Vries, letter to author, 1 December 1988.

76. Yagoda, "Peter De Vries," 44.

77. Hilliard, "Sophistication Sells," 136.

78. Andrews, *Chicago in Story*, 229, 257–58.

79. Peter De Vries, "The Man on the Street," *Esquire* 7 (April 1937): 100, 140, 142; "The Swede and Me," *Manuscript* 2 (September-October 1935): 45–49.

80. Yagoda, "Peter De Vries," 44.

81. Boyd, "The Novels of Peter De Vries," 2.

82. De Vries, interview by Hutchens, 5.

83. Hilliard, "Sophistication Sells," 134.

84. "News Notes," *Poetry* 52 (June 1938): 169.

85. De Vries, interview by Newquist, 148.

86. De Vries, interview by Nichols, 28.

87. Peter De Vries, "On Being Thirty," *Poetry* 61 (October 1942): 380.

88. Daryl Hine and Joseph Parisi, eds., *The Poetry Anthology 1912–1977* (Boston: Houghton Mifflin, 1978), 527.

89. Peter De Vries, "James Thurber: The Comic Prufrock," *Poetry* 63 (December 1943): 150.

90. Andrews, *Chicago in Story*, 211; see also *Twentieth Century Authors: A Biographical Dictionary of Modern Literature*, ed. Stanley J. Kunitz and Howard Haycraft (New York: The H. W. Wilson Co., 1942), s.v. "Dillon, George."

91. Hine, *The Poetry Anthology*, 527.

92. "News Notes," *Poetry* 52 (June 1938): 168.

93. Andrews, *Chicago in Story*, 253–54, 180–81, 257.

94. Ibid., 209–11, 213, 241–42, 247, 264, 280–81.

95. A prevalent view; see, e.g., Jellema, *Peter De Vries*, 14–15; Ter Maat, "Three Novelists," 139; Joseph M. De Roller, "The Lower-Case Absurd: A Study of the Novels of Peter De Vries" (Ph.D diss., University of Rochester, 1976), 22; and T. Jeff Evans, "Peter De Vries in American Humor," in Don L. F. Nilsen and Alleen Pace Nilsen, eds., *Whimsy VI* (Tempe: Arizona State University, 1988), 13.

96. "Adrift in a Laundromat," 100.

97. Hine, *The Poetry Anthology*, xliv.

98. Ibid., xliii.

99. For the *Daily Worker*'s wry reception of the Federal Poets' Number, see "News Notes," *Poetry* 52 (August 1938): 360–61.

100. De Vries, "On Being Thirty," 382.

101. See William Herber, "The Sign," *Poetry* 55 (February 1940): 243–45, 287 n.; and William Everson's letter and the rejoinder, *Poetry* 56 (May 1940): 108–9.

102. James Laughlin, ed., *New Directions in Prose & Poetry 1940* (Norfolk, Conn.: New Directions, 1940), 361.

103. H. R. Hays, "In the American Tradition," *Poetry* 62 (September 1943): 342.

104. *Poetry* 54 (April 1939): 59; Peter De Vries, letter to author, 20 October 1988. Roditi recalled meeting De Vries more than once in Chicago and then once in New York City. Edouard Roditi, letter to author, 19 September 1990.

105. *Poetry* 64 (May 1944): 104–5.

106. *Poetry* 52 (June 1938): 168–69.

107. Hine, *The Poetry Anthology*, xliii.

108. Peter De Vries, introduction to *Lanterns & Lances*, by James Thurber (New York: Time Inc., 1962), xv; "Chicagoans were always proud of the magazine's deficit," De Vries quips in "Peter De Vries & Katinka Loeser," interview by Sybil Steinberg, *Publishers Weekly*, 16 October 1981, 7.

109. *Poetry* 60 (September 1942): 349; *The Kenyon Review* has just barely been saved, *The Southern Review* has just died.

110. *Poetry* 54 (July 1939): 232.

111. Peter De Vries to Paul Engle, 9 July 1943, manuscript collection, University of Iowa Library.

112. De Vries, introduction to *Lanterns & Lances*, xvi; see also J. H. Bowden, *Peter De Vries*, 6.

113. Edwin Bowden, *A Bibliography*, 17.

114. See *New Republic*, 16 September 1940, 394; *New Yorker*, 7 September 1940, 57–58.

115. Ruth Hard Bonner, "Surrealist Fun: *But Who Wakes the Bugler*," *Boston Evening Transcript*, 7 September 1940, sec. 5, p. 1; Lisle Bell, "But Who Wakes the Bugler?" *New York Herald Tribune*, 1 September 1940, sec. 9, p. 8; Beatrice Sherman, "But Who Wakes the Bugler?" *New York Times Book Review*, 8 September 1940, 7; Fred Schwed, Jr., "Nightmares Are Fun," *Saturday Review*, 14 September 1940, 12; John Timmerman, "Mr. Thwing Is Not Pound-Proof," *The Calvin Forum*, October 1940, 54–55; and Sterling North, "Typewriter Bites Local Fantasist," *Chicago Daily News*, 9 October 1940, 20.

116. Edwin Bowden, *A Bibliography*, 17.

117. See Edwin Bowden, *A Bibliography*, 17–18, and T. A. Straayer, "Peter De Vries: A Bibliography of Secondary Sources, 1940–1981," *Bulletin of Bibliography* 39, no. 3 (September 1982): 152–53.

118. De Vries, interview by Hutchens, 5; Yagoda, "Peter De Vries," 45.

119. *Poetry* 57 (January 1941): 244–48 and *Poetry* 60 (April 1942): 27–29; Edwin McDowell, "Katinka Loeser, Story Writer, 77; Collections Told of Suburban Life," *New York Times*, 8 March 1991, sec. A, p. 22.

120. "Announcement of Awards," *Poetry* 61 (November 1942): 461.

121. De Vries and Loeser, interview by Steinberg, 7.

122. Yagoda, "Peter De Vries," 45.

123. Peter De Vries, "Portrait in Depth of Youth Suspended Between Worlds," review of *Dangling Man*, by Saul Bellow, *Chicago Sun Book Week*, 9 April 1944, 3; Saul Bellow, letter to author, 9 August 1991.

124. Yagoda, "Peter De Vries," 45.

125. Peter De Vries, "James Thurber: The Comic Prufrock," *Poetry* 63 (December 1943): 150–59.

126. Burton Bernstein, *Thurber: A Biography* (New York: Dodd, Mead & Co., 1975), 360.

127. Catherine McGehee Kenney, *Thurber's Anatomy of Confusion* (Hamden, Conn.: Archon Books, 1984), 86; Charles S. Holmes, *The Clocks of Columbus: The Literary Career of James Thurber* (New York: Atheneum, 1972), 241; Kenney, *Thurber's Anatomy*, 193.

128. Holmes, *Clocks*, 178.

129. Bernstein, *Thurber*, 362.

130. Holmes, *Clocks*, 241.

131. Yagoda, "Peter De Vries," 45.

132. De Vries, introduction to *Lanterns & Lances*, xv; Bernstein, *Thurber*, 361. Hutchens quotes De Vries as saying he did not meet Thurber until the latter arrived in Chicago.

133. Holmes, *Clocks*, 241–42.

134. De Vries, introduction to *Lanterns & Lances*, xvi.

135. Bernstein, *Thurber*, 361.

136. De Vries, introduction to *Lanterns & Lances*, xvi–xvii.

137. Holmes, *Clocks*, 242. Fanny Butcher, "The Literary Spotlight," *Chicago Sunday Tribune*, 16 April 1944, sec. 6, p. 12, guessed "a good half of the audience thought [De Vries] was Mr. Thurber"; "they aren't unlike in both being very tall, with hair that looks engagingly like a thatched roof on a skyscraper—a wonderful asset in a humorist."

138. Bernstein, *Thurber*, 362.

139. Yagoda, "Peter De Vries," 45; Holmes, *Clocks*, 243. There is warrant for Holmes's view in *Selected Letters of James Thurber*, ed. Helen Thurber and Edward Weeks (1981; reprint, New York: Penguin Books, 1982), 58–59.

140. James Thurber, *The Years with Ross* (1959; reprint, New York: Penguin Books, 1984), 90.

141. Yagoda, "Peter De Vries," 45.

142. Ibid.

143. Holmes, *Clocks*, 243; Bernstein, *Thurber*, 362.

144. Reading De Vries's life in his fiction is tempting. De Vries acknowledges that "Tulip" is "a reminiscence story" (interview by Newquist, 147). Jellema (*Peter De Vries*, 14) and T. Jeff Evans ("Peter De Vries in American Humor," 14) call "Tulip" and "Good Boy" autobiographical stories; many of the others in *No But I Saw the Movie* appear to be lightly embroidered autobiography. Jellema, Evans, and others avoid the implication in the early stories that a restrictive religious upbringing fosters hypocrisy. Similarly the writers who take later De Vries's characters' word for De Vries's when the characters poke fun at liberals and artists shy away from the stories' mordant satire of figures like Spiro Agnew. In any event, though it is fair to see much of De Vries in his characters—Andrew Mackerel resembles De Vries in coming from a Dutch Calvinist Chicago background and in uttering opinions like "the rarer human sensibility becomes, the closer it gets to the logic of insanity" (*The Mackerel Plaza*, 135) and Tillie Seltzer's favorite prayer, "the prayer by Robert Louis Stevenson . . . that might validly be uttered by people who didn't really think anyone was listening" (*Witch's Milk*, 263–64) is De Vries's favorite, too (Yagoda, "Peter De Vries," 56)—it is unwise to read from De Vries's fiction into his life.

145. J. H. Bowden, *Peter De Vries*, 7. The address is provided in Peter De Vries, letter to author, 1 December 1988. André Breton lived on West Eleventh Street for part of his sojourn in America (1941–46); see Anna Balakian, *André Breton* (New York: Oxford University Press, 1971), 173. But, as De Vries wrote me in his letter, he never met Breton.

146. J. H. Bowden, *Peter De Vries*, 7; Edwin Bowden, *A Bibliography*, 59.

147. J. H. Bowden, *Peter De Vries*, 7.

148. De Vries, interview by Nichols, 28; De Vries, interview by Newquist, 150 (according to "De Vries in Westport," *Newsweek*, 17 February 1964, 94, De Vries was down to two days in the office per week); Lewis Grossberger, "The Turf is Familiar. . . ." *People*, 29 September 1980, 42; Yagoda, "Peter De Vries," 46, 50.

149. Brendan Gill, *Here at the New Yorker* (New York: Random House, 1975); E. J. Kahn, Jr., *About the New Yorker and Me* (New York: G. P. Putnam's Sons, 1979). Neither is De Vries discussed in *Studies in American Humor* 3 (n.s.), no. 1 (Spring 1984), a special issue devoted to "The New Yorker from 1925 to 1950."

150. Wendy Lesser, "Runaway Glacier," *New York Times Book Review*, 16 October 1988, 32.

151. Brendan Gill, letter to author, 14 May 1989.

152. Eric Pace, "Peter De Vries, Writer, Is Dead; New Yorker Contributor Was 83," *New York Times*, 29 September 1993, sec. B, p. 11.

153. De Vries, interview by Steinberg, 7.

154. "Larder Ex Libris," *Esquire* 30 (December 1948): 130.

155. J. H. Bowden, *Peter De Vries*, "Chronology" (n.p.).

156. Girson, "The Author," 20.

157. De Vries, interview by Newquist, 148.

158. De Vries's letter to me of 1 December 1988 affirms that the De Vrieses lived in Greenwich Village until the move in 1948. J. H. Bowden's "Chronology" indicates 1946.

159. Thurber, *Selected Letters*, 42, 59.

160. John Malcolm Brinnin, *Dylan Thomas in America* (Boston: Little, Brown and Co., 1955), 34.

161. Peter De Vries, quoted by Paul Ferris in *Dylan Thomas* (New York: The Dial Press, 1977), 233.

162. Peter De Vries, letter to author, 20 October 1988.

163. Ferris, *Dylan Thomas*, 233.

164. Peter De Vries, "What's All That About Commuters?" *New York Herald Tribune Book Review*, 30 August 1959, 2.

165. De Vries, interview by Hutchens, 5. A few years later, it was reported that "De Vries's description of 'Woodsmoke' [in *Reuben, Reuben*] is acutely derisive but also warmly affectionate. . . . The Westport Town Crier last week pointed out the recognizable locale of the novel and commented: 'It's a howl'" ("De Vries in Westport," *Newsweek*, 17 February 1964, 93A–94).

166. Borden, "Peter De Vries," 460; Edwin Bowden, *A Bibliography*, 20–21.

167. Joseph Fields and Peter De Vries, *The Tunnel of Love* (Boston: Little, Brown and Co., 1957), "Cast" (n.p.).

168. Bernstein, *Thurber*, 452: "Thurber, in the words of another guest, was a 'horror.' 'It was Peter's night,' the other guest said, 'but all Thurber did was drunkenly talk about himself, the did-I-tell-you-about-the-time sort of thing. Nobody could get a word in—even Peter—and the evening was ruined for me and a lot of other people there." For Wolcott Gibbs's review, see "Low Jinks in Westport," *New Yorker*, 27 February 1957, 68.

169. Borden, "Peter De Vries," 460. De Vries complained that "They put Doris Day in the movie. . . . She was a superstar, so they had to take lines away from other characters and give them to her—when it made no sense" (quoted in Morris, "Delightful, Delicious, Delectable, De Vries," 8).

170. De Vries, interview by Nichols, 28; "Adrift in a Laundromat," 100; "Talk with the Author," *Newsweek*, 20 July 1959, 98 (earlier in 1959, Borden, in "Peter De Vries," had written that De Vries "is 6'2", 190 lb. His eyes are blue and his hair is brown, thick and wavy" [460]); De Vries, "What's All That About Commuters?" 2.

171. Peter De Vries, quoted in "Exurbia in a Dither," *Newsweek*, 28 September 1959, 107.

172. Holmes, *Clocks*, 256, 294, 314.

173. Bernstein, *Thurber*, 429; see also Holmes, *Clocks*, 276.

174. Bernstein, *Thurber*, 460, 486, 489, 496.

175. De Vries, introduction to *Lanterns & Lanterns*, xviii.

176. Peter De Vries, "An Interview with Peter De Vries," interview by Douglas M. Davis, *College English* 28, no. 7 (April 1967): 525.

177. See, for *Spofford, The New York Times Theater Reviews 1920–1970*, vol. 8, 1967–70 (New York: The New York Times and Arno Press, 1971); for *Reuben, Reuben*, Jerome S. Ozer, *Film Review Annual 1984* (Englewood, N.J.: Film Review Publications, 1984), 974–80; for *How Do I Love Thee?*, *Variety Film Reviews 1907–1980*, vol. 12 (New York: Garland Publishing, 1983); and for *Pete 'n' Tillie, The New York Times Film Reviews 1971–1972* (New York: The New York Times and Arno Press, 1973), 348; *Variety Film Reviews*, vol. 13; and Morris, "Delightful, Delicious, Delectable, De Vries," 8.

178. Peter De Vries, introduction to *Lions, Harts, Leaping Does and Other Stories*, by J. F. Powers; and Peter De Vries, introduction to *Three Men in a Boat*, by Jerome K. Jerome (New York: Time, Inc., 1964), xv–xix.

179. Peter De Vries, "Peter De Vries," in *Authors Take Sides on Vietnam*, ed. Cecil Woolf and John Bagguley (New York: Simon and Schuster, 1967), 32.

180. J. H. Bowden, *Peter De Vries*, 9. The Virginia and Villanova lectures have not been published; the Hopwood Lecture delivered at Michigan, "Exploring Inner Space," appears in *Michigan Quarterly Review* 9 (April 1969): 85–92.

181. Peter De Vries, "De Vries Finds Dreams Dull When He Can't Fall Asleep," interview by Israel Shenker, *New York Times*, 27 January 1969, 35, 64; reprinted as "Peter De Vries," in Israel Shenker, *Words and Their Masters* (Garden City, N.Y.: Doubleday & Co., Inc., 1974), 96–100.

182. Peter De Vries, interview by Newquist, 145; interview by Douglas M. Davis, 525; and "An Interview in New York with Peter De Vries," interview by Richard B. Sale, *Studies in the Novel* 1, no. 3 (Fall 1969): 364. Straayer has noted the edited nature of the interviews, in his "Bibliography," 151–52, as has J. H. Bowden, *Peter De Vries*, 1. De Vries reiterates some of his off-the-cuff remarks in his novels, where they resonate with the "found" quality of readymades. Thus, De Vries offers intentionalist and biographical critics much material to work with, despite his cameo appearance as a straw man in Janet Emig's *The Composing Process of Twelfth Graders* (Urbana, Ill.: National Council of Teachers of English, 1971): "On the established writer as a useful source of data about writing, an investigator can say simply with the novelist Peter de [*sic*] Vries, 'Don't ask the [*sic*] cow to analyze milk'; or he can examine this source" (8). Emig quotes only De Vries's quip from the interview by Newquist, in which De Vries says "Don't ask a cow to analyze milk" (147), even though De Vries goes on to speak revealingly about his work.

183. Peter De Vries, quoted in "Booze & the Writer," *Writer's Digest*, October 1978, 28–29.

184. Anthony Burgess, review of *Sauce for the Goose*, *New York*, 28 September 1981, 63–64.

185. McDowell, "Katinka Loeser," 22.

186. Pace, "Peter De Vries," 11; "Peter De Vries," *New Yorker*, 11 October 1993, 12; "Milestones," *Time*, 11 October 1993, 25; Donald Kaul, "Over the Coffee," *Des Moines Register*, 3 October 1993, sec. C. p. 3; "Deaths Last Week," *Chicago Tribune*, 3 October 1993, sec. 2, p. 6; "Newsletter," *Humor* 7 (1994): 301; Paul Theroux, "A Jolly Old Elf, A Master of Gloom: The Gifts of Peter De Vries," *New York Times Book Review*, 5 December 1993, 35, 38.

187. Grossberger, "The Turf is Familiar," 41.

188. J. H. Bowden, *Peter De Vries*, "Chronology" (n.p.), specifies chair no. 17, formerly that of John Cheever.

189. Yagoda, "Peter De Vries," 44.

190. Grossberger, "The Turf is Familiar," 42; Yagoda, "Peter De Vries," 42.

191. Yagoda, "Peter De Vries," 44.

192. Grossberger, "The Turf is Familiar," 41.

193. Straayer, "A Bibliography," 169.

Chapter 3. Peter De Vries and 1930s Surrealism

1. Caliban [pseud.], "Caliban Refuses to Collect His Thoughts," *Caliban*, no. 1 (1986): 142; the issue includes work by Edouard Roditi and Charles Henri Ford.

2. Peter De Vries, "Nahum, I Baptize Thee," *The Calithump* 1 (May 1934): 11–20; "Flight," *Bozart and Contemporary Verse* 8 (November-December 1934): 9.

3. Peter De Vries, "Rhapsody for a Girl on a Bar Stool," *Esquire* 8 (November 1937): 48–49; "Rooming House Anthology," *Coronet* 3 (February 1938): 12–13; "The

Floorwalker Attends a Slide Lecture on Gauguin," *Esquire* 12 (September 1939): 28; [as Carl Crane, pseud.] "The Reader Writes," *New Yorker,* 8 July 1939, 22.

4. Peter De Vries, "Late Song," *Poetry* 51 (January 1938): 196.

5. Peter De Vries, "Mirror," *Poetry* 53 (March 1939): 311; see M. H. Abrams, *The Mirror and the Lamp* (London: Oxford University Press, 1953) and James I. Wimsatt, "The Mirror as Metaphor for Literature," in *What Is Literature?* ed. Paul Hernadi (Bloomington: Indiana University Press, 1978), 127–41.

6. Peter De Vries, "Songs for Eight O'Clock," *Esquire* 9 (February 1938): 40–41.

7. Peter De Vries, "Song for a Bride," *Esquire* 9 (June 1938): 36; cf. Algernon Charles Swinburne, "A Forsaken Garden," in *Swinburne: Selected Poetry and Prose,* ed. John D. Rosenberg (New York: The Modern Library, 1968), 210–13.

8. Peter De Vries, "Men Marry Because They Are Tired," *The Calithump* 2 (July 1934): 22–25; "Eine Kleine Nacht," *Story* 6 (March 1935): 68–74; "Afterglow," *Vernier,* no. 5 (Fall 1936): 23–28; "I, Voluptuary," *Esquire* 6 (December 1936): 82, 245–46, 248, 250; "Pizzicato on the Heartstrings," *Story* 9 (August 1936): 87–94; "The Swede and Me," *Manuscript* 2 (September-October 1935): 45–49; "The Man on the Street," *Esquire* 7 (April 1937): 100, 140, 142.

9. Peter De Vries, "Art's a Funny Thing," *Esquire* 5 (February 1936): 59, 124, 127 (De Vries's first appearance in *Esquire*).

10. See George M. Cohen, *A History of American Art* (New York: Dell, 1971), 184–85.

11. Peter De Vries, "It Goes Like This," *Coronet* 5 (November 1938): 122–26.

12. André Breton, "Manifesto of Surrealism," in *Manifestoes of Surrealism,* trans. Richard Seaver and Helen R. Lane (Ann Arbor: University of Michigan Press, 1969), 10.

13. Edouard Roditi, "Poetry, Mysticism, and Magic," *Poetry* 53 (January 1939): 218–23; he includes Rimbaud and Lautréamont.

14. H. R. Hays, "Surrealist Influence in Contemporary English and American Poetry," *Poetry* 54 (July 1939): 202–9.

15. As Jack Kent Boyd in "The Novels of Peter De Vries: A Critical Introduction" (Ph.D. diss., University of Arkansas, 1971) and others have shown, De Vries's works bear comparison with Restoration wit comedies. In his 19 September 1990 letter to me, Edouard Roditi offers the opinion that De Vries's "writing is more ironical in a traditional sense than strictly Surrealist. Although he has much in common with Ambrose Bierce, Mark Twain, Artemus Ward and Petroleum V. Nasby, among nineteenth-century American masters of the absurd, he may actually have more in common with eighteenth-century satirists such as Voltaire in *Candide* or Sterne in *A Sentimental Journey* and *Tristran Shandy* [*sic*]. But this remains a moot point, above all because André Breton, in his definitions of Surrealism, always tended to stress the element of the Sublime rather than that of the Absurd." Hays's article shows the connections between the earlier traditions (and sublimity is surely not absent from, say, Sterne) and surrealism.

16. Hays, "Surrealist Influence," 203–4.

17. Ibid., 204–8.

18. Ibid., 209.

19. Delmore Schwartz, "Rimbaud in Our Time," *Poetry* 55 (December 1939): 148–54.

20. The classical concept of the poet as *vates,* reawakened by the Romantics, is central to Breton's idea of the surrealist; see, e.g., André Breton, "What Is Surrealism?" in *What Is Surrealism?* trans. David Gascoyne (1936; reprint, New York: Haskell

House, 1974), 65. During his *Poetry* years, De Vries often refers to the prognosticating powers of poets; see, e.g., "A Note on This Issue," *Poetry* 62 (August 1943): 272–77; "Poetry and the War," *College English* 5, no. 3 (December 1943): 113–20; and "James Thurber: The Comic Prufrock," *Poetry* 63 (December 1943): 150–59.

21. Eugene Jolas, "French Poetry and the Revival of Mysticism," *Poetry* 56 (August 1940): 264–65.

22. Eugene Jolas, "Toward a Metaphysical Renascence?" *Poetry* 57 (October 1940): 49–52.

23. David Daiches, "The Craftsman and the Poet," *Poetry* 64 (April 1944): 35–39.

24. Kimon Friar, "The Action of Incorrigible Tragedy," *Poetry* 64 (May 1944): 104–7.

25. Anna Balakian, *André Breton* (New York: Oxford University Press, 1971), 176.

26. Howard Blake, "There Is a Firbank in It," *Poetry* 60 (April 1942): 48–51. "The Overturned Lake," which appeared in *Poetry* 56 (April 1940): 19, had been turned down by the *Kenyon Review* with an arch note from John Crowe Ransome; see Charles Henri Ford, *Flag of Ecstasy: Selected Poems*, ed. Edward B. Germain (Los Angeles: Black Sparrow Press, 1972), 7.

27. Francis C. Golffing, "The Plain and the Stratosphere," *Poetry* 66 (September 1945): 340–43.

28. Edouard Roditi, "Surrealism Serves the State," *Poetry* 68 (April 1946): 54–56.

29. Oscar Williams, review of *New Directions 1942*, *Poetry* 61 (March 1943): 694. Williams's acerbity is the greater because he himself was identified with early surrealism.

30. Howard Moss, "Wrong Detour," *Poetry* 64 (April 1944): 46–48.

31. Peter De Vries, "Fusion and Confusion," *Poetry* 52 (July 1938): 237. Both books reviewed in this article contain introductions by William Carlos Williams, who was friendly to surrealism; see his *Something to Say*, ed. James E. B. Breslin (New York: New Directions, 1985).

32. De Vries, "Fusion and Confusion," 236–37.

33. Ibid., 237.

34. Ibid., 238.

35. Ibid. I have supplied the end of line 1, missing from the *Poetry* review, from the original edition: Charles Henri Ford, *The Garden of Disorder and Other Poems* (London: Europa Press, 1938), 60. In his introduction, Williams singles out the same poem for praise. Williams also likes Ford's "using the banal to escape the banal," a technique that De Vries adopts.

36. John Malcolm Brinnin, "Muriel Rukeyser: The Social Poet and the Problem of Communication," *Poetry* 61 (January 1943): 554–55.

37. See Karen L. Rood, "Charles Henri Ford," in *Dictionary of Literary Biography*, 2d ser., vol. 48, *American Poets, 1880–1945*, ed. Peter Quartermain (Detroit: Gale Research Co., 1986), 191–210.

38. De Vries, "Fusion and Confusion," 239.

39. Peter De Vries, "Voice in Babel," *Poetry* 62 (July 1943): 208–14.

40. Stephen Spender, review of *Heritage of Symbolism*, by C. M. Bowra, *Horizon* 7, no. 40 (April 1943): 288–89.

41. Stephen Spender, review of *Good and Evil*, by C. E. M. Joad, and *Man the Master*, by Gerald Heard, *Horizon* 7, no. 40 (April 1943): 277–82. On Picasso's surrealism, see Breton, "Surrealism and Painting," in *What Is Surrealism?* 9–24, and William S. Rubin, *Dada, Surrealism, and Their Heritage* (New York: The Museum of Modern Art, 1968), 124–27 and 216.

42. Cyril Connolly's *Horizon* (1940–49), an interesting item on De Vries's reading list, shows the affinities. It included work by George Barker and Dylan Thomas, artwork by René Magritte and Henry Moore, and articles on left-wing politics.

43. Balakian, *André Breton*, 20–21; De Vries, "Voice in Babel," 210.

44. Peter De Vries, "To Be," *Poetry* 64 (June 1944): 158–64. As Milton A. Cohen shows, Cummings had much in common with surrealism (*Poet and Painter: The Aesthetics of E. E. Cummings's Early Work* [Detroit: Wayne State University Press, 1987], 33–63, esp. 59–61). Jenny Penberthy notes that entries in Cummings's World War I notebooks are "indistinguishable from contemporary Dadaist or Surrealist jottings," in "E. E. Cummings," in *Dictionary of Literary Biography*, 2d ser., vol. 48, 122–23. See also Matthew Josephson, *Life among the Surrealists* (New York: Holt, Rinehart and Winston, 1962).

45. Spender, review of Joad and Heard, 281.

46. Peter De Vries, "A Note on This Issue," 272–77; the issue is composed of poems by servicemen.

47. Peter De Vries, "Poetry and the War," 113–20.

48. Thomas several times denied any surrealist influence yet had "almost certainly discussed Surrealist theory with [David Gascoyne] and others," published work in surrealist magazines, participated in the 1936 International Surrealist Exhibition, went to Arizona to visit Max Ernst and Dorothea Tanning, and, as De Vries pointed out, wrote poetry whose speaker "is a human atom dissolving itself, by an imagination almost deliriously vivid" ("Poetry and the War," 119). See John Malcolm Brinnin, *Dylan Thomas in America* (Boston: Little, Brown and Co., 1955), 163; Paul Ferris, *Dylan Thomas* (New York: The Dial Press, 1977), 134–35, 145, 276; and Constantine FitzGibbon, *The Life of Dylan Thomas* (Boston: Little, Brown and Co., 1965), 176–79, 192–96, 334–35.

49. Edmund Wilson, *Axel's Castle* (1931; reprint, New York: W. W. Norton & Co., 1984), 253–56, 304–12, 298.

50. "News Notes," *Poetry* 54 (September 1939): 350–51.

51. "News Notes," *Poetry* 54 (April 1939): 58.

52. See *London Bulletin: Complete Edition in Two Volumes*, Arno Series of Contemporary Art, no. 30 (New York: Arno Press, 1969); Thomas's listing appears in *London Bulletin*, no. 6 (October 1938): 1, reprinted in vol. 1 of the Arno edition.

53. See the Chronology in Rubin, *Dada, Surrealism*, 197–216.

54. Raymond Mortimer, "The Art of Displeasing," *The Living Age* 350 (August 1936): 529–32; "Marvelous & Fantastic," *Time*, 14 December 1936, 60–62; "Giddy Museum Exhibit Dizzies the Public With Dada," *News-Week*, 19 December 1936, 25–26; Barry Byrne, "Surrealism Passes," *The Commonweal*, 2 July 1937, 262–63; Charles W. Ferguson, "Art for Our Sake," *Harper's* 175 (July 1937): 218–20; Meyer Schapiro, "Blue Like an Orange," *The Nation*, 25 September 1937, 323–24; "Super," *Time*, 7 February 1938, 49; Jean Charlot, "Surrealism—Or, the Reason for Unreason," *The American Scholar* 7, no. 2 (April 1938): 230–48; Alex McGavick, "Weird Worlds," *The Commonweal*, 1 April 1938, 630–31; Northrop Frye, "Men as Trees Walking," *The Canadian Forum* 18 (October 1938): 208–10 (Frye shares De Vries's perception that the problem posed by surrealism is solipsism); Margaret Case Harriman, "A Dream Walking," *Reader's Digest* 35 (October 1939): 54–57; Eugene Jolas, "Beyond Surrealism," *The Living Age* 359 (September 1940): 93–95.

55. *New Directions in Prose and Poetry*, ed. James Laughlin IV (Norfolk, Conn.: New Directions, 1936), dedication; *New Directions in Prose & Poetry 1937*, ed. James Laughlin (Norfolk, Conn.: New Directions, 1937), xii; *New Directions in Prose & Poetry 1939*, ed. James Laughlin (Norfolk, Conn.: New Directions, 1939), x; "News

Notes," *Poetry* 54 (April 1939): 58; *New Directions in Prose & Poetry 1940* (Norfolk, Conn.: New Directions, 1940). The Calas, Muller, and Burke contributions are reprinted, with a new essay by Calas, as *Surrealism Pro and Con* (New York: Gotham Book Mart, 1973).

56. David Gascoyne, *A Short Survey of Surrealism* (1935; reprint, San Francisco: City Lights Books, 1982); André Breton, *What Is Surrealism?* trans. David Gascoyne (1936; reprint, New York: Haskell House, 1974); Herbert Read, ed., *Surrealism* (London: Faber and Faber Limited, 1936); Julien Levy, *Surrealism* (New York: The Black Sun Press, 1936), which ranges from Lautréamont to Freud to the Marx brothers.

57. Gascoyne, *Short Survey*, 61–62.

58. Breton, "Manifesto of Surrealism," 14; the statement appears as epigraph to Part II of Levy's *Surrealism* (9).

59. Gascoyne, *Short Survey*, viii; cf. 61.

60. See Gascoyne, *Short Survey*, 66, 61, 63, and Breton, "What Is Surrealism?" 64

61. Word games included the exquisite corpse—see Gascoyne, *Short Survey*, 78; for the psychological investigations, see Hugh Sykes Davies, "Surrealism at This Time and Place," in *Surrealism*, ed. Read, 138–48, and Breton, "What Is Surrealism?" 84–85; for the Gothic novels, see, e.g., André Breton, "Limits Not Frontiers of Surrealism," in *Surrealism*, ed. Read, 106–7.

62. Read, introduction to *Surrealism*, 63.

63. Gascoyne, *Short Survey*, 133–35.

64. See Breton, "What Is Surrealism?" 89, and Wayne Andrews, *The Surrealist Parade* (New York: New Directions, 1990), 130–45.

65. Breton, "What Is Surrealism?" 69–70.

66. Gascoyne, *Short Survey*, 66–67.

67. See Breton, "Limits Not Frontiers of Surrealism," 103–4; Mary Ann Caws, *André Breton* (New York: Twayne Publishers, 1971), 53–54, 118–19; and J. H. Matthews, *André Breton: Sketch for an Early Portrait* (Amsterdam: John Benjamins Publishing Co., 1986), 51–67.

68. Breton, "What Is Surrealism?" 85; Read, introduction to *Surrealism*, 90.

69. Breton, "What Is Surrealism?" 49, 52–53; Gascoyne, *Short Survey*, 80; Read, introduction to *Surrealism*, 21; Paul Eluard, "Poetic Evidence," in *Surrealism*, ed. Read, 174; Georges Hugnet, "1870 to 1936," in *Surrealism*, ed. Read, 188, 214; Levy, *Surrealism* 3, 5; Salvador Dali, quoted in Levy, *Surrealism*, 7; Davies, "Surrealism at This Time and Place," in *Surrealism*, ed. Read, 123.

70. Breton, "Exhibition X . . . Y . . ." in *What Is Surrealism?* 25; Gascoyne, *Short Survey*, 38, 7; Levy, *Surrealism*, 63, 65.

71. "Marvelous and Fantastic," 60; Byrne, "Surrealism Passes," 263 (Nicolas Calas proclaimed, "We can also claim in a sense as surrealist Barnum and his circus"—"The Meaning of Surrealism: An Interview with Nicolas Calas," in *Surrealism Pro and Con*, 16); Frye, "Men as Trees Walking," 208; McGavick, "Weird Worlds," 630–31; see also the general discussion in Kirk Varnedoe and Adam Gopnik, *High & Low: Modern Art and Popular Culture* (New York: The Museum of Modern Art, 1990).

72. Constance Rourke, *American Humor: A Study of the National Character* (New York: Harcourt, Brace and Co., 1931), 9, 297, 298, 67; for Rourke in Grand Rapids, see Samuel I. Bellman, *Constance M. Rourke* (Boston: Twayne Publishers, 1981), 17–33, and *Twentieth Century Authors*, ed. Stanley J. Kunitz and Howard Haycraft (New York: The H. W. Wilson Co., 1942), s.v. "Rourke, Constance Mayfield." De

Vries did not meet Rourke, however (Peter De Vries, letter to author, 15 March 1989).

73. Ralph Waldo Emerson, "The Poet," in *Essays: Second Series*, vol. 3 of *The Collected Works of Ralph Waldo Emerson*, ed. Joseph Slater and Douglas Emory Wilson (Cambridge: Harvard University Press, Belknap Press, 1983), 10.

74. Rourke, *American Humor*, 298–99.

75. Philip Lamantia, "Radio Voices—A Child's Bed of Sirens," in *Surrealism & Its Popular Accomplices*, ed. Franklin Rosemont (San Francisco: City Lights Books, 1980), 25; [Franklin Rosemont], "Editorial: Surrealism & Its Popular Accomplices," in *Surrealism & Its Popular Accomplices*, 3; Ado Kyrou, "Surrealism & Film," in *Surrealism & Its Popular Accomplices*, 46; Antonin Artaud, quoted in the "Surrealist Glossary" in André Breton, *What is Surrealism? Selected Writings*, ed. Franklin Rosemont (n.p.: Monad, 1978), 369. I am grateful to Ruedi Kuenzli for *Surrealism & Its Popular Accomplices*.

Chapter 4. A Reading of *But Who Wakes the Bugler?*

1. Julien Levy, *Surrealism* (New York: The Black Sun Press, 1936), 5.

2. Peter De Vries, *But Who Wakes the Bugler?* (Boston: Houghton Mifflin Co., 1940), hereafter *Bugler*.

3. An archetype of the surrealist collage novel is Max Ernst, *La femme 100 têtes* (Paris: Editions du Carrefour, 1929); the collage method is often referred to in 1930s commentaries on surrealism, e.g., Levy, *Surrealism*, 14. See, on unstable irony, Wayne Booth, *A Rhetoric of Irony* (Chicago: University of Chicago Press, 1974).

4. Fred Schwed, Jr., "Nightmares Are Fun," *Saturday Review*, 14 September 1940, 12.

5. Peter De Vries, "Poetry and the War," *College English* 5, no. 3 (December 1943): 117–18.

6. J. H. Matthews, *Surrealism and the Novel* (Ann Arbor: University of Michigan Press, 1966), 10.

7. André Breton, "Manifesto of Surrealism," in *Manifestoes of Surrealism*, trans. Richard Seaver and Helen R. Lane (Ann Arbor: University of Michigan Press, 1969), 14.

8. See on Ford *Contemporary Authors*, new rev. ser., vol. 13, ed. Linda Metzger (Detroit: Gale Research Co., 1984), and *Contemporary Poets*, 4th ed., ed. James Vinson and D. L. Kirkpatrick (New York: St. Martin's Press, 1985), s.v. "Ford, Charles Henri," and Karen L. Rood, "Charles Henri Ford," in *Dictionary of Literary Biography*, 2d ser., vol. 48, *American Poets, 1880–1945*, ed. Peter Quartermain (Detroit: Gale Research Co., 1986), 191–210.

9. Peter De Vries, letter to author, 20 October 1988.

10. *London Bulletin*, no. 7 (December 1938–January 1939): 5; reprinted in *London Bulletin: Complete Edition in Two Volumes*, Arno Series of Contemporary Art, no. 30 (New York: Arno Press, 1969), vol. 1: no. 1–9 (1938–39).

11. The description of Brezon tallies with various descriptions of Breton recorded in Anna Balakian, *André Breton* (New York: Oxford University Press, 1971).

12. Balakian, *André Breton*, 46–47. Proust nevertheless warmly proposed Breton for the Blumenthal prize. For further details, see Wayne Andrews, *The Surrealist Parade* (New York: New Directions, 1990), 34–35.

13. Balakian, *André Breton*, 173; Peter De Vries, letter to author, 1 December

1988. De Vries mentions Breton in two of his later novels, *Madder Music* (181) and *Slouching Towards Kalamazoo* (205).

14. Laughlin, on the strength of an endowment from his father, had already published twelve books when he graduated from Harvard in 1939; see John A. Harrison and Donald W. Faulkner, "James Laughlin," in *Dictionary of Literary Biography*, 2d ser., vol. 48, 275.

15. De Vries, "Poetry and the War," 118–19, esp. 119, where De Vries refers to Thomas's "free fantasia on a theme" and to psychoanalysis.

16. An actual "pioneer radio artist" who debuted in 1937 and whose soprano singing won her the Queen of Radio award eight years straight; see *Who's Who of American Women* 1, 1958–59 (Chicago: A. N. Marquis, 1958), s.v. "Dragonette, Jessica."

17. Cf. Breton, "Second Manifesto of Surrealism," in *Manifestoes*, 153, where Breton allows that surrealism is the "*amazingly prehensile tail*" of Romanticism; the characterization appears also in André Breton, "What Is Surrealism?" in *What Is Surrealism?* trans. David Gascoyne (1936; reprint, New York: Haskell House, 1974), 77.

18. See "Correspondence," *Poetry* 56 (May 1940): 108–9. This was the "proletarian poet" hoax mentioned in the preceding chapter. Charles W. Ferguson's "Art for Our Sake," *Harper's* 175 (July 1937): 219, discusses the ease with which hoaxes can be perpetrated in the age of surrealism.

19. Joseph M. De Roller, "The Lower-Case Absurd: A Study of the Novels of Peter De Vries" (Ph.D. diss., University of Rochester, 1976), 4.

20. Schwed, "Nightmares Are Fun," 12.

21. T. Jeff Evans, "The Apprentice Fiction of Peter De Vries," *Critique: Studies in Modern Fiction* 21, no. 3 (1980): 29.

22. Peter De Vries, "Universal Daydream," *Saturday Review*, 25 November 1961, 15–16.

23. See Linda Hutcheon, *A Theory of Parody* (New York: Methuen, 1985) for a discussion of modern parody as "trans-contextualizing."

24. For the Bidwell and Bruhl stories, see James Thurber, *The Middle-Aged Man on the Flying Trapeze* (New York: Harper & Brothers, 1935), 69–74 and 165–73; for Thurber's satire of pop psychology, see *Let Your Mind Alone!* (New York: Harper & Brothers, 1937).

25. Robert E. Morsberger, *James Thurber* (New York: Twayne Publishers, Inc., 1964), 58.

26. James Thurber, "The Secret Life of James Thurber," in *The Thurber Carnival* (New York: Harper & Brothers, 1945), 30–35.

27. Morsberger, *James Thurber*, 119–20.

28. Francis Hackett, quoted in Morsberger, *James Thurber*, 123.

29. Charles S. Holmes, *The Clocks of Columbus* (New York: Atheneum, 1972), 137, 149.

30. Catherine McGehee Kenney, *Thurber's Anatomy of Confusion* (Hamden, Conn.: Archon Books, 1984), 115.

31. Burton Bernstein, *Thurber: A Biography* (New York: Dodd, Mead & Co., 1975), 260.

32. Thurber, *The Middle-Aged Man*, 225.

33. Despite the parody, J. H. Bowden refers to Mr. Thwing as De Vries's agnostic "spokesman" in religious matters in his *Peter De Vries* (Boston: Twayne Publishers, 1983), 16. The real interest of the religious content of *Bugler* is its remarkable brevity in a supposedly religion-driven writer.

34. Matthews, *Surrealism and the Novel*, 77.

35. Ibid., 96.

36. Peter De Vries, "James Thurber: The Comic Prufrock," *Poetry* 63 (December 1943): 151.

37. Leonore Fleischer, "De Vries on Rewriting in the Supermarket," *Life*, 13 December 1968, 18; J. H. Bowden, *Peter De Vries*, 155.

38. Salvador Dali, "The Stinking Ass," in *Surrealists on Art*, ed. Lucy R. Lippard (Englewood Cliffs, N.J.: Prentice-Hall, Inc., 1970), 97–100; discussed in David Gascoyne, *A Short Survey of Surrealism* (1935; reprint, San Francisco: City Lights Books, 1982), 96–101.

39. Breton, "What Is Surrealism?" 83.

40. Gascoyne, *Short Survey*, 101.

41. Dali, "The Stinking Ass," 98.

42. Salvador Dali, quoted in Margaret Case Harriman, "A Dream Walking," *Reader's Digest* 35 (October 1939): 57.

43. Georges Hugnet, "1870 to 1936," in *Surrealism*, ed. Herbert Read (London: Faber and Faber Limited, 1936), 214–18; Paul Nougé, "Final Advice," *London Bulletin*, no. 1 (April 1938): 6, reprinted in *London Bulletin: Complete Edition*, vol. 1.

44. Evans, "The Apprentice Fiction," 33.

45. Constance Rourke, *American Humor: A Study of the National Character* (New York: Harcourt, Brace and Co., 1931), 202.

46. Kenneth Burke, "Surrealism," in *Surrealism Pro and Con* (New York: Gotham Book Mart, 1973), 77.

47. Hugh Sykes Davies, "Surrealism at This Time and Place," in *Surrealism*, ed. Read, 161.

48. See Jacqueline Chénieux-Gendron, *Surrealism*, trans. Vivian Folkenflik (New York: Columbia University Press, 1990), 88–93, for a recent exposition of "objective humor."

49. Burke, "Surrealism," 65–69.

50. Read, introduction to *Surrealism*, 23.

51. Paul Eluard, "Poetic Evidence," in *Surrealism*, ed. Read, 171.

52. René Magritte and Jean Scutenaire, "L'Art bourgeois," *London Bulletin*, no. 12 (15 March 1939): 13, reprinted in *London Bulletin: Complete Edition*, vol. 2.

53. Eluard, "Poetic Evidence," 171.

54. André Breton, "Exhibition X . . . Y . . ," in *What Is Surrealism?* 26.

55. Quoted by W. C. Fields's grandson Ronald J. Fields in *W. C. Fields: A Life on Film* (New York: St. Martin's Press, 1984), 221; *The Bank Dick* was released 29 November 1940 (229).

56. *The Jewish Encyclopedia* (New York: KTAV Publishing House, Inc. [1901]), s.v. "Jehoiakim"; cf. *The Universal Jewish Encyclopedia* (New York: Universal Jewish Encyclopedia Co., 1948), s.v. "Jehoiakim."

57. Breton, "What Is Surrealism?" in *What Is Surrealism?* trans. Gascoyne, 67; the segment of *The Communicating Vessels* on "The Phantom Object" also appears in this 1936 volume.

58. Levy, *Surrealism*, 5; Gascoyne, *Short Survey*, 123–24.

59. André Breton, "Beauty Will Be Convulsive," in *What Is Surrealism?* 42–43.

60. André Breton, quoted in *London Bulletin*, no. 1 (April 1938): 6; reprinted in *London Bulletin: Complete Edition*, vol. 1.

61. For Jubal, see Gen. 4:19–21. For Delia, cf. Pope, "The First Satire of the Second Book of Horace Imitated," l. 81: "Slander or Poyson, dread from *Delia's*

Rage." Charles Henri Ford's *Garden of Disorder* (London: Europa Press, 1938) also deals with freakish eccentricity; see Rood, "Charles Henri Ford."

62. See E. and M. A. Radford, "Robins," in *Encyclopedia of Superstitions*, ed. Christina Hole (London: Hutchinson, 1961).

63. Rourke, *American Humor*, 62.

64. Hugnet, "1870 to 1936," 206.

65. Walt Whitman, *An American Primer* (1904; reprint, Stevens Point, Wis.: Holy Cow! Press, 1987), 16. I am grateful to Jim Perlman for this book.

66. André Breton, "Surrealism and Painting," in *What Is Surrealism?* 11.

67. Read, introduction to *Surrealism*, 90.

68. Breton, "What Is Surrealism?" 49–50.

69. E.g., Gascoyne, *Short Survey*, 73.

70. Burke, "Surrealism," 64.

71. Breton, "Manifesto of Surrealism," 47; these concluding words of the first manifesto are often quoted—e.g., in Levy, *Surrealism*, 1.

72. Hugnet, "1870 to 1936," 200.

73. Tristan Tzara, quoted in Edmund Wilson, *Axel's Castle* (1931; reprint, New York: W. W. Norton & Co., 1984), 308.

74. André Breton, *Anthologie de l'humour noir* (1940; reprint, Paris: Editions du Sagittaire, 1950), 64–70; a note on 67 refers to *"Confessions d'un mangeur d'opium."*

75. André Breton, "Limits Not Frontiers of Surrealism," in *Surrealism*, ed. Read, 103.

76. James Thurber, quoted in Bernstein, *Thurber*, 237.

77. Cleanth Brooks, "Wit and High Seriousness," in *Modern Poetry and the Tradition* (Chapel Hill: University of North Carolina Press, 1939), 18–38.

78. Rourke, *American Humor*, 203, 299–302.

79. Clarence A. Andrews, *Chicago in Story* (Iowa City: Midwest Heritage Publishing Company, 1982), 225–27.

80. William Carlos Williams, preface to Ford's *Garden of Disorder*, 11.

81. Breton, quoting the "Second Manifesto of Surrealism" in "What Is Surrealism?" 82.

82. Nougé, "Final Advice," 6.

83. Breton, "Limits Not Frontiers," 111–12.

84. Read, introduction to *Surrealism*, 40.

85. Victor Shklovsky, "Sterne's *Tristram Shandy:* Stylistic Commentary," in *Russian Formalist Criticism*, trans. Lee T. Lemon and Marion J. Reis (Lincoln: University of Nebraska Press, 1965), 27.

86. "Marvelous & Fantastic," *Time*, 14 December 1936, 60.

87. *The Home Book of Proverbs, Maxims, and Familiar Phrases*, ed. Burton Stevenson (New York: Macmillan, 1956), v., 2499. The shape of the idea is traced, not very enlighteningly, through "Who shall keep the keepers?" (Thomas Fuller), "Yes, and who will ward the warders?" (Juvenal), and "It would be absurd that a guardian should need a guard" (Plato).

88. Evans, "The Apprentice Fiction," 42.

89. *The Girl on the Magazine Cover: Songs of Irving Berlin*, RCA Gold Seal recording AGL1–3704. Berlin's lyrics run far afield from De Vries's title. Mr. Thwing loves sleep but not militantly enough to go hunting for any bugler—anyway, he usually wakes up slowly and leisurely, ignoring the alarm clock. And Berlin's ditty, written for a 1918 Army review and not revived for World War II audiences until *This Is the Army* in 1942, refers specifically to military life, of which there is no trace in the novel. If Berlin's lyric had triggered the novel's title, wouldn't it be "But Who

Wakes Up the Bugler?" or "But Who Wakes the Bugler Up?" See Richard Lewine and Alfred Simon, *Songs of the American Theater* (New York: Dodd, Mead & Co., 1973), 360, and *The New Grove Dictionary of American Music*, vol. 1, ed. H. Wiley Hitchcock and Stanley Sadie (London: Macmillan Press, Ltd, 1986), s.v. "Berlin, Irving."

90. Schwed, "Nightmares Are Fun," 12.

91. Display ad, *New Yorker*, 7 September 1940, 56. The display ad in the *Chicago Daily News* of 2 October 1940, 15, more accurately promises "unreality" and "1940's most screwball book."

92. J. H. Bowden, *Peter De Vries*, 11.

93. Lewis Carroll, *The Annotated Alice* (New York: Bramhall House, 1960), 238–39.

94. Peter De Vries, "Conscript," *Poetry* 58 (July 1941): 184.

95. See William S. Rubin, *Dada, Surrealism, and Their Heritage* (New York: The Museum of Modern Art, 1968), 16, 19.

96. James Laughlin, in a letter to the author dated 16 June 1991, wrote of De Vries, "I don't think I ever met him, but I liked his stories."

97. "A Reader's List," *New Republic*, 16 September 1940, 394.

98. "Briefly Noted," *New Yorker*, 7 September 1940, 57–58.

99. Lisle Bell, "But Who Wakes the Bugler?" *New York Herald Tribune*, 1 September 1940, sec. 9, p. 8.

100. Beatrice Sherman, "But Who Wakes the Bugler?" *New York Times Book Review*, 8 September 1940, 7 (not, as in Straayer, 12).

101. Ruth Hard Bonner, "Surrealist Fun: *But Who Wakes the Bugler*," *Boston Evening Transcript*, 7 September 1940, sec. 5, p. 1.

102. Sterling North, "Typewriter Bites Local Fantasist," *Chicago Daily News*, 9 October 1940, 20.

103. Jack Conroy, "Love, Madness and Humor in Psychological Novel," *Chicago Sun Book Week*, 4 July 1943, 2. interestingly, the review is illustrated by the painting "The Madhouse" by Pavel Tchelitchew, Charles Henri Ford's companion.

104. Schwed, "Nightmares Are Fun," 12; this extraordinary lead sentence is quoted with fondness by students of De Vries, but only once have I seen it remarked that Mr. Schwed should have "blocked that metaphor!" See Roderick H. Jellema, "Peter De Vries: The Decline and Fall of Moot Point," *The Reformed Journal* 13, no. 3 (April 1963): 9; Jellema notes the mixed metaphors but also misquotes Schwed.

105. Breton, "Second Manifesto of Surrealism," 179.

106. Schwed, "Nightmares Are Fun," 12.

107. Peter De Vries, "A Note on This Issue," *Poetry* 62 (August 1943): 274.

108. John J. Timmerman, "Mr. Thwing Is Not Pound-Proof," *The Calvin Forum*, October 1940, 54–55.

109. Herbert J. Muller, "Surrealism: A Dissenting Opinion," in *Surrealism Pro and Con*, 59.

110. Peter De Vries, "'You Hear Cliches, and Dislodge Them': An Interview with Peter De Vries," interview by John K. Hutchens, *New York Herald Tribune Book Review*, 18 March 1962, 5.

111. Sybil S. Steinberg, "Peter De Vries & Katinka Loeser," *Publishers Weekly*, 16 October 1981, 7–8. In Van Allen Bradley's *Book Collector's Handbook of Values, 1982–1983 Edition* (New York: G. P. Putnam's Sons, 1982), the "fledgling work" is listed at seventy-five to one hundred dollars (137).

112. Peter De Vries, "Peter De Vries," interview by Roy Newquist, in *Counterpoint* (Chicago: Rand McNally & Co., 1964), 148.

113. Cornelius John Ter Maat, "Three Novelists and a Community: A Study of American Novelists with Dutch Calvinist Origins" (Ed.D. diss., University of Michigan, 1963) and Arnold Ray Hoffman, "The Sense of Place: Peter De Vries, J. F. Powers, and Flannery O'Connor" (Ph.D. diss., Michigan State University, 1970) do not mention *Bugler.* Nancy Down, "The Search for Authenticity in the Satiric Worlds of Nathanael West and Peter De Vries" (Ph.D. diss., Drew University, 1986) mentions "surrealism" but uses the word as a synonym for "bizarre" and says little about *Bugler.* Jack Kent Boyd, "The Novels of Peter De Vries: A Critical Introduction" (Ph.D. diss., University of Arkansas, 1971) merely mentions the first three novels. Roderick Jellema, *Peter De Vries: A Critical Essay* (Grand Rapids, Mich.: William B. Eerdmans Publishing Co., 1966), dismisses them as "now out of print and relatively unimportant" (15); Jellema had earlier called the novels merely "the products of a competent apprenticeship," in "The Decline and Fall of Moot Point," 9. Fred Rodewald, "The Comic *Eiron* in the Novels of Peter De Vries," *Quartet* 6, no. 41 (Winter 1973), begins, "Any critical discussion of the work of Peter De Vries . . . reasonably ignores his three apprentice novels of the 1940s" (34); Rodewald cites the interview by Hutchens.

114. Israel Shenker, *Words and Their Masters* (Garden City, N.Y.: Doubleday & Co., Inc., 1974), 96; Thomas L. Kilpatrick and Patsy-Rose Hoshiko, *Illinois! Illinois! An Annotated Bibliography of Fiction* (Metuchen, N.J.: The Scarecrow Press, Inc., 1979), 360.

115. De Roller, "The Lower-Case Absurd," 6–7.

116. T. Jeff Evans, "Peter De Vries: A Retrospective," *American Humor* 7, no. 2 (Fall 1980): 14–15.

117. Evans, "The Apprentice Fiction," 34. Evans claims he is "forsaking the viscera of biography" but not before he has ventured that "the roots of De Vries's concern with the self in relation to an authoritarian system probably lie somewhere in his strict Dutch Reformed Church background" (28).

118. J. H. Bowden, *Peter De Vries*, 15–16, 1.

119. Malcolm Bradbury, *The Modern American Novel* (1983; reprint, Oxford: Oxford University Press, 1984), 121.

120. Ibid., 100, 66.

121. Ibid., 121–22.

122. Mary Ann Caws, *Surrealism and the Literary Imagination* (The Hague: Mouton & Co., 1966), 79.

123. "Surrealism aims to destroy by the denial of reason . . . the evidence of evil design is everywhere. . . . The question is, what have we, plain American people, done to deserve this sore affliction that has been visited upon us so direly; who has brought down this curse upon us; who has let into our homeland this horde of germ-carrying art vermin?" A congressman's speech, quoted in Franklin Rosemont, "André Breton and the First Principles of Surrealism," introduction to André Breton, *What is Surrealism? Selected Writings* (n.p.: Monad, 1978), 138, n. 93. Such vehemency can be heard from the first appearance of dada in America; see "Articles on New York Dada from New York Newspapers," in *New York Dada*, ed. Rudolf E. Kuenzli (New York: Willis Locker & Owens, 1986), 127–45.

124. Rosemont, "André Breton and the First Principles of Surrealism," 119–20. David S. Reynolds, in *Beneath the American Renaissance: The Subversive Imagination in the Age of Emerson and Melville* (Cambridge: Harvard University Press, 1988), records a variety of discoveries in what he terms "a presurrealistic American style" (453).

125. Caws, *André Breton*, 25.

126. Jellema, *Peter De Vries*, 44; Kathleen Verduin, in "Teaching *Moby-Dick* in a

Calvinist Setting," in *Approaches to Teaching Melville's* Moby-Dick, ed. Martin Bickman (New York: The Modern Language Association of America, 1985), likens De Vries to Captain Ahab himself: "Like De Vries, whose novels endlessly explore the same pattern, the same confrontation between religion and irreligion, . . . Ahab simply can't let it alone" (82).

127. Jellema, *Peter De Vries*, 44.

128. J. H. Matthews, *André Breton* (New York: Columbia University Press, 1967), 23.

129. Burke, "Surrealism," 70. Not all readers will accept Burke's epithets, but they do seem to fit De Vries's experience of both philosophies.

130. Books by J. H. Matthews and Mary Ann Caws and such studies as Jack J. Spector, *The Aesthetics of Freud* (New York: Praeger Publishers, 1972); Morton Gurewitch, *Comedy: The Irrational Vision* (Ithaca: Cornell University Press, 1975); and Linda Hutcheon, *A Theory of Parody* (New York: Methuen, 1985) have assisted my approach to *But Who Wakes the Bugler?*

Chapter 5. Surrealizations: The Unofficial Career of Peter De Vries

1. Peter De Vries, "Perelmania," *New Yorker*, 13 August 1984, 88–91. I am grateful to Renee Huntley for this article.

2. Malcolm Cowley, blurb in the Penguin paperback edition of Peter De Vries, *Consenting Adults* (New York: Penguin Books, 1981), [i]. The compliment "is simply a quote [Cowley] sent to the publishers" (Peter De Vries, letter to author, 26 June 1989).

3. Rochelle Girson, "The Author," *Saturday Review*, 24 March 1962, 20.

4. Peter De Vries, "An Interview with Peter De Vries," interview by Douglas M. Davis, *College English* 28, no. 7 (April 1967): 528.

5. André Breton, "Manifesto of Surrealism," in *Manifestoes of Surrealism*, trans. Richard Seaver and Helen R. Lane (Ann Arbor: University of Michigan Press, 1969), 10.

6. Peter De Vries, "The Children's Hour; or, Hopscotch and Soda," *New Yorker*, 18 August 1956, 20–22; reprinted in *Without a Stitch in Time* (Little, Brown and Co., 1972), 240–46.

7. Peter De Vries, "Peter De Vries," interview by Roy Newquist, in *Counterpoint* (Chicago: Rand McNally & Co., 1964), 149.

8. Breton, "Manifesto of Surrealism," 24.

9. Peter De Vries, "'You Hear Cliches, and Dislodge Them': An Interview with Peter De Vries," interview by John K. Hutchens, *New York Herald Tribune Book Review*, 18 March 1962, 5.

10. Peter De Vries, "An Interview in New York with Peter De Vries," interview by Richard B. Sale, *Studies in the Novel* 1, no. 3 (Fall 1969): 365–66; see also Leonore Fleischer, "De Vries on Rewriting in the Supermarket," *Life*, 13 December 1968, 18; and Girson, "The Author," 20.

11. Peter De Vries, "Exploring Inner Space," *Michigan Quarterly Review* 9 (April 1969): 86, 91.

12. Peter De Vries, "Peter De Vries: Being Seriously Funny," interview by Ben Yagoda, *New York Times Magazine*, 12 June 1983, 54. Peter De Vries, "Fusion and Confusion," *Poetry* 52 (July 1938): 236–40.

13. Peter De Vries, "What's All That About Commuters?" *New York Herald Tribune Book Review*, 30 August 1959, 2.

14. De Vries, interview by Newquist, 153; cf. [Douglas M. Davis], "My Stuff Is Really Over My Head," *National Observer*, 9 August 1965, 19.

15. De Vries, interview by Yagoda, 55.

16. See, e.g., *Through the Fields of Clover*, 256–57 and *The Blood of the Lamb*, 32.

17. Peter De Vries, "James Thurber: The Comic Prufrock," *Poetry* 63 (December 1943): 157–58; the theme also appears in De Vries's "A Note on This Issue," *Poetry* 62 (August 1943): 272–77, and "Poetry and the War," *College English* 5, no. 3 (December 1943): 113–20.

18. De Vries, interview by Newquist, 154.

19. Richard Boston, *An Anatomy of Laughter* (London: Collins, 1974), 230–31.

20. See, for example, Patrick Brantlinger, *Bread and Circuses: Theories of Mass Culture as Social Decay* (Ithaca: Cornell University Press, 1983).

21. See *The International Directory of Literary Magazines and Small Presses*, 23rd ed., 1987–88, ed. Len Fulton (Paradise, Calif.: Dustbooks, 1987), 202.

22. Paul Theroux, "Groucho Redivivus," *New York Times Book Review*, 16 October 1977, 15, 42.

23. Girson, "The Author," 20.

24. Respectively, De Vries, interview by Newquist, 148–49; interview by Davis, 525; interview by Sale, 368; and "An Interview with Peter De Vries," interview by Jean W. Ross, in *DLB Yearbook*, 1982, ed. Richard Ziegfeld (Detroit: Gale Research Co., 1983), 136.

25. Respectively, Peter De Vries, interview by Newquist, 149; interview by Davis, 525; interview by Sale, 368–69; interview by Ross, 136; and "Peter De Vries & Katinka Loeser," interview by Sybil Steinberg, *Publishers Weekly*, 16 October 1981, 8.

26. De Vries, interview by Sale, 369.

27. De Vries, interview by Newquist, 149.

28. De Vries, interview by Davis, 525.

29. Peter De Vries, "The Turf is Familiar," interview by Lewis Grossberger, *People*, 29 September 1980, 42.

30. De Vries, interview by Steinberg, 6.

31. De Vries, interview by Hutchens, 5; cf. interview by Newquist, 153, and Allen B. Borden, "Peter De Vries," *Wilson Library Bulletin* 33, no. 7 (March 1959): 460.

32. De Vries, interview by Ross, 137.

33. See James Tucker, *The Novels of Anthony Powell* (New York: Columbia University Press, 1976), esp. 1–5.

34. De Vries, interview by Davis, 525; cf. interview by Newquist, 153, and T. A. Straayer, "Peter De Vries: A Bibliography of Secondary Sources, 1940–1981," *Bulletin of Bibliography* 39, no. 3 (September 1982): 151, item C-6.

35. De Vries, interview by Yagoda, 50; cf. interview by Hutchens, 5; interview by Ross, 137.

36. Walter Blair and Hamlin Hill, *America's Humor* (New York: Oxford University Press, 1978), 503.

37. De Vries, interview by Yagoda, 45; cf. Girson, "The Author," 20; interview by Newquist, 147; *World Authors 1950–1970*, ed. John Wakeman (New York: The H. W. Wilson Company, 1975), s.v. "De Vries, Peter"; interview by Grossberger, 41–42.

38. Whitney Balliett, quoted in Jean W. Ross, "Peter De Vries," *DLB Yearbook, 1982,* ed. Richard Ziegfeld (Detroit: Gale Research Co., 1983), 135–36.

39. De Vries, interview by Newquist, 152; interview by Davis, 525; "Laughter in Theory and Practice," Calvin College Lecture Series, Grand Rapids, Mich., 10 April 1979, quoted in Straayer, 147.

40. Melvin Maddocks, "Galloping Lust, Crawling Remorse," *Time,* 21 September 1981, 81.

41. Breton, "Second Manifesto of Surrealism," 125.

42. Edouard Roditi, "The Unspoken Word," *Poetry* 63 (October 1943): 50.

43. Dudley Fitts, "Mighty Lak a Whale," *Poetry* 64 (April 1944): 44. Edouard Roditi makes a similar point in "Translator's Dilemma," *Poetry* 67 (February 1946): 278–82.

44. John Gross, review of *The Prick of Noon, New York Times,* 5 April 1985, sec. C., p. 25, reprinted in "De Vries, Peter," in *Contemporary Literary Criticism,* vol. 46, ed. Daniel G. Marowski and Roger Matuz (Detroit: Gale Research Co., 1988); Gross does not follow up on the implications.

45. Lautréamont, *Maldoror (Les Chants de Maldoror),* trans. Guy Wernham (1943; reprint, New York: New Directions, 1965).

46. "*Ulalume* is a surrealist poem if there ever was one," wrote John Peale Bishop introducing Ford's "Chainpoems" section of *New Directions in Prose & Poetry 1940,* ed. James Laughlin (Norfolk, Conn.: New Directions, 1940), 365. Breton expressed admiration for "Ulalume" in an interview by Ford published in *View* in August 1941; see André Breton, "Interview with Charles Henri Ford," in *Conversations: The Autobiography of Surrealism* (New York: Paragon House, 1993), 183.

47. Frederic Raphael, introduction to *The Mackerel Plaza* (New York: Penguin Books, 1986), xi; Raphael's acute remark is unaccompanied by discussion of its implications.

48. Jack Kent Boyd, "The Novels of Peter De Vries: A Critical Introduction" (Ph.D. diss., University of Arkansas, 1971), 60–61. The source of De Vries's epigraph for the second part of *The Tents of Wickedness* ("Convention has always more heroes than revolt"), Ben Hecht, was scarcely a hero of convention. Dubbed "Ben-Dada" by his Berlin Dadaist friends, Hecht jeers at convention in the source text, his scandalous best-selling novel *A Jew in Love,* where conformists are described as being "mutilated" by their conformity. Doug Fetherling sees "the influence of [Hecht's] imagery . . . in writers like Peter De Vries." See *The Dada Almanac,* ed. Richard Huelsenbeck, English edition presented by Malcolm Green, Atlas Arkhive 1 (London: Atlas Press, 1993), 64; Ben Hecht, *A Jew in Love* (1931; reprint, New York: Triangle Books, 1938), 208; and Doug Fetherling, *The Five Lives of Ben Hecht* (Toronto: Lester and Orpen Limited, 1977), 16.

49. "La beauté sera CONVULSIVE ou ne sera pas"; the last sentence in André Breton, *Nadja* (Paris: Editions Gallimard, 1964), 187; see Breton's "Beauty Will Be Convulsive," in *What Is Surrealism?* trans. David Gascoyne (1936; reprint, New York: Haskell House, 1974), 37–43.

50. Boyd remarks this unusual pairing as evidence of De Vries's "protean" nature ("The Novels of Peter De Vries," 16); for the publication history of the novel, see Edwin T. Bowden, *Peter De Vries: A Bibliography 1934–1977* (Austin: Humanities Research Center, The University of Texas at Austin, 1978), 29–32.

51. Joseph M. De Roller, "The Lower-Case Absurd: A Study of the Novels of Peter De Vries" (Ph.D. diss., University of Rochester, 1976), 60.

52. Arthur Kroker, Marilouise Kroker, and David Cook, *Panic Encyclopedia* (New York: St. Martin's Press, 1989), 215.

53. Craig Challender, "Peter De Vries: The Case for Comic Seriousness," *Studies in American Humor* 1, no. 1 (April 1974): 50.

54. André Breton, quoted in the "Surrealist Glossary" in *What is Surrealism? Selected Writings*, ed. Franklin Rosemont (n.p.: Monad, 1978), 376.

55. Breton, "Manifesto of Surrealism," 27.

56. Elton Trueblood, *The Humor of Christ* (New York: Harper and Row, 1964); Richard Boston, *An Anatomy of Laughter* (London: Collins, 1974), 45.

57. Boston, *An Anatomy of Laughter*, 47.

58. One who noticed the association was Joseph M. De Roller, who writes, "Repeatedly in *Let Me Count the Ways*, De Vries blends slapstick with surrealism to create a tension between reassurance and anxiety which is at once exhilarating and disturbing" in "The Lower-Case Absurd," 77–78.

59. Lautréamont, *Maldoror*, 263.

60. F. Scott Fitzgerald, *The Great Gatsby* (New York: Charles Scribner's Sons, 1925), 20–21.

61. Breton, "Manifesto of Surrealism," 32–35. Tom Waltz indulges in other gestures of disdain for conventional reality: as Chester Eisinger says, "One of [De Vries's] humorous devices . . . as in the Tom Waltz section of *Let Me Count the Ways*, is to counter the world's madness with the most extravagant and wildest kind of individual action"; see *Contemporary Novelists*, 3d ed., ed. James Vinson (New York: St. Martin's Press, 1982), s.v. "De Vries, Peter."

62. J. J. Lamberts, "I Love You Just the Same," *The Banner*, 4 October 1974, 15.

63. *DAB*, Supplement Five, 1951–55, ed. John A. Garraty (New York: Charles Scribner's Sons, 1977), s.v. "Blodgett, John Wood."

64. Roland Barthes, "To Write: An Intransitive Verb?" in *The Structuralists from Marx to Levi-Strauss*, ed. Richard T. De George and Fernande M. De George (Garden City, N.Y.: Anchor Books, 1972), 161–62.

65. E.g., Peter De Vries, "Art's a Funny Thing," *Esquire* 5 (February 1936): 59, 124, 127; "American Primitive," *Story* 29 (September-October 1946): 28–33.

66. Salvador Dali, "Playboy Interview: Salvador Dali," *Playboy* 11, no. 7 (July 1964): 41, 44.

67. Malcolm Cowley, *Exile's Return* (New York: Viking, 1951).

68. See M. H. Abrams, *Natural Supernaturalism* (New York: W. W. Norton & Co., 1971).

69. This is Charles Baudelaire, *Flowers of Evil*, trans. George Dillon and Edna St. Vincent Millay (New York: Harper & Brothers, 1936). "Abstract me, silent ships!" appears in "Maestra et Errabunda," 42–43.

70. H. L. Mencken, "On Being an American," in *Prejudices: A Selection*, ed. James T. Farrell (New York: Vintage Books, 1958), 93.

Chapter 6. In "The Extravagant Vein in American Humor"

1. In "The Lower-Case Absurd: A Study of the Novels of Peter De Vries" (Ph.D. diss., University of Rochester, 1976), Joseph M. De Roller discusses De Vries's "juxtaposed mutually illuminating scenes" (53) and "juxtaposing works . . . not only his own but those of other writers as well" (72). It is only a small step from this vision of intertextuality into *les champs magnetiques*.

2. Richard Keller Simon, *The Labyrinth of the Comic* (Tallahassee: Florida State University Press, 1985), 239.

3. Arthur Koestler, *The Act of Creation* (New York: Dell, 1967), 27.

4. Ibid., 35, 317.

5. John Allen Paulos, *Mathematics and Humor* (Chicago: University of Chicago Press, 1980), 26–27, 80–99.

6. Kenneth Burke, quoted in Robert McMahon, "Kenneth Burke's Divine Comedy: The Literary Form of *The Rhetoric of Religion*," *PMLA* 104, no. 1 (January 1989): 59.

7. See "The Technique of Jokes," in Sigmund Freud, *Jokes and Their Relation to the Unconscious*, trans. and ed. James Strachey (New York: W. W. Norton & Co., 1960), 16–89.

8. Sigmund Freud, "Humour," in *Collected Papers*, vol. 5, ed. James Strachey, The International Psycho-Analytical Library, no. 37, ed. Ernest Jones (London: The Hogarth Press and the Institute of Psycho-Analysis, 1950), 215–21.

9. Freud, "Jokes," 86–88.

10. Jacqueline Chénieux-Gendron, *Surrealism*, trans. Vivian Folkenflik (New York: Columbia University Press, 1990), 185.

11. H. R. Hays, "Surrealist Influence in Contemporary English and American Poetry," *Poetry* 54 (July 1939): 202–9.

12. Edouard Roditi, "Oscar Wilde's Poetry as Art History," *Poetry* 67 (March 1946): 322–38.

13. J. H. Bowden, *Peter De Vries* (Boston: Twayne Publishers, 1983), 134–35.

14. E.g., Patrick Brantlinger, *Bread and Circuses* (Ithaca: Cornell University Press, 1983), 154–83.

15. William Skaff, *The Philosophy of T. S. Eliot: From Skepticism to a Surrealist Poetic, 1909–1927* (Philadelphia: University of Pennsylvania Press, 1986), 3, 131–32.

16. For the affinity between the early Eliot and the American avant-garde, see Matthew Josephson, *Life among the Surrealists* (New York: Holt, Rinehart and Winston, 1962).

17. Chénieux-Gendron, *Surrealism*, 16.

18. Jesse Bier, *The Rise and Fall of American Humor* (New York: Holt, Rinehart and Winston, 1968), 284, 319.

19. Walter Blair and Hamlin Hill, *American Humor: From Poor Richard to Doonesbury* (New York: Oxford University Press, 1978), 416. See also Albert Sonnenfeld, "The Last of the Red-Hot Dadas: Ring Lardner, American Playwright," *Dada/Surrealism*, no. 8 (1978): 36–44.

20. Blair and Hill, *American Humor*, 427, 434, 444, 500–503.

21. J. H. Matthews, *The Imagery of Surrealism* (Syracuse, N.Y.: Syracuse University Press, 1977), xiv–xv.

22. Ibid., xv.

23. Peter De Vries, letter to author, 15 March 1989.

24. See *Dictionary of Literary Themes and Motifs*, ed. Jean-Charles Seigneuret (New York: Greenwood Press, 1988), s.v. "Alchemy," "Alienation," "Nihilism," and "Seduction."

25. See André Breton, "Interview with Professor Freud," in *Freud As We Knew Him*, ed. Hendrik M. Ruitenbeek (Detroit: Wayne State University Press, 1973), 63–64, and Jack S. Spector, *The Aesthetics of Freud* (New York: Praeger Publishers, 1972), 148, 153–54.

26. Ernest Jones, M. D., *The Life and Work of Sigmund Freud*, vol. 3 (New York: Basic Books, 1957), 235.

27. Gerald Graff, preface to Charles Newman, *The Post-Modern Aura* (Evanston, Ill.: Northwestern University Press, 1985), ii.

28. Bier, *Rise and Fall*, 303.

29. Dan Quayle, quoted in *Newsweek*, 22 May 1989, 33.

30. Hays, "Surrealist Influence," 209.

31. See J. H. Matthews, "André Breton and Painting: The Case of Arshile Gorky," *Dada/Surrealism*, no. 17 (1988): 44.

32. Newman, *The Post-Modern Aura*, 188.

33. There is, in any event, debunking within surrealism: some theoreticians "believe that Bretonian hypocrisy must be unmasked, and authenticity tracked down amid the make-believe," and Lautréamont himself "multiplies the enigmas: the violence of absolute derision and revolt [in *Maldoror*] is then, in the *Poésies*, itself derided" (Chénieux-Gendron, *Surrealism*, 8, 17).

34. J. H. Matthews, *Surrealism and the Novel* (Ann Arbor: University of Michigan Press, 1966), 5–6; cf. 89.

35. Matthews, *Imagery of Surrealism*, 5.

36. Matthews, *Surrealism and the Novel*, 3, 171–73, 176.

37. Matthews, *Imagery of Surrealism*, 29.

38. Ibid., 58.

39. Mary Ann Caws, *André Breton* (New York: Twayne, 1971), 17–18, 51–52, 16, 34–35, 55–56, 60.

40. Matthews, *Surrealism and the Novel*, 10.

41. Stamos Metzidakis, "Breton and Poetic Originality," *Dada/Surrealism*, no. 17 (1988): 32.

42. André Breton, quoted in Matthews, "André Breton and Painting," 40.

43. Ibid., 44.

44. André Breton, "Second Manifesto of Surrealism," in *Manifestoes of Surrealism*, trans. Richard Seaver and Helen R. Lane (Ann Arbor: University of Michigan Press, 1969), 153.

45. Chénieux-Gendron, *Surrealism*, 30.

46. Ibid., 1.

47. Ibid., 187.

48. Alexis de Tocqueville, *Democracy in America*, vol. 2 (New York: Vintage Books, 1945), 106.

49. Newman, *The Post-Modern Aura*, 79.

50. Kenneth Burke, quoted in Spector, *Aesthetics of Freud*, 158–59.

51. See Darcy O'Brien's "Critique of Psychoanalytic Criticism, or What Joyce Did and Did Not Do," *James Joyce Quarterly* (Spring 1976): 275–91. I am grateful to Jim Bass for this article. "'In classic paintings,' Freud declared, 'I look for the subconscious—in a surrealist painting for the conscious'"; quoted in Wayne Andrews, *The Surrealist Parade* (New York: New Directions, 1990), 109.

52. Freud, "Humour," 217.

53. Ibid., 218.

54. Blair and Hill, *American Humor*, 221.

55. Freud, "Humour," 220.

56. Ibid., 216.

57. Bier, *Rise and Fall*, 254.

58. Linda Hutcheon, *A Theory of Parody* (New York: Methuen, 1985), 11.

59. Ibid., 20.

60. Ibid., 101.

61. Ibid., 103; this is not to deny that the parodied text sometimes *is* under attack; George A. Test, in *Satire: Spirit and Art* (Tampa: University of South Florida

Press, 1991), cites De Vries's "Requiem for a Noun" as a paradigmatic "satiric attack" (160–61).

62. Hutcheon, *A Theory of Parody*, 101.

63. Ibid., 23.

64. Matei Calinescu, "Parody and Intertextuality," *Semiotica* 65, nos. 1–2 (1987): 187.

65. Wayne Booth, *Critical Understanding* (Chicago: University of Chicago Press, 1979), 232–62, 339, 349, appendix.

66. Anthony Burgess, review of *Sauce for the Goose*, *New York*, 28 September 1981, 64.

67. On this problem, see Rudolf E. Kuenzli, "Derridada," *L'esprit créatur* 20, no. 2 (Summer 1980): 12–21.

68. Walter Redfern, *Puns* (1984; reprint, Oxford: Basil Blackwell and Andre Deutsch, 1986), 111, 123. Ben Yagoda, in "Peter De Vries: Being Seriously Funny," *New York Times Magazine*, 12 June 1983, mentions "the De Vriesism—a locution in which the literal and the metaphorical are paradoxically merged. Husband: 'Come to bed.' Wife: 'I'm too tired'" (54).

69. *The Oxter English Dictionary*, ed. George Stone Saussy III (New York: Facts on File, 1984).

70. John Ellison Kahn, "Polysemania, Semantic Taint, and Related Conditions," *Verbatim* 12, no. 3 (Winter 1986): 1–3.

71. Peter De Vries, "Different Cultural Levels Eat Here," *New Yorker* 22 (16 November 1946): 26–28; reprinted in *No But I Saw the Movie* and *Without a Stitch in Time*.

72. Sigmund Freud, *Civilization and Its Discontents*, trans. and ed. James Strachey (New York: W. W. Norton & Co., 1961), 92.

73. Peter De Vries, "Delightful, Delicious, Delectable, De Vries," interview by Edward Morris, *Writer's Digest*, January 1978, 8.

74. Newman, *The Post-Modern Aura*, 96–99.

75. Burgess, review of *Sauce for the Goose*, 64.

76. Allen Bloom, *The Closing of the American Mind* (New York: Simon and Schuster, 1987); E. D. Hirsch, Jr., *Cultural Literacy* (Boston: Houghton Mifflin Company, 1987).

77. I. A. Richards, *Practical Criticism* (New York: Harcourt, Brace & World, Inc., 1929).

78. Peter De Vries, quoted in *The Portable Curmudgeon*, ed. Jon Winokur (New York: New American Library, 1987), 7, 269.

79. Peter De Vries, "Exploring Inner Space," *Michigan Quarterly Review* 9 (April 1969): 85–87. Not long after first reading this piece, I enjoyed watching De Vries's son Jon in a lead role as a clone in an episode of the television series *Star Trek: The Next Generation*.

80. Peter De Vries, "The Turf is Familiar," interview by Lewis Grossberger, *People*, 29 September 1980, 41.

81. Kenneth Burke, *Language as Symbolic Action* (Berkeley and Los Angeles: University of California Press, 1966), 20.

82. McMahon, "Kenneth Burke's Divine Comedy," 53, 61–62.

83. Peter De Vries, "Peter De Vries," interview by Roy Newquist, in *Counterpoint* (Chicago: Rand McNally & Co., 1964), 150.

84. Richard Boston, *An Anatomy of Laughter* (London: Collins, 1974), 229–36.

85. William R. Higgins, "Peter De Vries," in *Dictionary of Literary Biography*, 2d

ser., vol. 6, *American Novelists Since World War II*, ed. James E. Kibler, Jr. (Detroit: Gale Research Co., 1980), 83.

86. Paul Theroux, "Peter De Vries: What Is the Thinking Man's Cereal? Joyce Carol Oates," *New York Times Book Review*, 27 October 1974, 6–7.

87. Melvin Maddocks, "Chase Scenes by Kafka," *Christian Science Monitor*, 22 July 1965, 11.

88. De Vries frequently refers to the Nietzschian dialectic of Apollonian and Dionysian, most prominently in *Reuben, Reuben*. Leonore Fleischer wrote that in *The Cat's Pajamas & Witch's Milk* De Vries "tells a Dionysiac tale in Apollonian terms." Vice versa. See Fleischer, "A Master Sharpens His Comic Focus," *Life*, 13 December 1968, 16.

89. Yagoda, "Peter De Vries," 42.

90. Paul Gray, "How the Sexual Revolution Began," *Time*, 11 July 1983, 68.

91. The phrase is Morton Gurewitch's, in *Comedy: The Irrational Vision* (Ithaca: Cornell University Press, 1975).

92. Burke, *Language as Symbolic Action*, 20.

Works Cited

Edwin T. Bowden provides a thorough bibliography of Peter De Vries's works through 1977 in *Peter De Vries: A Bibliography 1934–1977*, Tower Bibliographical Series, no. 14 (Austin: Humanities Research Center, The University of Texas at Austin, 1978), and T. A. Straayer gives an invaluable annotated guide to the secondary sources through 1981 in "Peter De Vries: A Bibliography of Secondary Sources, 1940–1981," *Bulletin of Bibliography* 39, no. 3 (September 1982): 146–69; their classification systems are followed in sections I and II below. Section III lists works primarily concerned with surrealism, and section IV lists other works cited.

I. Works by Peter De Vries

A. BOOKS

But Who Wakes the Bugler? Boston: Houghton Mifflin Co., 1940.

The Handsome Heart. New York: Coward-McCann, Inc., 1943.

Angels Can't Do Better. New York: Coward-McCann, Inc., 1944.

No But I Saw the Movie. Boston: Little, Brown and Co., 1952.

The Tunnel of Love. Boston: Little, Brown and Co., 1954.

Comfort Me With Apples. Boston: Little, Brown and Co., 1956.

The Tunnel of Love, A Play. By Joseph Fields and Peter De Vries. Boston: Little, Brown and Co., 1957.

The Mackerel Plaza. Boston: Little, Brown and Co., 1958.

The Tents of Wickedness. Boston: Little, Brown and Co., 1959.

Through the Fields of Clover. Boston: Little, Brown and Co., 1961.

The Blood of the Lamb. Boston: Little, Brown and Co., 1962.

Reuben, Reuben. Boston: Little, Brown and Co., 1964.

Let Me Count the Ways. Boston: Little, Brown and Co., 1965.

The Vale of Laughter. Boston: Little, Brown and Co., 1967.

The Cat's Pajamas & Witch's Milk. Boston: Little, Brown and Co., 1968.

Mrs. Wallop. Boston: Little, Brown and Co., 1970.

Into Your Tent I'll Creep. Boston: Little, Brown and Co., 1971.

Without a Stitch in Time: A Selection of the Best Humorous Short Pieces. Boston: Little, Brown and Co., 1972.

Forever Panting. Boston: Little, Brown and Co., 1973.

The Glory of the Hummingbird. Boston: Little, Brown and Co., 1974.

I Hear America Swinging. Boston: Little, Brown and Co., 1976.

Madder Music. Boston: Little, Brown and Co., 1977.

Consenting Adults, or The Duchess Will Be Furious. Boston: Little, Brown and Co., 1980.

Sauce for the Goose. Boston: Little, Brown and Co., 1981.

Slouching Towards Kalamazoo. Boston: Little, Brown and Co., 1983.

The Prick of Noon. Boston: Little, Brown and Co., 1985.

Peckham's Marbles. New York: G. P. Putnam's Sons, 1986.

B. ORIGINAL CONTRIBUTIONS TO OTHER BOOKS

Introduction to *Lanterns & Lances,* by James Thurber. New York: Time Inc., 1962.

Introduction to *Lions, Harts, Leaping Does and Other Stories,* by J. F. Powers. New York: Time Inc., 1963.

Introduction to *Three Men in a Boat,* by Jerome K. Jerome. New York: Time, Inc., 1964.

"Peter De Vries." In *Authors Take Sides on Vietnam.* New York: Simon and Schuster, 1967.

C. CONTRIBUTIONS TO PERIODICALS

"Nahum, I Baptize Thee." *The Calithump* 1 (May 1934): 11–20.

"Men Marry Because They Are Tired." *The Calithump* 2 (July 1934): 22–25.

"Flight." *Bozart and Contemporary Verse* 8 (November-December 1934): 9.

"Eine Kleine Nacht." *Story* 6 (March 1935): 68–74.

"The Swede and Me." *Manuscript* 2 (September-October 1935): 45-49.

"Art's a Funny Thing." *Esquire* 5 (February 1936): 59, 124, 127.

"Pizzicato on the Heartstrings." *Story* 9 (August 1936): 87–94.

"Afterglow." *Vernier: A Quarterly Magazine of Salient Short Stories,* no. 5 (Fall 1936): 23–28.

"I, Voluptuary." *Esquire* 6 (December 1936): 82, 245–46, 248, 250.

"The Man on the Street." *Esquire* 7 (April 1937): 100, 140, 142.

"Rhapsody for a Girl on a Bar Stool." *Esquire* 8 (November 1937): 48–49.

"Late Song." *Poetry* 51 (January 1938): 196.

"Songs for Eight O'Clock." *Esquire* 9 (February 1938): 40–41.

"Rooming House Anthology." *Coronet* 3 (February 1938): 12–13.

"Song for a Bride." *Esquire* 9 (June 1938): 36.

"Fusion and Confusion." Review of *The Garden of Disorder and Other Poems,* by Charles Henri Ford, and *Christopher Columbus and Other Poems,* by Sydney Salt. *Poetry* 52 (July 1938): 236–40.

"It Goes Like This." *Coronet* 5 (November 1938): 122–26.

"Mirror." *Poetry* 53 (March 1938): 311.

Crane, Carl [Peter De Vries]. "The Reader Writes." *New Yorker,* 8 July 1939, 22.

"The Floorwalker Attends a Slide Lecture on Gauguin." *Esquire* 12 (September 1939): 28.

"Conscript." *Poetry* 58 (July 1941): 184–88.

"On Being Thirty." *Poetry* 61 (October 1942): 380–83.

"Voice in Babel." *Poetry* 62 (July 1943): 208–14.

"A Note on This Issue." *Poetry* 62 (August 1943): 272–77.

"Poetry and the War." *College English* 5, no. 3 (December 1943): 113–20.

"James Thurber: The Comic Prufrock." *Poetry* 63 (December 1943): 150–59.

"Portrait in Depth of Youth Suspended Between Worlds." Review of *Dangling Man*, by Saul Bellow. *Chicago Sun Book Week*, 9 April 1944, 3.

"To Be." Review of *One Times One*, by E. E. Cummings. *Poetry* 64 (June 1944): 158–64.

"American Primitive." *Story* 29 (September-October 1946): 28–33.

"Different Cultural Levels Eat Here." *New Yorker*, 16 November 1946, 26–28.

"Good Boy." *New Yorker*, 27 December 1947, 49–50, 53–54.

"Larder Ex Libris." *Esquire* 30 (December 1948): 130.

"Tulip." *New Yorker*, 29 January 1949, 27–28.

"The Children's Hour; or, Hopscotch and Soda." *New Yorker*, 18 August 1956, 20–22.

"Universal Daydream." *Saturday Review*, 25 November 1961, 15–16.

"Exploring Inner Space." *Michigan Quarterly Review* 9 (April 1969): 85–92.

"The Iridescence of Mrs. Pulsifer." *New Yorker*, 26 March 1979, 32–36.

"Perelmania." *New Yorker*, 13 August 1984, 88–91.

II. Works about Peter De Vries

A. BIOGRAPHICAL INFORMATION

"Adrift in a Laundromat." *Time*, 20 July 1959, 100.

Bellow, Saul. Letter to author, 9 August 1991.

Borden, Allen B. "Peter De Vries." *Wilson Library Bulletin* 33, no. 7 (March 1959): 460.

Contemporary Authors: A Bio-Bibliographical Guide to Current Authors and Their Works. Vol. 17–20, 1st rev. Edited by Clare D. Kinsman. Detroit: Gale Research Co., 1976.

"Deaths Last Week." *Chicago Tribune*, 3 October 1993, sec. 2, p. 6.

De Vries, Jan. Letter to author, 4 December 1994.

De Vries, Peter. Letters to author, 20 October 1988, 23 November 1988, 1 December 1988, 15 March 1989, 26 June 1989.

———. Letter to Paul Engle, 9 July 1943. University of Iowa Special Collections Department.

"De Vries in Westport." *Newsweek*, 17 February 1964, 93A-94.

Gill, Brendan. Letter to author, 14 May 1989.

Girson, Rochelle. "The Author." *Saturday Review*, 24 March 1962, 20.

Higgins, William R. "Peter De Vries." In *Dictionary of Literary Biography*. 2d ser., vol. 6. *American Novelists Since World War II*, edited by James E. Kibler, Jr. Detroit: Gale Research Co., 1980.

Kaul, Donald. "Over the Coffee." *Des Moines Register*, 3 October 1993, sec. C, p. 3.

"The Literary Club." *Violet and Maize* 7 (June 1927): 67.

Manfred, Frederick. "An Interview With Frederick Manfred Conducted by Leslie T. Whipp, May 7, 1987." By Leslie T. Whipp. East Lansing, Mich.: The Midwestern Press, The Society for the Study of Midwestern Literature, Michigan State University, 1992.

———. *The Selected Letters of Frederick Manfred 1932–1954*. Edited by Arthur R. Huseboe and Nancy Owen Nelson. Lincoln: University of Nebraska Press, 1988.

McDowell, Edwin. "Katinka Loeser, Story Writer, 77; Collections Told of Suburban Life." *New York Times*, 8 March 1991, sec. A, p. 22.

"Milestones." *Time*, 11 October 1993, 25.

"Newsletter." *Humor: International Journal of Humor Research* 7 (1994): 301.

Pace, Eric. "Peter De Vries, Writer, Is Dead: New Yorker Contributor Was 83," *New York Times*, 29 September 1993, sec. B, p. 11.

"Peter De Vries." *New Yorker*, 11 October 1993, 12.

Roditi, Edouard. Letter to author, 19 September 1990.

Theroux, Paul. "A Jolly Old Elf, A Master of Gloom: The Gifts of Peter De Vries." *New York Times Book Review*, 5 December 1993, 35, 38.

Timmerman, John J. "As I Knew Them." *Dialogue*, April 1975, 20–22.

Who's Who in America. 45th ed., 1988–89, vol. 1. Wilmette, Ill.: Marquis Who's Who, 1988.

World Authors 1950–1970. Edited by John Wakeman. New York: The H. W. Wilson Company, 1975.

Yearbook 1930–31, Calvin College and Seminary (Grand Rapids, Mich., 1931).

B. GENERAL CRITICISM

Amis, Kingsley. "What We Need Is Savage Laughter." In *Opinions and Perspectives from the New York Times Book Review*, edited by Francis Brown, 279–83. Boston: Houghton Mifflin Co., 1964.

Boston, Richard. *An Anatomy of Laughter*. London: Collins, 1974.

Bowden, J. H. *Peter De Vries*. Twayne's United States Authors Series, no. 448. Boston: Twayne Publishers, 1983.

Boyd, Jack Kent. "The Novels of Peter De Vries: A Critical Introduction." Ph.D. diss., University of Arkansas, 1971.

Bratt, James D. *Dutch Calvinism in Modern America: A History of a Conservative Subculture*. Grand Rapids, Mich.: W. B. Eerdmans Publishing Co., 1984.

Burgess, Anthony. *The Novel Now: A Guide to Contemporary Fiction*. New York: W. W. Norton & Company, Inc., 1967.

Byrd, Max. "Reconsideration." *New Republic*, 23 October 1976, 29–31.

Campion, Daniel Ray. "Running on the Surrealist Ticket: The Extravagant Peter De Vries." Ph.D. diss., University of Iowa, 1989.

Challender, Craig. "Peter De Vries: The Case for Comic Seriousness." *Studies in American Humor* 1, no. 1 (April 1974): 40–51.

The Chelsea House Library of Literary Criticism. Vol. 2, *Twentieth-Century American Literature*. Gen. ed. Harold Bloom. New York: Chelsea House Publishers, 1986.

Contemporary Literary Criticism. Vol. 46, edited by Daniel G. Marowski and Roger Matuz. Detroit: Gale Research Co., 1988.

Davies, Horton. *The Mirror of the Ministry in Modern Novels*. New York: Oxford University Press, 1959.

Davies, Marie-Helene. "Fools for Christ's Sake: A Study of Clerical Figures in De

Vries, Updike and Buechner." *Thalia: Studies in Literary Humor* 6, no. 1 (Spring and Summer 1983): 60–72.

De Roller, Joseph Michael. "The Lower-Case Absurd: A Study of the Novels of Peter De Vries." Ph.D. diss., University of Rochester, 1976.

De Vries, Calvin. "Peter De Vries: The Vale of Laughter." *Theology Today* 32 (April 1975): 10–20.

Down, Nancy. "The Search for Authenticity in the Satiric Worlds of Nathanael West and Peter De Vries." Ph.D. diss., Drew University, 1986.

Eisinger, Chester E. "De Vries, Peter." In *Contemporary Novelists*. 3d ed. Edited by James Vinson. New York: St. Martin's Press, 1982.

Evans, T. Jeff. "The Apprentice Fiction of Peter De Vries." *Critique: Studies in Modern Fiction* 21, no. 3 (1980): 28–42.

———. "The Madder Music of Peter De Vries." *Studies in Contemporary Satire* 8 (1981): 21–29.

———. "Peter De Vries: A Retrospective." *American Humor: An Interdisciplinary Newsletter* 7, no. 2 (Fall 1980): 13–16.

———. "Peter De Vries in American Humor." In *Whimsy VI*. Proceedings of the Sixth (1987) Conference on International Humor, edited by Don L. F. Nilsen and Alleen Pace Nilsen, 13–15. Tempe: Arizona State University, 1988.

Film Review Annual 1984. Englewood, N.J.: Film Review Publications, 1984.

Frohock, Wilbur Merril. *Strangers to This Ground*. Dallas: Southern Methodist University Press, 1961.

Hamblen, Abigail Ann. "Peter De Vries: Calvinist Gone Underground." *Trace* 48 (1963): 20–24.

Hoffman, Arnold Roy. "The Sense of Place: Peter De Vries, J. F. Powers, and Flannery O'Connor." Ph.D. diss., Michigan State University, 1970.

H[ook], A[ndrew], and E[ric] M[ottram]. "Peter De Vries." In *The Penguin Companion to American Literature*, edited by Malcolm Bradbury, Eric Mottram, and Jean Franc. New York: McGraw-Hill, 1971.

Jellema, Roderick. *Peter De Vries: A Critical Essay*. Contemporary Writers in Christian Perspective Series. Edited by Roderick Jellema. Grand Rapids, Mich.: William B. Eerdmans Publishing Co., 1966.

———. "Peter De Vries: The Decline and Fall of Moot Point." *The Reformed Journal* 13, no. 3 (April 1963): 9–15.

Kort, Wesley. *Shriven Selves*. Philadelphia: Fortress Press, 1972.

Raphael, Frederic. Introduction to *The Mackerel Plaza*, by Peter De Vries, v–xi. New York: Penguin Books, 1986.

Rodewald, Fred. "The Comic *Eiron* in the Novels of Peter De Vries." *Quartet* 6, no. 41 (Winter 1973): 34–39.

Rome, Joy. "Peter De Vries: Compassionate Satirist." *Unisa English Studies* 9, no. 3 (September 1971): 23–29.

Ross, Jean W. "Peter De Vries." In *DLB Yearbook, 1982*, edited by Richard Ziegfeld, 133–36. Detroit, Mich.: Gale Research Co., 1983.

Sanders, David. "De Vries, Peter." In *Contemporary Novelists*. 4th ed. Edited by D. L. Kirkpatrick. London: St. James Press, 1986.

Ter Maat, Cornelius John. "Three Novelists and a Community: A Study of American

Novelists with Dutch Calvinist Origins." Ed.D. diss., University of Michigan, 1963.

Timmerman, John H. "Tragicomedy and Saving Grace." *Christian Century*, 26 November 1975, 1076–80.

Walcutt, Charles Child. *Man's Changing Mask: Modes and Methods of Communication in Fiction*. Minneapolis: University of Minnesota Press, 1966.

Walsh, William. "The Combination in the Safe." *Encounter* 40, no. 1 (January 1973): 74–80.

Will, George. "D is for Dodo." *Newsweek*, 9 February 1976, 84.

Wolcott, James. "Naughty Old Men: Two Veteran Novelists Who Can Still Bounce the Bedsprings." *Harper's* 265 (October 1982): 60–63.

Wood, Ralph C. *The Comedy of Redemption: Christian Faith and Comic Vision in Four American Novelists*. Notre Dame, Ind.: University of Notre Dame Press, 1988.

C. INTERVIEWS (LISTED ALPHABETICALLY BY INTERVIEWER)

Davis, Douglas M. "An Interview with Peter De Vries." *College English* 28, no. 7 (April 1967): 524–28.

[Davis, Douglas M.]. "My Stuff Is Really Over My Head." *National Observer*, 9 August 1965, 19.

Fleisher, Leonore. "De Vries on Rewriting in the Supermarket." *Life*, 13 December 1968, 18.

Hutchens, John K. "'You Hear Cliches, and Dislodge Them': An Interview with Peter De Vries." *New York Herald Tribune Book Review*, 18 March 1962, 5.

Morris, Edward. "Delightful, Delicious, Delectable, De Vries." *Writer's Digest*, January 1978, 8.

Newquist, Roy. "Peter De Vries." In *Counterpoint*, 145–54. Chicago: Rand McNally & Co., 1964.

Nichols, Lewis. "Talk with Peter De Vries." *New York Times Book Review*, 29 April 1956, 28.

Ross, Jean W. "An Interview with Peter De Vries." In *DLB Yearbook, 1982*, edited by Richard Ziegfeld, 136–37. Detroit: Gale Research Co., 1983.

Sale, Richard B. "An Interview in New York with Peter De Vries." *Studies in the Novel* 1, no. 3 (Fall 1969): 364–69.

Shenker, Israel. "Peter De Vries." In *Words and Their Masters*, 96–100. Garden City, N.Y.: Doubleday & Co., Inc., 1974.

Steinberg, Sybil S. "Peter De Vries & Katinka Loeser." *Publishers Weekly*, 16 October 1981, 6–8.

"Talk with the Author." *Newsweek*, 20 July 1959, 98–99.

Yagoda, Ben. "Peter De Vries: Being Seriously Funny." *New York Times Magazine*, 12 June 1983, 42–56.

D. BOOK REVIEWS

Selections are available in *Contemporary Literary Criticism: Excerpts from Criticism of the Works of Today's Novelists, Poets, Playwrights, and Other Creative Writers*. 46 vols. Detroit: Gale Research Co., 1973–88. The listings below under *Sauce for the Goose* and later novels include several reviews not cited in the text, but which are listed here as a supplement to T. A. Straayer's bibliography.

But Who Wakes the Bugler?

Bell, Lisle. Review in *New York Herald Tribune*, 1 September 1940, sec. 9, p. 8.

Bonner, Ruth Hard. "Surrealist Fun: *But Who Wakes the Bugler*." *Boston Evening Transcript*, 7 September 1940, sec. 5, p. 1.

North, Sterling. "Typewriter Bites Local Fantasist." *Chicago Daily News*, 9 October 1940, 20.

Review in *New Republic*, 16 September 1940, 394.

Review in *New Yorker*, 7 September 1940, 57–58.

Schwed, Fred. "Nightmares Are Fun." *Saturday Review of Literature*, 14 September 1940, 12.

Sherman, Beatrice. Review in *New York Times Book Review*, 8 September 1940, 7.

Timmerman, John J. "Mr. Thwing Is Not Pound-Proof." *The Calvin Forum*, October 1940, 54–55.

The Handsome Heart

Conroy, Jack. "Love, Madness and Humor in Psychological Novel." *Chicago Sun Book Week*, 4 July 1943, 2.

The Tunnel of Love

Hine, Al. "Serious Frivolity." *Saturday Review*, 15 May 1954, 14.

Comfort Me With Apples

Balliett, Whitney. "The Egg in the Omelet." *New Yorker*, 12 May 1956, 157–59.

Hine, Al. "Exurbia Impaled." *Saturday Review*, 5 May 1956, 19–20.

Let Me Count the Ways

Coray, Don. "Only When I Laugh." *The Reformed Journal* 15, no. 9 (November 1965): 21–34.

Maddocks, Melvin. "Chase Scenes by Kafka." *Christian Science Monitor*, 22 July 1965, 11.

The Cat's Pajamas & Witch's Milk

Fleischer, Leonore. "A Master Sharpens His Comic Focus." *Life*, 13 December 1968, 16–18.

Mrs. Wallop

Gilliatt, Penelope. "Art, the Always-with-Us." *New Yorker*, 16 January 1971, 95–98.

Without a Stitch in Time

Showers, Paul. Review in *New York Times Book Review*, 24 December 1972, 3, 17.

Forever Panting

Gilliatt, Penelope. "The Unbudgeable Blodgett." *New Yorker*, 16 July 1973, 76–78.

Green, Alan. "The Giddy Heights of Humor." *World*, 17 July 1973, 39.

The Glory of the Hummingbird

Theroux, Paul. "Peter De Vries: What Is the Thinking Man's Cereal? Joyce Carol Oates." *New York Times Book Review*, 27 October 1974, 6–7.

I Hear America Swinging

Strozier, Robert M. Review in *New York Times Book Review*, 9 May 1976, 5.

Madder Music

Theroux, Paul. "Groucho Redivivus." *New York Times Book Review*, 16 October 1977, 15, 42.

Consenting Adults

Sutherland, Stuart. "The Comedy of the Commonplace." *Times Literary Supplement*, 30 January 1981, 107.

Sauce for the Goose

Balliett, Whitney. "Convulsive Merriment." *New Yorker*, 19 October 1981, 200–204.

Burgess, Anthony. Review in *New York*, 28 September 1981, 63–64.

Craig, George. "An Terrific Nice Girl." *Times Literary Supplement*, 22 January 1982, 76.

Koenig, Rhoda. "A Satire on Feminism." *New Republic*, 14 October 1981, 38–39.

Maddocks, Melvin. "Galloping Lust, Crawling Remorse." *Time*, 21 September 1981, 81.

Shapiro, Anna. Review in *Saturday Review*, September 1981, 60.

Teachout, Terry. "Books in Brief." *National Review*, 20 August 1981, 1038.

Slouching Towards Kalamazoo

Campion, Dan. Review in *Iowa Journal of Literary Studies* 6 (1985): 132–35.

Crane, Lucille. Review in *Best Sellers* 43, no. 6 (September 1983): 201.

Gilbert, Harriett. "A+." *New Statesman*, 19 August 1983, 26.

Gray, Paul. "How the Sexual Revolution Began." *Time*, 11 July 1983, 68.

Kakutani, Michiko. Review in *New York Times*, 22 July 1983, sec. C, p. 23.

Korn, Eric. "Double Everything." *Times Literary Supplement*, 26 August 1983, 898.

Lyons, Gene. "Scarlet A Plus." *Newsweek*, 1 August 1983, 68–69.

Macfarlane, David. "The Architect of Chuckles." *Maclean's*, 25 July 1983, 54.

Review in *Publishers Weekly*, 3 June 1983, 65.

"Upfront: Advance Reviews, Adult Fiction." *Booklist* 79 (15 March 1983): 929.

The Prick of Noon

Balliett, Whitney. "Climbers." *New Yorker*, 10 June 1985, 139.

Dyer, Geoff. "Tanglewood Tales." *New Statesman*, 24 January 1986, 28.

Ewart, Gavin. "Acting Upwardly." *Times Literary Supplement*, 24 January 1986, 82.

Gross, John. Review in *New York Times*, 5 April 1985, sec. C, p. 25.

Review in *Library Journal*, 15 May 1985, 78.

Sheppard, R. Z. "Uncle Gatsby in Connecticut." *Time*, 22 April 1985, 69.

Sigal, Clancy. "Paronomasiamania." *New York Times Book Review*, 19 May 1985, 16.

Peckham's Marbles

Review in *Library Journal*, 1 October 1986, 108.

Review in *Time*, 13 October 1986, 102.

E. MISCELLANY

Biles, Roger. *Big City Boss in Depression and War: Mayor Edward J. Kelly of Chicago*. DeKalb: Northern Illinois University Press, 1984.

"Booze & The Writer." *Writer's Digest*, October 1978, 28–29.

Brinnin, John Malcolm. *Dylan Thomas in America: An Intimate Journal*. Boston: Little, Brown and Co., 1955.

Butcher, Fanny. "The Literary Spotlight." *Chicago Sunday Tribune*, 16 April 1944, sec. 6, p. 12.

De Vries, Peter. "What's All That About Commuters?" *New York Herald Tribune Book Review*, 30 August 1959, 2.

"De Vries, Peter." In *The New Encyclopaedia Britannica*. 15th ed. Chicago: Encyclopaedia Britannica, Inc., 1990.

Emig, Janet. *The Composing Process of Twelfth Graders*. Urbana, Ill.: National Council of Teachers of English, 1971.

Evans, Arthur. "479,825 for Kelly; A Record." *Chicago Daily Tribune*, 27 February 1935, 1.

"Exurbia in a Dither," *Newsweek*, 28 September 1959, 107.

Ferris, Paul, ed. *The Collected Letters of Dylan Thomas*. London: J. M. Dent & Sons, Ltd., 1985.

———. *Dylan Thomas*. New York: The Dial Press, 1977.

"Fusion in Chicago Will Run Douglas." *New York Times*, 16 February 1935, 7.

Gibbs, Wolcott. "Low Jinks in Westport." *New Yorker*, 27 February 1957, 68.

Grossberger, Lewis. "The Turf is Familiar. . . ." *People*, 29 September 1980, 41–42.

Hilliard, Celia. "Sophistication Sells: *Esquire*'s Chicago Success Story." *Chicago*, May 1980, 134–40.

Kakutani, Michiko. Review of *Are You Listening Rabbi Löw*, by J. P. Donleavy. *New York Times*, 12 October 1988, sec. C, p. 21.

Lamberts, J. J. "I Love You Just the Same." *The Banner*, 4 October 1974, 14–15.

Muir, Frank, ed. *The Oxford Book of Humorous Prose*. Oxford: Oxford University Press, 1990.

New York Times Film Reviews 1971–72. New York: The New York Times and Arno Press, 1973.

New York Times Theater Reviews 1920–1970. Vol. 8, 1967–70. New York: The New York Times and Arno Press, 1971.

Queenan, Joe. "Then the Spoon Speaks Up." Review of *Skinny Legs and All*, by Tom Robbins. *New York Times Book Review*, 15 April 1990, 12.

Test, George A. *Satire: Spirit and Art*. Tampa: University of South Florida Press, 1991.

Variety Film Reviews 1907–1980. Vols. 12–13. New York: Garland Publishing, 1983.

Verduin, Kathleen. "Teaching *Moby-Dick* in a Calvinist Setting." In *Approaches to Teaching Melville's* Moby-Dick, edited by Martin Bickman, 75–84. New York: The Modern Language Association of America, 1985.

III. Works Related to Surrealism

Andrews, Wayne. *The Surrealist Parade.* New York: New Directions, 1990.

Balakian, Anna. *André Breton: Magus of Surrealism.* New York: Oxford University Press, 1971.

Blake, Howard. "There Is a Firbank in It." Review of *The Overturned Lake,* by Charles Henri Ford. *Poetry* 60 (April 1942): 48–51.

Breton, André. *Anthologie de l'humour noir.* 1940. Reprint, Paris: Editions du Sagittaire, 1950.

———. *Conversations: The Autobiography of Surrealism.* Translated by Mark Polizzotti. New York: Paragon House, 1993.

———. "Interview with Professor Freud." In *Freud As We Knew Him,* edited by Hendrik M. Ruitenbeek. Detroit: Wayne State University Press, 1973.

———. *Manifestoes of Surrealism.* Translated by Richard Seaver and Helen R. Lane. Ann Arbor: University of Michigan Press, 1969.

———. *Nadja.* Paris: Editions Gallimard, 1964.

———. *What Is Surrealism?* Translated by David Gascoyne. 1936. Reprint, New York: Haskell House, 1974.

———. *What is Surrealism? Selected Writings.* Edited by Franklin Rosemont. N.p.: Monad, 1978.

Brinnin, John Malcolm. "Muriel Rukeyser: The Social Poet and the Problem of Communication." *Poetry* 61 (January 1943): 554–75.

Byrne, Barry. "Surrealism Passes." *The Commonweal,* 2 July 1937, 262–63.

Charlot, Jean. "Surrealism—Or, the Reason for Unreason." *The American Scholar* 7, no. 2 (April 1938): 230–48.

Calas, Nicolas, Herbert J. Muller, and Kenneth Burke. *Surrealism Pro and Con.* New York: Gotham Book Mart, 1973.

Caliban [pseud]. "Caliban Refuses to Collect His Thoughts." *Caliban,* no. 1 (1986): 141–46.

Caws, Mary Ann. *André Breton.* New York: Twayne Publishers, 1971.

———. *Surrealism and the Literary Imagination: A Study of Breton and Bachelard.* The Hague: Mouton & Co., 1966.

Chénieux-Gendron, Jacqueline. *Surrealism.* Translated by Vivian Folkenflik. New York: Columbia University Press, 1990.

The Dada Almanac. Edited by Richard Huelsenbeck. English edition presented by Malcolm Green. Atlas Arkhive 1. London: Atlas Press, 1993.

Daiches, David. "The Craftsman and the Poet." Review of *The Violent,* by Harry Brown, and *Sacred and Secular Elegies,* by George Barker. *Poetry* 64 (April 1944): 35–39.

Dali, Salvador. "Playboy Interview: Salvador Dali." *Playboy* 11, no. 7 (July 1964): 41–48.

————. "The Stinking Ass." In *Surrealists on Art*, edited by Lucy R. Lippard. Englewood Cliffs, N.J.: Prentice-Hall, Inc., 1970.

De Jonge, Alex. *Nightmare Culture: Lautréamont and Les Chants de Maldoror.* New York: St. Martin's Press, 1973.

Ernst, Max. *La femme 100 têtes*. Paris: Editions du Carrefour, 1929.

Ferguson, Charles W. "Art for Our Sake." *Harper's* 175 (July 1937): 218–20.

Fitts, Dudley. "Mighty Lak a Whale." Review of *Prose Poems from "The Illuminations" of Arthur Rimbaud*, translated by Helen Rootham. *Poetry* 64 (April 1944): 44–45.

Ford, Charles Henri. *Flag of Ecstasy: Selected Poems.* Edited by Edward B. Germain. Los Angeles: Black Sparrow Press, 1972.

————. *The Garden of Disorder and Other Poems.* London: Europa Press, 1938.

————. *The Overturned Lake.* Cincinnati: The Little Man Press, 1941.

Fowlie, Wallace. *Lautréamont.* Twayne's World Authors Series, no. 284. New York: Twayne Publishers, Inc., 1973.

Friar, Kimon. "The Action of Incorrigible Tragedy." *Poetry* 64 (May 1944): 86–107.

Frye, Northrop. "Men as Trees Walking." *The Canadian Forum* 18 (October 1938): 208–10.

Gascoyne, David. *A Short Survey of Surrealism.* 1935. Reprint, San Francisco: City Lights Books, 1982.

"Giddy Museum Exhibit Dizzies the Public With Dada." *News-Week*, 19 December 1936, 25–26.

Golffing, Francis C. "The Plain and the Stratosphere." Review of *Generation of Journey*, by Jacob Sloan, and *Poems for Painters*, by Charles Henri Ford. *Poetry* 66 (September 1945): 340–43.

Harriman, Margaret Case. "A Dream Walking." *Reader's Digest* 35 (October 1939): 54–57.

Hays, H. R. "Surrealist Influence in Contemporary English and American Poetry." *Poetry* 54 (July 1939): 202–9.

————. "In the American Tradition." Review of *Trance Above the Streets*, by Harold Rosenberg. *Poetry* 62 (September 1943): 342–44.

Jolas, Eugene. "Beyond Surrealism." *The Living Age* 359 (September 1940): 93–95.

————. "French Poetry and the Revival of Mysticism." *Poetry* 56 (August 1940): 264–71.

————. "Toward a Metaphysical Renascence?" Review of *The Spiritual Aspects of the New Poetry*, by Amos N. Wilder. *Poetry* 57 (October 1940): 49–52.

Josephson, Matthew. *Life among the Surrealists.* New York: Holt, Rinehart and Winston, 1962.

Kuenzli, Rudolf E. "Derridada." *L'esprit créatur* 20, no. 2 (Summer 1980): 12–21.

————, ed. *New York Dada.* New York: Willis Locker & Owens, 1986.

Lautréamont. *Lautréamont's Maldoror.* Translated by Alexis Lykiard. London: Allison & Busby, 1970.

————. *Maldoror (Les Chants de Maldoror).* Translated by Guy Wernham. 1943. Reprint, New York: New Directions, 1965.

Levy, Julien. *Surrealism.* New York: The Black Sun Press, 1936.

London Bulletin: Complete Edition in Two Volumes. Arno Series of Contemporary Art, no. 30. New York: Arno Press, 1969.

"Marvelous & Fantastic." *Time*, 14 December 1936, 60–62.

Matthews, J. H. *André Breton*. New York: Columbia University Press, 1967.

———. "André Breton and Painting: The Case of Arshile Gorky." *Dada/Surrealism*, no. 17 (1988): 36–45.

———. *André Breton: Sketch for an Early Portrait*. Purdue University Monographs in Romance Languages, vol. 52. Amsterdam: John Benjamins Publishing Co., 1986.

———. *The Imagery of Surrealism*. Syracuse, N.Y.: Syracuse University Press, 1977.

———. *Surrealism and the Novel*. Ann Arbor: University of Michigan Press, 1966.

McGavick, Alex. "Weird Worlds." *The Commonweal*, 1 April 1938, 630–31.

Metzidakis, Stamos. "Breton and Poetic Originality." *Dada/Surrealism*, no. 17 (1988): 28–35.

Mortimer, Raymond. "The Art of Displeasing." *The Living Age* 350 (August 1936): 529–32.

Moss, Howard. "Wrong Detour." Review of *New Road 1943*, edited by Alex Comfort and John Bayliss. *Poetry* 64 (April 1944): 46–48.

Roditi, Edouard. "Oscar Wilde's Poetry as Art History." *Poetry* 67 (March 1946): 322–38.

———. "Poetry, Mysticism, and Magic." Review of *L'Expérience poétique*, by Rolland de Renéville, and *Situation de la Poésie*, by Jacques et Raïsa Maritain. *Poetry* 53 (January 1939): 218–23.

———. "Surrealism Serves the State." Review of *Ode to Bombed London*, by Philippe Soupault, and *Three Prayers for Pilots*, by Jules Roy. *Poetry* 68 (April 1946): 54–56.

———. "Translator's Dilemma." Review of *A Season in Hell*, by Arthur Rimbaud, translated by Louise Varèse. *Poetry* 67 (February 1946): 278–82.

———. "The Unspoken Word." Review of *New Poems*, by Dylan Thomas. *Poetry* 63 (October 1943): 48–50.

Rosemont, Franklin, ed. *Surrealism & Its Popular Accomplices*. San Francisco: City Lights Books, 1980.

Rubin, William S. *Dada, Surrealism, and Their Heritage*. New York: The Museum of Modern Art, 1968.

Schapiro, Meyer. "Blue Like an Orange." *The Nation*, 25 September 1937, 323–34.

Schwartz, Delmore. "Rimbaud in Our Time." *Poetry* 55 (December 1939): 148–54.

Skaff, William. *The Philosophy of T. S. Eliot: From Skepticism to a Surrealist Poetic, 1909–1927*. Philadelphia: University of Pennsylvania Press, 1986.

Sonnenfeld, Albert. "The Last of the Red-Hot Dadas: Ring Lardner, American Playwright." *Dada/Surrealism*, no. 8 (1978): 36–44.

"Super." *Time*, 7 February 1938, 49.

Surrealism. Edited by Herbert Read. London: Faber and Faber Limited, 1936.

Varnedoe, Kirk, and Adam Gopnik. *High & Low: Modern Art and Popular Culture*. New York: The Museum of Modern Art, 1990.

Williams, Oscar. Review of *New Directions 1942*, edited by James Laughlin. *Poetry* 61 (March 1943): 694.

Zweig, Paul. *Lautréamont: The Violent Narcissus*. National University Publications Series on Literary Criticism. Port Washington, N.Y.: Kennikat Press, 1972.

IV. Other Works Cited

Abrams, M. H. *The Mirror and the Lamp: Romantic Theory and the Critical Tradition*. London: Oxford University Press, 1953.

———. *Natural Supernaturalism: Tradition and Revolution in Romantic Literature*. New York: W. W. Norton & Co., 1971.

Andrews, Clarence A. *Chicago in Story: A Literary History*. Iowa City: Midwest Heritage Publishing Company, 1982.

Barthes, Roland. "To Write: An Intransitive Verb?" In *The Structuralists from Marx to Lévi-Strauss*, edited by Richard T. De George and Fernande M. De George. Garden City, N.Y.: Anchor Books, 1972.

Baudelaire, Charles. *Flowers of Evil*. Translated by George Dillon and Edna St. Vincent Millay. New York: Harper & Brothers, 1936.

Bellman, Samuel I. *Constance M. Rourke*. Twayne's United States Authors Series, no. 412. Boston: Twayne Publishers, 1981.

Bernstein, Burton. *Thurber: A Biography*. New York: Dodd, Mead & Co., 1975.

Bier, Jesse. *The Rise and Fall of American Humor*. New York: Holt, Rinehart and Winston, 1968.

Blair, Walter, and Hamlin Hill. *America's Humor: From Poor Richard to Doonesbury*. New York: Oxford University Press, 1978.

Bloom, Allen. *The Closing of the American Mind*. New York: Simon and Schuster, 1987.

Booth, Wayne. *Critical Understanding: The Powers and Limits of Pluralism*. Chicago: University of Chicago Press, 1979.

———. *A Rhetoric of Irony*. Chicago: University of Chicago Press, 1974.

Bradbury, Malçolm. *The Modern American Novel*. 1983. Reprint, Oxford: Oxford University Press, 1984.

Bradley, Van Allen. *Book Collector's Handbook of Values, 1982-1983 Edition*. New York: G. P. Putnam's Sons, 1982.

Brantlinger, Patrick. *Bread and Circuses: Theories of Mass Culture as Social Decay*. Ithaca: Cornell University Press, 1983.

Brooks, Cleanth. *Modern Poetry and the Tradition*. Chapel Hill: University of North Carolina Press, 1939.

Burke, Kenneth. *Language as Symbolic Action: Essays on Life, Literature, and Method*. Berkeley and Los Angeles: University of California Press, 1966.

Byron, George Gordon, Lord. *The Complete Poetical Works*. Vol. 1. Edited by Jerome J. McGann. Oxford: The Clarendon Press, 1980.

Calinescu, Matei. "Parody and Intertextuality." *Semiotica* 65, nos. 1–2 (1987): 187.

Carroll, Lewis. *The Annotated Alice*. Introduction and notes by Martin Gardner. New York: Bramhall House, 1960.

Cohen, George M. *A History of American Art*. New York: Dell, 1971.

Cohen, Milton A. *Poet and Painter: The Aesthetics of E. E. Cummings's Early Work*. Detroit: Wayne State University Press, 1987.

Contemporary Authors. New rev. ser., vol. 13. Edited by Linda Metzger. Detroit: Gale Research Co., 1984.

Contemporary Poets. 4th ed. Edited by James Vinson and D. L. Kirkpatrick. New York: St Martin's Press, 1985.

Cowley, Malcolm. *Exile's Return: A Literary Odyssey of the 1920s*. New York: Viking, 1951.

Davis, Douglas. *The World of Black Humor*. New York: E. P. Dutton & Co. Inc., 1967.

De Quincey, Thomas. *The Confessions of an English Opium-Eater*. London: J. M. Dent, 1907.

Dictionary of Literary Biography. 2d ser., vol. 48, *American Poets, 1880–1945,* edited by Peter Quartermain. Detroit: Gale Research Co., 1986.

Dictionary of Literary Themes and Motifs. Edited by Jean-Charles Seigneuret. New York: Greenwood Press, 1988.

Eliot, T. S. *Selected Poems.* New York: Harcourt, Brace & World, Inc., 1964.

Emerson, Ralph Waldo. *Essays: Second Series.* Vol. 3 of *The Collected Works of Ralph Waldo Emerson.* Cambridge: Harvard University Press, Belknap Press, 1983.

Fetherling, Doug. *The Five Lives of Ben Hecht.* Toronto: Lester and Orpen Limited, 1977.

Fields, Ronald J. *W. C. Fields: A Life on Film.* New York: St. Martin's Press, 1984.

Fitzgerald, F. Scott. *The Great Gatsby.* New York: Charles Scribner's Sons, 1925.

FitzGibbon, Constantine. *The Life of Dylan Thomas.* Boston: Little, Brown and Co., 1965.

Forster, E. M. *The Art of the Novel.* New York: Harcourt, Brace & World, Inc., 1927.

Freud, Sigmund. *Civilization and Its Discontents.* Translated and edited by James Strachey. New York: W. W. Norton & Co., 1961.

———. *Collected Papers.* Vol. 5. Edited by James Strachey. The International Psycho-Analytical Library, no. 37, edited by Ernest Jones. London: The Hogarth Press and the Institute of Psycho-Analysis, 1950.

———. *Jokes and Their Relation to the Unconscious.* Translated and edited by James Strachey. New York: W. W. Norton & Co., 1960.

Gill, Brendan. *Here at the New Yorker.* New York: Random House, 1975.

Gordon, Lyndall. "Love With Its Trousers Rolled." *New York Times Book Review,* 21 August 1988, 1, 28.

Gurewitch, Morton. *Comedy: The Irrational Vision.* Ithaca: Cornell University Press, 1975.

Hecht, Ben. *A Jew in Love.* 1931. Reprint, New York: Triangle Books, 1938.

Hine, Daryl, and Joseph Parisi, eds. *The Poetry Anthology 1912–1977: Sixty-Five Years of America's Most Distinguished Verse Magazine.* Boston: Houghton Mifflin, 1978.

Hirsch, E. D., Jr. *Cultural Literacy: What Every American Needs to Know.* Boston: Houghton Mifflin Company, 1987.

Holmes, Charles S. *The Clocks of Columbus: The Literary Career of James Thurber.* New York: Atheneum, 1972.

The Home Book of Proverbs, Maxims, and Familiar Phrases. Edited by Burton Stevenson. New York: Macmillan, 1956.

Hutcheon, Linda. *A Theory of Parody: The Teachings of Twentieth-Century Art Forms.* New York: Methuen, 1985.

The International Directory of Little Magazines and Small Presses. 23rd ed., 1987–88. Edited by Len Fulton. Paradise, Calif.: Dustbooks, 1987.

"John Wood Blodgett." *Dictionary of American Biography,* Supplement 5, 1951–55. Edited by John A. Garraty. New York: Charles Scribner's Sons, 1977.

Jones, Ernest, M.D. *The Life and Work of Sigmund Freud.* Vol. 3. New York: Basic Books, 1957.

Kahn, E. J., Jr. *About the New Yorker and Me: A Sentimental Journal.* New York: G. P. Putnam's Sons, 1979.

Kahn, John Ellison. "Polysemania, Semantic Taint, and Related Conditions." *Verbatim* 12, no. 3 (Winter 1986): 1–3.

Kenney, Catherine McGehee. *Thurber's Anatomy of Confusion.* Hamden, Conn.: Archon Books, 1984.

Kilpatrick, Thomas L., and Patsy-Rose Hoshiko. *Illinois! Illinois! An Annotated Bibliography of Fiction.* Metuchen, N.J.: The Scarecrow Press, Inc., 1979.

Koestler, Arthur. *The Act of Creation.* New York: Dell, 1967.

Kroker, Arthur, Marilouise Kroker, and David Cook. *Panic Encyclopedia: The Definitive Guide to the Postmodern Scene.* New York: St. Martin's Press, 1989.

Laughlin, James, IV, ed. *New Directions in Prose and Poetry.* Vols. 1–5. Norfolk, Conn.: New Directions, 1936–40.

Leopold, Aldo. *A Sand County Almanac.* 1949. Reprint, New York: Ballantine, 1984.

Lesser, Wendy. "Runaway Glacier." *New York Times Book Review,* 16 October 1988, 32.

McMahon, Robert. "Kenneth Burke's Divine Comedy: The Literary Form of *The Rhetoric of Religion.*" *PMLA* 104, no. 1 (January 1989): 53–63.

Mencken, H. L. *Prejudices: A Selection.* Edited by James T. Farrell. New York: Vintage Books, 1958.

Morsberger, Robert E. *James Thurber.* Twayne's United States Authors Series, no. 62. New York: Twayne Publishers, Inc., 1964.

Newman, Charles. *The Post-Modern Aura: The Act of Fiction in an Age of Inflation.* Evanston, Ill.: Northwestern University Press, 1985.

O'Brien, Darcy. "Critique of Psychoanalytic Criticism, or What Joyce Did and Did Not Do." *James Joyce Quarterly,* Spring 1976, 275–91.

The Oxter English Dictionary. Edited by George Stone Saussy, III. New York: Facts on File, 1984.

Ozer, Jerome S. *Film Review Annual 1984.* Englewood, N.J.: Film Review Publications, 1984.

Paulos, John Allen. *Mathematics and Humor.* Chicago: University of Chicago Press, 1980.

Perkins, David, ed. *English Romantic Writers.* New York: Harcourt, Brace, and World, Inc., 1967.

Poetry: A Magazine of Verse. Vols. 52–67 (April 1938–March 1946).

Redfern, Walter. *Puns.* 1984. Reprint, Oxford: Basil Blackwell and Andre Deutsch, 1986.

Reynolds, David S. *Beneath the American Renaissance: The Subversive Imagination in the Age of Emerson and Melville.* Cambridge: Harvard University Press, 1988.

Richards, I. A. *Practical Criticism: A Study of Literary Judgment.* New York: Harcourt, Brace & World, Inc., 1929.

Rourke, Constance. *American Humor: A Study of the National Character.* New York: Harcourt, Brace and Co., 1931.

Russian Formalist Criticism: Four Essays. Translated by Lee T. Lemon and Marion J. Reis. Regents Critics Series. Lincoln: University of Nebraska Press, 1965.

"St. Leo the Great Parish." [Chicago, 1985].

Simon, Richard Keller. *The Labyrinth of the Comic: Theory and Practice from Fielding to Freud.* Tallahassee: Florida State University Press, 1985.

Smith, Elsdon C. *New Dictionary of American Family Names.* New York: Harper and Row, 1956.

Spector, Jack J. *The Aesthetics of Freud: A Study in Psychoanalysis and Art.* New York: Praeger Publishers, 1972.

Spender, Stephen. "Selected Notices." *Horizon* 7, no. 40 (April 1943): 277–89.

Studies in American Humor 3 (n.s.), no. 1 (Spring 1984): special issue on "The New Yorker from 1925 to 1950."

Swinburne, Algernon Charles. *Swinburne: Selected Poetry and Prose.* Edited by John D. Rosenberg. New York: The Modern Library, 1968.

Thoreau, Henry David. *The Writings of Henry David Thoreau.* Vol. 5. *Excursions and Poems.* Boston: Houghton Mifflin and Co., 1906.

Thurber, James. *Let Your Mind Alone! And Other More or Less Inspirational Pieces.* New York: Harper & Brothers, 1937.

———. *The Middle-Aged Man on the Flying Trapeze.* New York: Harper & Brothers, 1935.

———. *Selected Letters of James Thurber.* Edited by Helen Thurber and Edward Weeks. 1981. Reprint, New York: Penguin Books, 1982.

———. *The Thurber Carnival.* New York: Harper & Brothers, 1945.

———. *The Years with Ross.* 1959. Reprint, New York: Penguin Books, 1984.

Tocqueville, Alexis de. *Democracy in America.* Vol. 2 New York: Vintage Books, 1945.

Trueblood, Elton. *The Humor of Christ.* New York: Harper and Row, 1964.

Tucker, James. *The Novels of Anthony Powell.* New York: Columbia University Press, 1976.

Twentieth Century Authors: A Biographical Dictionary of Modern Literature. Edited by Stanley J. Kunitz and Howard Haycraft. New York: The H. W. Wilson Co., 1942.

Whitman, Walt. *An American Primer.* 1904. Reprint, Stevens Point, Wis.: Holy Cow! Press, 1987.

Williams, William Carlos. *Something to Say: William Carlos Williams on Younger Poets.* The William Carlos Williams Archive Series, vol. 1. Edited by James E. B. Breslin. New York: New Directions, 1985.

Wilson, Edmund. *Axel's Castle: A Study in the Imaginative Literature of 1870–1930.* 1931. Reprint, New York: W. W. Norton & Co., 1984.

Wimsatt, James I. "The Mirror as Metaphor for Literature." In *What Is Literature?* edited by Paul Hernadi, 127–41. Bloomington: Indiana University Press, 1978.

Winoker, Jon, ed. *The Portable Curmudgeon.* New York: New American Library, 1987.

Index